The Suspect

'An instant classic. No other book portrays the traumatising effects of British state violence with more power or lucidity. Sabir's struggle to resist and overcome injustice is an inspiration.'
—Arun Kundnani, author of *The Muslims Are Coming!*
Islamophobia, Extremism, and the Domestic War on Terror

'Discussions of Islamophobia are greatly deficient when they fail to tackle the ways in which the Muslim community has been perpetually securitised in uniquely nefarious ways. Rizwaan offers a compelling breakdown of what that has looked like through his own tragic experience.'
—Omar Suleiman, scholar, civil rights leader,
writer and public speaker

'Rizwaan Sabir's captivating recollection of his Kafkaesque experiences with the British counterterrorism apparatus illustrates with devastating clarity the long-term consequences of the Prevent program.'
—Lisa Stampnitzky, University of Sheffield and author of
Disciplining Terror: How Experts Invented Terrorism

'A raw, compelling account of the profound trauma, social harms and human costs generated by counter-terrorism policy.'
—Professor Joe Sim, Liverpool John Moores University

The Suspect

Counterterrorism, Islam, and the Security State

Rizwaan Sabir

Foreword by Hicham Yezza
Afterword by Aamer Anwar

PLUTO PRESS

First published 2022 by Pluto Press
New Wing, Somerset House, Strand, London WC2R 1LA

www.plutobooks.com

Copyright © Rizwaan Sabir 2022
Foreword © Hicham Yezza 2022; Afterword © Aamer Anwar 2022

The right of Rizwaan Sabir to be identified as the author of this work has been
asserted in accordance with the Copyright, Designs and Patents Act 1988.

British Library Cataloguing in Publication Data
A catalogue record for this book is available from the British Library

ISBN 978 0 7453 3849 1   Hardback
ISBN 978 0 7453 3848 4   Paperback
ISBN 978 1 786807 17 5   PDF
ISBN 978 1 786807 18 2   EPUB

Typeset by Stanford DTP Services, Northampton, England

Simultaneously printed in the United Kingdom and United States of America

In the Name of Allah, the Most Beneficent, the Most Merciful.

Contents

Acknowledgements

I owe a debt of gratitude to a number of people over the years for their love, support, and trust – all of which have allowed me to successfully complete this book.

My mum and dad, my brothers Irfan and Hamaad, and my sister Aneesa. Without their patience, understanding, and love, especially when matters got really difficult in 2013 and 2018, I would not have made it this far. Thank you.

Thank you to Rod Thornton for his bravery, support, and encouragement over the last decade. Rod's courage and quest to hold power to account, no matter what the personal and professional costs were to him, have been more inspirational than words can convey.

Thank you to Professor Joe Sim, Ghulam Haydar, Hicham Yezza, and Fahid Qurashi for taking time out of their busy lives to comment on early drafts of the manuscript. Also, thank you to Will Jackson, Adam Elliot-Cooper, Tanzil Chowdhury, Nadya Ali, Tarek Younis, Zishan Khawaja, Yassir Morsi, Zirwa Raza, Sadia Habib, and Shabnam Mayet for reading chapters and extracts over the years. You helped me synthesise my thinking when it all stopped making sense.

I owe a special note of gratitude to Asim Qureshi for his friendship and generosity over the past four years. Asim found the time to read entire drafts of the manuscript when they made little sense, helped me recognise the role and relevance of trauma, and supported me in getting it all down on paper with empathy and without judgement. He stopped me from downplaying the significance of my experiences when I compared myself to those who had suffered a far worse fate at the hands of power and kept reminding me about the importance of finishing this book when I had wanted to give up.

Thank you to Arun Kundnani for reviewing the manuscript and going above and beyond what was expected of him. Through his meticulous and constructive feedback, he helped me tighten and focus the text. He also gave me the confidence to talk about resistance. Any mistakes or shortcomings are mine alone.

My heartfelt thanks to some friends and family members who have been by my side through thick and thin. In particular, and in no order of importance, Amreez Akhtar and Amjad Hussain for keeping me grounded and always real. Shazad Khawaja and Zafran Zaman for their unconditional friendship for almost two decades. Aunty Shaheena for adopting me as a son, Mohsin Hussain for adopting me as a brother, and both of them for giving me a home away from home. Omayr Ghani for his good company, banter, and his spare room. Sadia Habib and Ghulam Haydar for opening their home and hearts to me. Haaris Kadri for always providing an empathetic listening ear. Katy Sian for helping me intellectually and conceptually grow. Tarek Younis for being a wise sounding board despite being inundated with his own work, research, and family commitments. Thank you to the 'Muslim Academics' for offering me a sanctuary to express myself without the fear of being judged. Your support, positivity, and jokes have kept me sane in some testing times. A huge thank you to the apes – Aftab Zahoor, Lydia Leboutillier, Zirwa Raza, Haaris Raza, Hamaad Sabir, Safaa Raza, and Aneesa Sabir. Over the years, and especially the last two, your love, presence, and support has made me appreciate what Caesar in *Rise of the Planet of the Apes* meant when he said, 'ape stronger together'.

Finally, I am grateful to the team at Pluto Press and, in particular, the Editorial Director David Castle who believed in this book from the get-go and patiently stood by as my requests for extensions filled his inbox.

Foreword

Hicham Yezza

More than a decade after our wrongful arrests on that beautiful morning of May 2008, I still find it very difficult to think and talk about 'the events'. There is both too much and too little to say.

I have especially struggled to convey to others the extent to which such an event can have repercussions far beyond its immediate and obvious confines, to explain just *how deep* this sort of wound goes.

This book is a necessary and salutary corrective in that regard.

It tells a human story: a story of pain and trauma, but also of generosity, kindness and empathy, written by someone uniquely placed to tell the tale in all its myriad colours and complexities.

It delineates with great dexterity the contours of the intricate lattice of personal, institutional, political, and ideological forces that led to our absurd, preposterous arrests on our university campus for suspected terrorism, and their long-drawn aftermath.

The book paints a lucid and sharp-eyed portrait of just how irretrievably damaging crossing the line into 'suspect-land' can be, and how these were traumatic events not just for Rizwaan and me, but for an entire community; a trauma which has irreparably fractured and distorted the personal and professional trajectories of countless lives, starting with our own.

And this, for me, is the book's signal message: trauma does not live on the surface of things, it branches deep to the very core of one's being, and remains there for months, years, and decades; creeping up and triggering us when we least expect it.

Rizwaan and I took parallel but divergent approaches in our return to 'normalcy', and his path was far braver than mine. Instead of retreating away from the pain, he returned to it again and again, epitomising what George Orwell called 'the power of facing'. He was the guy signing up to become a scuba diver after a near-drowning.

But, as he documents in heart-wrenching detail, this has come at a dear price. While our public discourse around mental health has certainly made commendable strides in the past decade, psychiatric trauma remains all too easy to dismiss. Unless one is paying attention, it is still largely invisible and silent, rarely manifesting itself and only doing so once it is too late.

Anyone who knows Rizwaan will recognise the infectious joviality at the core of his character. This makes the darknesses he chronicles in the pages ahead even more poignant, resonant, and harrowing.

In the pages that follow, Rizwaan eloquently articulates what it feels like to be on the other side of political and institutional blindness, and what it means to be what Liz Fekete calls a 'suitable enemy' or what Stan Cohen dubbed 'impure victims'.

Through forensic examination and argument, and marshalling over a decade's worth of scholarly research and engagement as an academic, Rizwaan compellingly shows us the consequences of reducing entire communities to a threat-level chart.

Reading Rizwaan's words, I was constantly reminded of Fanon's quip in his introduction to *Black Skin, White Masks*: 'not many people asked me to write this book, certainly not the ones to whom it is addressed...'.

I have no doubt that many of those most in need of reading the book – officials, academics, thinktank wonks – will be among those most reluctant to hear and engage with its message.

And yet, amid the pain and trauma, this is a book that is remarkably generous in its attempt to understand and engage with its critics on the issues it diagnoses and interrogates so cogently.

Whether they agree with its arguments or not, few readers will finish this book without having their understanding of the dialectic between high-level policy and raw trauma, both personal and communal, significantly deepened, nuanced, and enriched.

By excavating the emotional and psychiatric impact of a highly racialised and securitised counterterrorism infrastructure, the book also serves as an exemplary act of intellectual and political resistance, as well as of true civic engagement, in the best tradition traced by luminaries such as Bertrand Russell, A. Sivanandan and Stuart Hall.

Above all, this book is an act of pedagogic public service, and should be an essential read for anyone seeking to understand what it means to be a Muslim living in twenty-first-century Britain.

I hope all readers will approach the book with the same sense of empathy and generosity of spirit that Rizwaan has shown in writing it.

London
July 2021

1
Awakening

Like hundreds of millions of people around the world, especially in the West, I can recall the day the 11 September 2001 attacks (9/11) happened with a great deal of clarity. I had spent the day in lessons at sixth form and hung out with friends in the common room as I eased myself into the start of my A-Levels. When the day ended, I left to take the bus to my uncle's. My first cousin Aftab and I were helping him paint his home as we awaited news on the arrival of his newborn daughter Hafsa. Near the bus stop, I bumped into my friend Majid. We greeted one another. 'Have you seen the news?,' Majid asked. 'No. Why?,' I replied. 'America is under attack,' he said. 'The World Trade Centre in New York has been hit by two airplanes and so has the Pentagon in Washington DC.' As soon as I walked into my uncle's home, I immediately turned on the news. The images that have become embedded into the minds and memories of tens of millions of people around the world were on display for all to see. Smoke was billowing from the rubble of the twin towers, which had collapsed by this stage, and overshadowed the New York skyline. The news broadcasts kept repeating footage of the planes flying into the buildings, the collapsing towers, and interviews and testimonies with terrified witnesses.

Growing up, I was no stranger to images of war or talk of it. As a six-year-old boy, I remember watching news broadcasts containing night-vision images of American fighter jets taking off and landing on a naval vessel as part of the first Gulf War in 1991. I also recall countless political conversations around the dinner table with my dad and older brother discussing Indian-Hindutva atrocities against Muslims in Gujarat and Kashmir, and the never-ending atrocities committed by Israelis against defenceless Palestinians. In the mid-1990s, a few Muslim families had resettled in my hometown of Nottingham after fleeing the war in Bosnia.

Given the central role that Islam and Muslims began to play in the news coverage and the policy statements of politicians in the US and UK after 9/11, I began to become more curious. Before this, references to 'otherness' seemed focused on nationalist identifiers such as Pakistani, Bengali, and so forth. But the post-9/11 world had seemingly done away with these labels and catapulted the figure of the 'Muslim' into popular consciousness with a speed and intensity that could not be ignored.

By the time Afghanistan had been invaded by the American-led coalition to 'smoke' al-Qaeda out of the mountains of Tora Bora, as President Bush repeatedly said, and the resistance to the US and UK invasion and occupation of Iraq in 2003 had started to gain momentum, I started a degree in Management Systems and Multimedia Technology at Manchester Metropolitan University. Though I was interested in current affairs, the concept of studying a subject in the social sciences had not really registered with me. Like most other working-class Muslims I knew, I thought education was about getting qualifications that would secure me a well-paid job. Learning about history, politics, and war was to be done outside of formal educational spaces. As the degree got underway, my interest started to quickly diminish. The degree was excruciatingly boring and, without my parents to keep me in check, I spent the nights smoking pot, going clubbing or being at a house party. In the summer of 2004, I was unsurprised to discover that I had failed the first year.

When the new academic year started, I returned to Manchester and moved into a student home with Aftab and my friends Nas and Zafran. The news at this stage was filled with reports of the Iraq War. Questions were being asked about the integrity of the intelligence the Blair government had cited to take the UK into war. One evening, my schoolfriend Nadia, who was going into her final year of sociology, was visiting. I told her that I had failed my year and was looking to study something different; something I was interested in. Nadia suggested sociology. I prodded her for details, and she outlined the sorts of topics I could study. Within a few days, I was sat opposite the admissions tutor for the humanities. But there was a problem. There were no more spaces left on the sociology degree. There was, however, some spaces available to study politics.

My understanding of politics was pretty much restricted to images from the BBC Parliament channel that consisted of pale males debating each other in a room that either had red or green leather benches. On the few occasions I had followed parliamentary debates, I found the tone and language quite privileged, alien, and boring. With this image running in my mind, I asked the admissions tutor why anybody would study politics. Without saying a word, he opened a light-green booklet he had before him and pointed to a list of subjects and modules, including US foreign policy, war, terrorism, humanitarian intervention, narco-terrorism, Israel–Palestine, the conflict in Northern Ireland, and, crucially, the 9/11 attacks that I would study as part of the degree. Everything I had become curious about over the last three years could be formally studied on this politics degree. I needed no further convincing.

As the semester got underway, the demographics on the Politics degree were visibly different. There were only a handful of students of colour, and even fewer were Muslim. Within a short time, I had found my routine. There was no more clubbing, house parties, or pot. I needed to keep my mind focused, and I was not going to repeat the mistakes I had made the previous year. My circle of friends also reduced in size. On the days I had my lectures or seminars, I arrived on campus early so I could read my newspaper with my coffee and cigarette, and prepare for the seminars by reading journal articles. Studying for a degree that interested me seemed to have a positive effect on my lifestyle.

During lectures, I listened attentively to every word that was uttered by my professors and tried to capture them in my notebook, even though I wrote so quickly that most of them were unreadable by the end. I enjoyed various parts of the degree, but the most fulfilling was studying the wars and conflicts that had been fuelled by the American–Soviet Union rivalry, including the latter's invasion of Afghanistan where Osama bin Laden and his fellow mujahideen fought with weapons and money supplied by the Americans and Saudis via the Pakistanis. The academic who lectured on this topic, Steve Hurst, was a specialist on US foreign policy and was inspiring. He was middle-aged, wore thick, black spectacles, and donned a dark goatee beard. He was eccentric, reserved, smart, and, to top it off, funny in a very dry way. He would make remarks in the lecture that frequently had the entire theatre break out into laughter. He once described Russian President Boris Yeltsin as 'a part-time President and a full-time drunk'.

In one of his lectures, a question crossed my mind: how do academics come to work, get to talk about so many interesting things, and get paid to do this job? For me, employment was something you were compelled to do, usually in a job that you didn't want to be in so you could make a living; an inevitable reality for able adults. How was it therefore possible that academics got to do something they were interested in and passionate about but were being paid a salary for it? In that moment, as a nineteen-year-old man who was sat in the lecture theatre listening to Steve speak, I knew exactly what I wanted to do for the rest of my life.

I started to inquire what the process of becoming an academic was, and asked Steve for guidance. He explained that an ordinary route would require me to complete my Politics degree to a good standard, then complete a Master's degree in a relevant subject, and then complete a PhD, where I could research a subject of my own choosing for three years. By the end of it, I would be a 'specialist' in the area I had researched and could start applying for lectureships.

The process seemed simple, and there was no better option on the horizon for me. I therefore studied tirelessly for the next three years, and graduated with my degree in Politics in the summer of 2007. By September of the same year, I had moved back to my parents' home in Nottingham and started studying for my Master's degree in International Relations at the University of Nottingham. Soon after, I was putting together applications for a PhD scholarship to research political Islam and al-Qaeda. Finally, it felt as if I was edging closer to working on a topic that had been driving my curiosity for the previous six years. I thought I was on a pathway to a respectable career as an academic. I saw myself as projecting a positive image on behalf of my Pakistani and Muslim community. I felt I had a future in the country where I had been born and raised. I believed in its institutions, its police, its courts, and its civil servants. Everything, it seemed, was going to plan.

2

A Divine Signal

By the time I reached the top of the stairs at my parents' home to see what the shouting was, the front door had already been forced open. Three policemen – wearing white shirts with collar badges showing their ID numbers, black ties, black trousers, and shiny black shoes – were stood in the hallway. They wore blank expressions on their face. The morning sun was beaming through the broken door and the smoked glass panels that surrounded it. On hitting the oak flooring, the sun created a blinding reflection. One of the policemen was watching me stood at the top of the staircase as I looked at him with a mix of fear and confusion. The other two walked into the kitchen and were now out of sight. One of the officers remained in the hallway and continued staring. He raised a blue piece of paper in my direction; his way of inviting me downstairs. But, without moving, I already knew what the sheet of paper was. It was a warrant for my arrest on suspicion of being a terrorist and laid out the legal grounds on which the police were going to search my home. Before I could do or say anything, I found myself sat in a chair in the centre of a large room which had extremely bright ceiling lights and white walls that seemed to go on forever. Around ten police officers, who stood around me loudly talking over one another, filled the room. I silently sat there trying to decipher what they were saying but to no avail. And then, I awoke from my sleep in my bedroom. It was all a dream.

It was the end of April 2008 and I had been living with my parents for almost a year by this stage. I had a simple yet productive routine that centred my studies. It was exam season at the University of Nottingham, and though this brought its own anxiety, the time was quite memorable. I spent most of the time studying in the Graduate Centre with course mates who had moved to Nottingham from various parts of the world – from Panama City, Beirut, Dublin, Los Angeles, Erbil, Cairo, London, and Chicago – and would spend hours talking with them about geopolitics as part of our exam revision and drink copious amounts of coffee. The weather was also beginning to heat up and the sunshine made everything seem less daunting.

In the eight months I had been at the University of Nottingham, I had become far more academically and politically active compared to my days as an undergraduate student. I was in my element amongst students who seemed more politically engaged and plugged-in. There were more seminars and lectures taking place with external speakers invited to talk about a whole host of topics concerning US foreign policy, the Middle East, and Muslim issues. There were more student demonstrations and protests on campus. Having attended protests against the Iraq War as well as Israel's bombing of Lebanon in 2006, I was comfortable being in such circles and made friends with quite a few student activists, many of whom were active in the anti-war movement and Palestinian society. In the week prior to my dream, a couple of my activist friends had been camped outside the university's main Hallward Library to protest the institution's involvement in the arms trade. They had staged a forty-eight-hour hunger strike as part of their campaign. I spent a fair amount of time with them in solidarity, and when their protest ended, volunteered to transport their tents home, which were emblazoned with anti-war graffiti. However, I had not found the time to do so and the tents lay dormant in the boot of my 1997 sky-blue Toyota.

Before leaving the house every morning, it was routine to say goodbye to my mum and tell her what time I would return. The morning of my dream was no different. She was sat watching television and eating her breakfast in the lounge. The dream had sort of spooked me because of its vividness and also because I did not know what to make of it. Dreams can carry a divine meaning and may be considered premonitions and signs sent by God, but they can also more simply be expressions of the mind processing subconscious thoughts. Before walking out of the lounge, I told my mum how I had dreamt the police had come to the house to arrest me for terrorism. In a reassuring motherly tone, she told me not to worry. 'Allah Maalik hai,' she said in her native Urdu. 'Allah is the Master.'

3
Suspected Terrorist

Around a fortnight had passed since my dream, and I had forgotten all about it. Life carried on as normal. Like most other days, I arrived at the University of Nottingham and parked my car in my usual spot at the west entrance. I walked through the leafy campus towards the Graduate Centre, which is located in the iconic Trent Building. The views on my walk were no less than spectacular. I could see a tall clocktower up ahead, a boating lake to the right, open fields ahead of me, tall trees to my left, and eventually a courtyard, which was basked in sunshine, that I would walk through to enter the building.

On the staircase just outside of the Graduate Centre, a man who I had never seen or spoken to before approached me. He introduced himself as an academic and a friend of Hicham Yezza. He wanted to know if I had spoken with Hicham. I did not ask him how he knew I was Hicham's friend, assuming he had probably seen us together in the lower-ground café where we often met and talked about history, politics, and the PhD proposal he was helping me write. Plus, I was far more curious to know why he was asking me about Hicham. 'I haven't spoken with him, but why do you ask?,' I inquired. The academic explained that university security guards were outside Hicham's office but would not tell him what they were doing or why they were there. He was asking me in case I knew something. Slightly confused but more intrigued by his claim, I said I would try to find out.

As I made my way towards Hicham's office, which was located on the opposite end of the corridor where the Graduate Centre is situated, I could see a uniformed university security officer standing guard. I recognised him and had exchanged pleasantries with him in the past. 'How you doing?,' I asked. 'What's happening here? Is everything okay?' The security guard, who had always been pleasant whenever he spoke with me sounded different. 'I am not at liberty to tell you,' he said in a formal and somewhat cold tone. 'Come on now,' I replied. 'I won't tell anyone. What's happening?' But the security guard was having none of it. 'I'm sorry,' he said, 'but I'm not at liberty to tell you.' Rather than prod him any further, I took a few steps back from Hicham's office door and observed what may be happening.

In the two or so minutes I stood there, I witnessed the deputy head of the university's security team speaking with a man who was casually dressed in light jeans and a dark blue sports jacket. Around the same time, the door to Hicham's office opened and I saw two people in his office wearing white overalls, facemasks, hoods, and blue rubber gloves. The only other time I had seen people dressed this way was in student accommodation a few years earlier. A middle-aged neighbour of mine, Paul, had unexpectedly died after suffering a brain haemorrhage. The people who arrived to remove his body in a black private ambulance were dressed in exactly the same way. Were these people in Hicham's office because he was dead?

I had no calling-credit on my mobile telephone and therefore went straight to the Graduate Centre and panickily asked a staff member if I could use her phone to make an urgent call. The staff member, who I was friendly with, probably heard the desperation in my voice and agreed without asking any questions. I stood next to her and dialled Hicham's telephone number. The phone rang but there was no answer and so I left a message asking Hicham to call me back as soon as possible. I thanked the staff member and headed for the café on the ground floor for my routine morning coffee. As I took a seat in the outdoor area, I was joined by a German course mate. We sipped our coffees, smoked cigarettes, and talked about the German welfare system. Hicham had still not returned my call. I sent him a text message: 'Hicham, are you okay? Call me when you get this please.'

The outdoor seating area of the café, which overlooks a lake and tall trees, was quiet. The only other person sat outside was a young man who was already seated when we arrived. Arriving slightly after us was a middle-aged white man and woman, both casually dressed, who sat two tables away from us. The Trent Building, with its mostly administrative and management offices, often has random people coming and going, but this pair seemed slightly out of place. They were too casual to be attending a formal meeting and too old to be typical students. Still, I thought nothing of them and carried on talking with my course-mate. As the minutes passed, I kept glancing over at my telephone but there was still no message or call from Hicham. 'Hich,' I texted again, 'please call me when you get this message. Are you okay? I'm really worried.' Within a few minutes of sending the second message, Hicham called back.

'Hey, comrade,' he said in his softly spoken tone before offering a long-winded apology for not returning my call or texts sooner. 'I am unwell and off sick from work,' he explained. 'What's up, anyway?' Not wanting to embarrass myself by telling him that I thought he was dead, I told him the truth: that university security officers were at his office but they would not tell me anything. I speculated that his office may have been burgled. There had been a few instances of burglaries in the Trent Building, which I had come to discover through my conversations with staff members in the Graduate Centre given how much time I spent in this space, and since Hicham was alive, the people in forensics uniforms may be examining his office for clues. Hicham said he would make his way onto campus and see what was happening for himself. My course-mate and I finished our coffees and walked upstairs to the Graduate Centre to start revision for our exams, which were due to take place later that week. I went to my desk, put down my belongings, and then walked back out into the hallway and straight into the men's toilets.

*   *   *

As soon as I walked in, the door was aggressively pushed open behind me. I immediately turned around and saw three men, two white and one Sikh, standing there dressed in jeans and jackets. One of them was the man I had seen earlier speaking with the deputy head of security outside of Hicham's office in the blue sports jacket. 'Don't move! Don't move!' he shouted aggressively at me. I froze in my step. I did not see these men on my way in. Where did they suddenly appear from? 'Who are you?,' the man asked me in a very firm voice. 'I'm a student,' I replied, and immediately produced my university ID card which was in my pocket.

'Who are *you*?,' I asked in return. The man pulled out a black leather warrant card and said, 'I'm a police officer.'

The officer explained that he was looking for a person of a similar description to me and felt that I may be able to help the police with their inquiries, which I agreed to do. He asked me to take him to the space where I was studying. When we reached my desk, he looked at my laptop bag and books and asked if I had met with anybody this morning. 'I had coffee with a course-mate earlier on, who's sat over there,' I said pointing towards the opposite end of the Graduate Centre. 'Can you take me to your friend?' We walked to my course-mate's desk and I pointed him out. My course-mate, who was tall, white, and balding, had been engrossed in his revision. He looked up confusedly towards the officer and me, but before he could say or ask anything, the officer said, 'That's fine' and turned away. This young white man did not excite the curiosity of the police. As we walked back towards my desk, the officer told me to collect my belongings and accompany him to his car. 'I need to ask you some questions,' he said. At this stage, I was under the impression that I was being asked to help the police solve some sort of crime, and even though a part of me felt a little anxious, I was curious to know more so agreed to go along with him.

We walked out of the Trent Building through a side entrance and into the main car park, where a blue unmarked Vauxhall Vectra was stationed. I sat in the passenger seat and the officer sat in the driver seat. He reached over to the back seat and grabbed an A4 notebook with a red cover and a pen from his pocket. It was the sort of notebook you use in high school. The officer wanted my full name, my home address, date of birth, and details of the course I was studying. I provided all and he made a note of them in his notebook. However, I was beginning to feel a little apprehensive. I was providing my information to the police but I was not being told what was happening or why. Every time I asked the officer to explain, he refused to tell me anything.

Feeling frustrated, and seeking to evoke a response, I told the officer that I knew his presence on campus had something to do with Hicham. 'Do you know Hicham?,' he asked. 'Have you spoken with him?' I told the officer that I did know Hicham and that I had sent him two text messages a little earlier on, and that I had also spoken with him over the telephone a short while ago. 'Can I read the text messages you sent to him?,' the officer asked. I decided to use the text messages as leverage to see if I could get him to explain what had happened. I felt I had a right to know seeing as though I was answering his questions. 'I won't show you until you tell me what is happening and why you are asking me these questions,' I said. But the officer was having none of it. 'So, you're refusing to cooperate?,' he menacingly asked. 'I'm not refusing to cooperate,' I explained, 'but I will not show you the text messages unless you tell me what is happening and why you are asking me these questions.' Within a matter of seconds, the officer's tone and persona had changed, and so began the threats. 'Well, maybe I should arrest you for perverting the course of justice or maybe arrest you for wasting police time?' And so, under the threat of arrest, I handed my battered maroon Nokia telephone over to him.

I was observing that he went straight to my text messages, and began looking through them. As he made a note of the messages in his red notebook, he asked if had ever been in trouble with the police before and, if so, on what grounds. I explained that I had once been arrested at a student protest in support of Palestine. 'That place is a right mess, isn't it?,' he casually said. 'All those Jews taking over more and more land. What do you make of the whole Palestine thing anyway?' I was gobsmacked. Up until this moment, I had suspected that the police presence on campus was connected to a burglary that had something to do with Hicham's office, but the politically charged nature of the officer's comment, and his attempt to bait me in such a vulgar manner to perhaps say something anti-Semitic suggested there was something bigger, something more political, at play. 'That's an extremely weird thing to say,' I told him. 'Are you from counterterrorism?' Without even giving it a thought, the officer said 'No.'

*   *   *

We had been sat in the car for around ten minutes when a black Vauxhall Vectra pulled up beside us. It parked so close, in fact, that I was no longer able to open my car door. I had been boxed in of sorts. Sitting in the car were the middle-aged man and woman I had spotted earlier in the café. 'I saw you in the café earlier on,'

I said to them through the open window. 'Are you following me?' The female officer, who was in the driver's seat, flatly said 'No.' The officer in whose blue car I was sitting, exited to take a call on his mobile telephone, and I used this opportunity to ask the newly arrived officers what was happening. But they, too, refused to go into any detail.

The officer finished his call and approached me at the passenger side of the car where I was sitting. 'Can I go, please? I have exams to revise for,' I pleaded. 'Rizwaan Sabir,' the officer said, 'from this moment onwards, you are under arrest under Section 41 of the Terrorism Act 2000 on suspicion of being involved in the commission, preparation or instigation of acts of terrorism.' I could not believe the words I was hearing and thought the officer was joking. 'Are you having a laugh?,' I asked him. 'Does it look like I'm having a laugh?' I fell silent as I tried to read his facial expressions, expecting him to break out into laughter before saying something like 'Fooled you' or 'Just kidding. Thanks for your help, you're free to go.' But nothing of the sort happened. 'You do not have to say anything,' the officer cautioned. 'But it may harm your defence if you fail to mention when questioned something which you may later rely on in court. Anything you do say may be given in evidence.'

I was told to step out of the car, was searched, and ordered to sit in the back of the blue car. The male officer from the café came and sat next to me as the car fell silent whilst the arresting officer tried to figure out how to use his satellite navigation system so he could start his journey. Meanwhile, my thoughts were racing. I had not done anything remotely related to 'terrorism', so why had I been arrested? It must be Hicham, I thought to myself; not realising that within a matter of minutes, the police, through their legal powers and threats, can turn friends and community members against each other and make them doubt their innocence. Is Hicham a terrorist? Has Hicham done something related to terrorism? Maybe it was connected to him being Algerian, I thought. He's not part of the Armed Islamic Group (GIA), is he? What does it have to do with me though? When the chance comes, I reassured myself, I will explain everything to the police honestly and openly, and they will soon realise that this is all one big mistake. My racing thoughts and doubts about Hicham, and my predicament, were interrupted by a loud frustrated sigh from the officer, who was still struggling to work the navigation system. 'Where are we going?,' I asked. Looking at me through the rear-view mirror, 'Bridewell Police Station,' he answered. 'I know where that is so I can direct you if you want.' He immediately gave up on his feeble attempt at using the navigation system and, without saying a word, began driving. 'By the way,' he added, 'I didn't tell you before but I am Detective Constable Richard West and I'm from the West Midlands Counter-Terrorism Unit.'

4
Detention

Bridewell Police Station was only around four miles from the university campus, and, after directing the officer for the short journey, we arrived at around 11:00 am. After passing an external security barrier that was manned by a uniformed guard, we drove into a shuttered unit and parked. We could not exit the vehicle straight away. We had to wait for the shutter to fully close and a prison officer to open my door. I was then escorted to the second floor of the station through a back-entrance staircase. On entry to the second floor, a uniformed police officer, holding a clipboard, was stood there. His job was to register the details of every person entering or leaving the second floor for the entire time of my detention. I was then told to take a seat in the reception area for a few minutes, before being escorted through a door into a deserted cell block. All the windows and glass doors of the second floor, including in the reception area, had been covered with brown paper that was held up with duct tape. The floor was dark green and had recently been cleaned with bleach, which I could still smell. All the lights were switched off, and the only light entering the cell block came via the smoked windows of the ten or so empty prison cells which had their doors wide open. To see the cell block deserted and unlit in this way made me feel quite intimidated and scared, especially since nobody knew that I had been arrested and brought here.

I was told to stand in the doorway of a cell marked 'B3', so as to face an observation table and two chairs that had been positioned directly outside of the cell door looking in. A custody officer sat on one chair and a uniformed police sergeant sat on the second. Flanking them were around five police officers who were all dressed in civilian clothing, including DC West and the male officer from the cafe. 'Do you know why you have been arrested?,' the uniformed police sergeant asked me. 'No, I don't. Can you please explain?' He looked down at his paperwork and began reading: 'You have been arrested under Section 41 of the Terrorism Act 2000 on suspicion of being involved in the commission, preparation, or instigation of acts of terrorism.' But I was already aware of the legal grounds being invoked for the arrest. 'What have I actually done?', I asked. 'What's my crime?' But once again, there were no answers. The police sergeant would not go into any detail. 'Everything will become clearer to you once you are interviewed,' he said, and then asked if I would like legal advice from a lawyer who was independent of the police. 'No,' I naively replied. 'I do not need one since I am going to answer everything honestly.' I would later discover that the police sergeant wrote my reply word-for-word in the custody record. He also asked if I wanted anybody informed that I had been arrested and was in police custody. Not realising the seriousness of the situation, and not wanting to alarm my family, I gave the details of my friend Waqar who was a little older than me and could, if the need arose, communicate with my family. I was under the impression that I would be in and out of custody after I had given my side of the story, and by the end of the day at the latest. There was, I felt, no reason to cause my family alarm by telling them I was under arrest for suspected terrorism. I was searched again and told to enter the prison cell.

The cell was around 10 square feet in surface, and the walls were made entirely of breezeblocks that had been painted white. The cell window, at the back of the cell, was heavily smoked and I could see nothing out of it. Under the window, a dark grey blanket had been neatly folded and placed on a thin blue mattress. If you looked up, you could see a tube light omitting a bright white light, the sort you would expect to find in a laboratory. Near the dark green metal door was a steel toilet and sink. The door remained wide open as I paced around the cell trying to think what Hicham had done that had led me to be arrested. The police sergeant and the custody officer remained seated at the desk immediately outside, observing and recording all of my actions, words, and moves in the custody log. In fact, they would do this for twenty-four hours a day for the first two days because I was on suicide watch. And then, the monitoring and checks would be reduced to thirty-minute intervals.

After a short while of pacing and sitting in my cell, DC West arrived. He had changed his clothes and was now dressed in a dark suit, green shirt, and tie. He sat down next to me on the blue mattress and said that he was concerned that I was absent from university. His priority, he claimed, was to make sure that I could sit my exams on time and that if I cooperated with the police I could get on with my life as normal. By this stage, I had no idea what was happening or what would happen next, and I was feeling extremely anxious and afraid. DC West's words therefore felt quite reassuring. I told him that I had done nothing wrong, had nothing to hide, and would be happy to help the police with their inquiries. As he left, I felt a little better, though I still paced around the cell trying to remain patient and make sense of what was happening and why.

*　　*　　*

Around an hour had passed when another officer arrived. I was standing in the doorway making small talk with the custody sergeant and the custody officer. The new officer was tall; he had white hair and a white beard. Out of all the officers I had seen until this moment, this officer was the one I thought looked least like a policeman. He looked more like a geography teacher than somebody who worked in counterterrorism. After introducing himself, he showed me a set of keys he was holding in his hand. 'Are these your car and house keys?,' he asked. 'Yes,' I confirmed, adding 'why do you need to know?' He explained that a warrant had been issued by the court giving police the authorisation to seize and search my car and search my family home for items they deemed relevant to their inquiries. Until this moment, I had assumed everything would be revealed as a big mistake and I would be released within a matter of hours. I had also instructed the police not to share news of my arrest with my family, reasoning that I could explain whatever needed explaining to them on my release. But now that my family home, where my parents, two teenage siblings, and elderly grandmother lived was going to be searched, I understood that irrespective of whether the police had made an error by arresting me or not, matters were extremely serious and my attempts to protect my family from the inevitable stress and shock they would feel were in vain. I began to panic. 'Please don't kick my door down or hurt my family,' I begged the officer. 'My family are decent, law-abiding people who have never done anything wrong or broken any laws. If you kick our door down and start searching the house, you are going to terrorise them.' The officer told me not to panic. 'Let me explain how this will work,' he said. 'We will knock on the door. If nobody answers, we will use your house key, and if we still can't gain access, we will force entry.'

On the evening of my first day in detention, the police knocked on my parents' door. When my mother, who was cooking, opened it, they produced a search warrant and ushered her, my grandmother, my teenage brother and sister, Hamaad and Aneesa, into the front room. They would not allow them to leave. My dad was still at work at this stage. The police began searching the house but would not tell my family anything; only that a warrant had been issued by the court under the Terrorism Act 2000, and that they had authorisation to seize any items they thought were connected to terrorism, especially 'terrorism propaganda'.[1] When my mum and Aneesa asked the police whether their presence had something to do with me since they could not reach me on my mobile telephone, the police refused to give them any information, adding to their frustration, anxiety, and stress.

After a few hours into the search, my family were ordered to leave their home whilst the police would continue with their search. They were offered temporary accommodation but they chose to stay with my dad's youngest sister, aunty Sofia, instead. Throughout the entire forty-eight-hour period that the search lasted, an officer stood guard outside of our front door and controlled entry and exit to our home. With the knowledge that my home was being searched, I felt powerless, guilt, and anger in equal measure. When the officer left with my house keys, I went back into my cell and sobbed like a helpless child, unbothered by the police sergeant and custody officer who were both watching.

Though my family had each other for support, they were all faced with their own challenges and fears that were made worse given they are all law-abiding people who therefore have no experience nor understanding of the mechanics or processes of policing and the criminal justice system. When they eventually found out that I had been arrested for suspected terrorism, they were shocked and confused. How can this happen to *us*? How was

I, a student of International Relations, being suspected of terrorism? None of my family ever doubted my innocence. They were convinced that I had been picked up by the police because of my association with somebody else. When they discovered that Hicham, who nobody knew at the time except my girlfriend and Aftab, had been arrested with me, they assumed it was association with him that had landed me in trouble. Aftab telephoned my girlfriend and arranged to meet with her. He was trying to find out more about Hicham but they were too afraid to speak over the phone. In fact, my whole family were convinced that their phones were being monitored and that saying something out of turn could be manipulated or used by the police and create more trouble for me. When Aftab met with her, they spoke only after they had both switched off their phones. It quickly transpired that she, like Aftab, knew very little about Hicham other than what I had told them; that Hicham worked at the university, was friends with me, and was helping me with my studies.

As time went on, and once my family began to get a clearer picture of what had transpired, their impression of Hicham quickly improved but they were deeply worried about the consequences of being arrested for terrorism. Like so many Muslim families, they were aware of the rampant Islamophobia that was driving government policies in the aftermath of the 9/11 attacks and especially the London bombings that happened three years earlier in 2005. They knew there was a different set of rules that applied to Muslims when it came to matters of terrorism, especially in terror raids that were being executed up and down the UK in which young Muslims, especially men, were being detained and, seemingly, never released from custody. The reason for this false impression concerns media coverage. A lot of counterterror raids are reported with full media fanfare and headline coverage when they are executed but their 'news-value' and 'news-worthiness' quickly diminishes if a person is released without charge. By not centring a person's release with the same degree of interest and coverage, irrespective of the reasons, the news media contribute to creating a false impression of the threat and downplay the fact that 49 per cent of people arrested from 9/11 until March 2021 have been released without charge.[2]

My family were not free from the anxieties and stresses this partial media-reporting creates. They were convinced between themselves that Hicham and my prospects for release were looking bleak; so bleak, in fact, that Aftab and Lydia, who were set to get married in exactly one week – on 21 May 2008 – were both considering calling off their wedding. Both of them felt guilty that they would be celebrating whilst I was in a prison cell with my future hanging in the balance. When I learned of this, I asked the police if I could speak with Aftab over the telephone, and they agreed. He was driving his car and pulled over to take my call. I told him in no uncertain terms that no matter what the outcome was, Lydia and he had to go ahead with their wedding. They had spent far too much time, energy, and money on wedding preparations over the last year, and had invited hundreds of family members and friends from all over the UK to simply cancel or delay. Aftab, who is my first cousin, is one year older than me and my confidant in pretty much all matters. He is a cool-headed, poker-faced character who very rarely, if ever, shows emotion or vulnerability. Throughout my entire life of growing up with him, attending the same school and university, I have never seen Aftab display any extremeness in any emotion he feels; be it joy, anger, or frustration. But, when he told Lydia and his parents what I said to him, he cried. The police had managed not only to break me but my nearest and dearest too.

*　　*　　*

Around four hours had passed since I had been taken into custody when a police officer wearing a black police uniform arrived at my cell, holding a camera in his hand. I was ordered to stand against a wall in the corridor so photographs of me, from three different distances, could be taken for police records. My face and shoulders were photographed from the front, the left, and the right. Photos were also taken of the back of my head and my shoulders. I obediently complied with every instruction the officer gave, and as the photos were being taken, all I could think of was how such photos are shared with the media and paraded all over the internet, in newspapers, and on evening news bulletins, as the public is informed that somebody has been charged with terrorism. Would I become one of these 'faces'? How many times had I

seen these types of photos of people who were accused of terrorism, and how long did I spend reflecting upon the fact some of
these faces may actually be innocent? How long would somebody
who may potentially see these photos of me spend considering
whether I was innocent? As a Muslim person of colour, I thought
I knew what racism, Islamophobia, and stereotyping were, but I
began to experience the meaning of these things in ways that I had
never imagined. But I still had no idea why I was in custody and
being treated like this.

A short while after the photographs had been taken, DC West
and his Irish colleague, DC Shankey, arrived with a female officer
whose job title was 'Counter-Terrorism trained Fingerprint
Expert'. I was now being taken for DNA swabbing so I could be
entered onto the DNA-database and to have my fingerprints and
footprints taken with ink. Electronic prints, I was told by DC
Shankey, were not as detailed as ink and therefore all individuals
arrested for suspected terrorism had to give their fingerprints and
footprints in this way. 'If you do not consent to giving your fingerprints,' DC Shankey had warned me at the start of the process, 'we
have the right to use reasonable force to take your prints'. But protesting or resisting this process was not on my mind. I wanted this
process to be over as soon as possible. I wanted to go into the interview room and find out why I had been arrested and detained as
a suspected terrorist. What my 'crime' was. Why my family home
was being searched and my family probably traumatised. I signed
the consent form and the fingerprinting began.

I quickly realised that this was going to be an extremely lengthy
process, and a painful one too. The officers were bending and
twisting my fingers for the entire practice, which lasted for around
two and a half hours, in order to ensure that every print was as
detailed as possible and to the satisfaction of the female fingerprint expert. Her role was to examine every single print with a
magnifying glass for detail and accuracy. She would then either
accept the print or instruct the officers to retake it. This frustrated
me because it not only meant more pain and sorer fingers but,
more importantly, having to wait longer for the interview to take
place. It also frustrated DC West too. At one stage, she was examining the prints and had her back turned to us. DC West stuck two
fingers up to her in frustration. When he noticed I had seen him,

his face turned red and I smiled. In this one moment, DC West and I were on the same side. Or so I thought.

After the prints had been taken, I was finally permitted to go into an exercise yard on the second floor, accompanied by a custody officer, for a much-needed and overdue smoke. The yard was small and had very high walls. It was impossible to see anything other than the sky, which was interrupted by a metal cage that served as the ceiling. It was a warm evening, and it felt good being in the yard where I could hear the passing traffic, the distant sound of people chatting, and the sound of music coming from the nearby waterfront bars and cafes. The walls were extremely thick in the cell block, and the window was so heavily smoked that it wasn't really possible to hear or see anything. As I sat there and took long, drawn out drags on my cigarette, I reflected on how everyday life was continuing for so many people outside, yet, here I was, invisible and powerless to do anything other than be at the mercy of the security state. I also realised how much I took for granted in ordinary life. For example, in the exercise yard, I was never allowed to use a lighter to spark my cigarette. The custody officer escorting me would always light it for me. I was unsure why I was denied this liberty but it made me realise how often I took the smallest privileges and liberties for granted, and only came to appreciate them now that they had been taken from me.

A short while after I had returned from the exercise yard, I was in my cell. The custody sergeant had brought me a sandwich and an apple to eat but I had no appetite so it laid untouched on the table outside of my cell. The only thing I wanted was to go into the interview room and learn what I was meant to have done. And then, within a short space of time, DC West appeared at my cell door, which was wide open. 'It's time for the interview.'

5
Suspicious Documents

Two days prior to my arrest, on 12 May 2008, senior management at the University of Nottingham had tipped off the police that three 'suspicious' documents had been discovered on the computer of Hicham Yezza consisting of an article from the journal *Foreign Affairs*,[1] an article from the *Middle East Policy Council Journal*,[2] and a document called the Al-Qaeda Training Manual. Hicham is an Algerian Muslim man who had studied at the university at both undergraduate and PhD levels. At the time of the arrest in 2008, Hicham was the Principal Administrator in the university's Department of Modern Languages, an appropriate fit for somebody who is fluent in Arabic, English, French, and some Spanish. He was also the Editor-in-Chief of the political magazine *Ceasefire*. When I met him in the Trent Building in early October 2007, it was his work at *Ceasefire* that formed the basis of our subsequent friendship.

The tip-off by the university was made in an unusual way. Conventionally, a report of this sort would be made to uniformed officers who would ordinarily escalate it to senior police officers, CID, and then onto Special Branch. However, the university, through an existing relationship between the Head of Security and Special Branch, tipped off Special Branch directly.[3] On receipt of the tip-off, Special Branch assessed the three documents and felt they warranted an investigation. However, since Special Branch had a limited set of resources at their disposal, the West Midlands Counter-Terrorism Unit was called in for support. This unit, part of the national counterterrorism network created in 2008, houses specialist officers who work full-time on counterterrorism cases. A decision was subsequently made that a joint police operation between West Midlands Counter-Terrorism Unit and Nottinghamshire Police would to be launched. The codename given to the operation was 'Minerva' after the Roman Goddess of Wisdom.

Covert police inquiries were initially made into Hicham for a period of forty-eight hours before the next phase of the operation was triggered: executing his arrest under Section 41 of the Terrorism Act 2000. On the morning of 14 May 2008, Hicham was arrested upon his arrival at the university's Trent Building, where his office was located, and taken into custody. He was marked as 'Detainee 1'. When I arrived on campus that same morning, I too was arrested and became 'Detainee 2'. As we were being detained, the Senior Coordinator for Counter-Terrorism at New Scotland Yard in London, as well as the Office for Security and Counter-Terrorism (OSCT) at the Home Office, were both being briefed about Operation Minerva and our arrests.

At the time of the arrest, I was researching al-Qaeda in Iraq for my Master's dissertation. I had already been accepted to research armed Muslim groups for my PhD at the University of Nottingham. As part of this research and preparation for the upcoming PhD, five months earlier in January 2008, I was working on my laptop in the Graduate Centre. I came across a document called the 'Al-Qaeda Training Manual' that was available for download on the US Department of Justice website. I knew this document existed through my studies but I had no idea it was available for download courtesy of the US government. On opening it, I could see there was a stamp that said: 'Government Exhibit ID 1677-T.' I immediately understood that the US government had declassified the document and placed it into the public domain. Believing the document would serve as a useful reference source, I saved a copy to a folder on my laptop which contained hundreds of primary documents, government and NGO reports, and journal articles related to armed Muslim groups, counterterrorism, and human rights.

During this period, I was in routine communication with Hicham and must have sent him hundreds of journal articles, reports, and drafts of my written work via the Microsoft MSN chat service as well as email. An intellectual in every sense of the word, and an avid reader, Hicham has been the Editor-in-Chief of *Ceasefire* since 2002, and has a meticulous understanding of political theory, philosophy, and geopolitics, amongst other subjects. In addition to drawing on his knowledge and asking for his feedback on my PhD proposal, in what had essentially become a 'student–mentor' friendship, I shared documents and articles I felt would be of interest to him. Occasionally, I would ask if he could print a paper or article for me on his office printer. The student–mentor friendship between Hicham and I continued for around six months without any issues, but on 12 May 2008 everything was about to change.

Hicham was away from work after falling sick. A member of staff at the school contacted him with regards to some documents relating to urgent school business she needed to access. Hicham told her that these could be found on his office computer, which did not require a password. The colleague went into Hicham's office and, while searching on his computer for the school documents, noticed the two journal articles and the Al-Qaeda Training Manual on his desktop. Hicham's colleague sought advice from a more senior member of the school. After some discussion, the documents were reported to the University of Nottingham's management until they landed on the desk of the Registrar, the person responsible for the operational running of the university.

Based purely on its title, the Al-Qaeda Training Manual sounds dangerous. How could it not be when it apparently belongs to the group that executed, amongst a long list of attacks, the 9/11 attacks, the Madrid bombing, and the London bombings of 2005? This is why due diligence is so critical and had the University of Nottingham bothered to carry it out, they would have immediately recognised that this so-called 'Al-Qaeda Training Manual', in actual fact, has nothing to do with al-Qaeda.[4] The manual's original (i.e. real) title is 'Military Studies in the Jihad against the Tyrants'. A copy was discovered during a police search of the home of a Libyan terror suspect, Anas al-Liby, in Manchester eight years earlier, in May 2000. The manual was handed by the British to American prosecutors who gave it its contemporary title – *Al-Qaeda Training Manual* – and then used it in the New York trial of suspects who stood accused of the US Embassy bombings in Nairobi, Kenya and Dar-es-Salaam, Tanzania in 1998. On page 2 of the document, it actually says in handwritten form: 'Entered as evidence in trial of Africa embassy bombings.'

The decision by US prosecutors to change the name of the document was evidently a way of connecting those who were found in possession of it to Al-Qaeda, and, if the need arose, to increase the likelihood that people in possession of it in the future would have a higher chance of being successfully prosecuted in the courts. But the document itself has nothing to do with Al-Qaeda, other than the new title it was given by US prosecutors.[5] In fact, the document is nothing more than 'a compilation of material drawn from various military, intelligence and law enforcement manuals ... and thus is not unique for its alleged sponsorship by Al Qaeda – which is not mentioned in the manual'.[6]

The version of the Al-Qaeda Training Manual which Hicham and I possessed was a heavily redacted and truncated version. It had Chapters 5 to 11 completely missing. As it happens, the full, non-redacted version of the manual, I later found out, was obtainable from the University of Nottingham's own library via the inter-library loan system at the time (class mark HV6431). At the time of writing, the full version of the manual is also available to purchase from Blackwell's bookstore for just £19.36.[7] This same version, which is published by the US Air Force's Counterproliferation Center in Alabama, can also be downloaded free of charge from the Center's website, where readers can follow a running commentary by Jerrold M. Post, the late American psychologist and CIA profiler who is listed as the 'editor' of the manual.[8] There also seems to be an endless stream of academic books that cite the manual.[9] To reiterate: not only was the document that Hicham and I were arrested, detained and investigated for a document that had been given the title of 'Al-Qaeda Training Manual' by the US government, but it was also an incomplete and truncated version compared to the fuller, longer versions that were, at the time, publicly available via the university's library and can be downloaded or purchased until this day from high-street bookshops and US military websites.

But none of these facts were sought out by the university management or Registrar, and none seem to have mattered. The university had neither bothered to conduct even the most cursory of checks to assess the nature of the document before calling the police, nor did they consult the in-house university expert, Dr Rod Thornton, who specialises in the study of terrorism and insurgency, for advice or counsel on the matter. The university had also failed to conduct anything even remotely resembling a formal 'risk assessment', as one might expect from a responsible institution about to trigger a 'national security' investigation.[10] Based simply on the title of a document discovered on the computer of an Algerian Muslim member of staff, the university had made all sorts of assumptions and contributed to Hicham and me being arrested and detained as suspected terrorists.

6
Interrogation

The interview room was in the same wing of the cell block I was being detained in. It was small, around 10 square feet, and had a very surreal feel to it because it had been soundproofed. This deadened any echoes and created an unnatural acoustic that made the room feel claustrophobic and smaller than it was. In one corner of the room was a cassette-based device to record the interview. On the ceiling were tube lights that emitted a laboratory-style white light and a fixed-surveillance camera, which I was told was being live-monitored by police officers elsewhere. There were three chairs, two for the interviewing officers and one for me. The floor was made up of a dark carpet, possibly a shade of red. My eyes felt sore from the crying that I had done on discovering the police were searching my family home. My mind and body felt exhausted from trying to work out why I was under arrest for suspected terrorism. DC West busied himself with loading up the recording equipment and DC Shankey arranged his papers. He then offered me a glass of water and told me not to worry. 'Just be honest,' he said. 'Nobody is trying to trip you up.' After a long beep on the cassette recorder, the interview started. The original charge for which I was arrested was read out to me again and I was then cautioned. This was standard procedure and was repeated at the beginning of every interview.

'Documentation, including the Al-Qaeda Training Manual was recovered on Hicham Yezza's work computer,' DC Shankey said. 'Can you tell us about that, please?' Without even a split-second's thought, I began talking. I explained to the officers how I had come across the Al-Qaeda Training Manual when I was collecting reading and referencing material for my dissertation, which was on al-Qaeda. 'I thought this document is brilliant for my research,' I told them. 'If I can reference it for my dissertation, then it's going to get me some really good marks because it's a primary document that I thought wasn't even available.' The officers seemed surprised as well as confused. 'Are you saying there is a link between you downloading the Al-Qaeda Training Manual [and] that manual being on Hicham's workstation?' I explained to the officers that I had discussed the discovery of the manual with Hicham since I did not realise that such a document was available online but I could not remember sending it to him. I explained that I very routinely sent Hicham drafts of my university work and academic articles and reports over Microsoft MSN messenger and how this was connected to the student–mentor friendship we had and the printing he sometimes did for me. I also gave a very comprehensive summary of my relationship to Hicham and how I had come to know him. However, during the interview, I could not remember with any certainty whether I had sent Hicham the Al-Qaeda Training Manual. Over the course of the six or so months that I had known Hicham, we had exchanged hundreds of documents, reports, and articles, and so recalling whether I had sent him this one specific document was extremely difficult. However, I was open with the police that *I* had downloaded the Al-Qaeda Training Manual for my studies and research.

After talk of the Al-Qaeda Training Manual had concluded in the first interview, the remainder of the questioning was about whether I was a practising Muslim, whether I prayed, what Hicham's and my political, ideological, and religious outlook on the world was, what modules and courses I was studying as part of my Master's in International Relations, and where I had studied for my Politics degree. By the time the first interview was terminated, and the tape-recording stopped, forty-five minutes had passed. The officers began arranging their paperwork and I was going to be led back to my cell. I was under the impression that once the interview had concluded, and I had given my side of the story, I would be free to leave. Here, I discovered that this was not the end of the process but rather the start. But what had Hicham or I done that had landed us in this situation? From the focus of the interview questions, it seemed that the entire inquiry, and our arrests, were connected to the Al-Qaeda Training Manual. But this left me more confused than anything else: how is it even possible to be arrested for having a declassified government document freely available on an American government website that is being used for my studies? In the entire interview, there was no opportunity for me to ask this question. I had assumed at some stage I would have the chance to ask but the interview had ended without the opportunity being given to me. As I was being escorted back to my cell, I asked DC West outside of the interview room: 'What will happen now? Have you arrested and detained me because I downloaded the Al-Qaeda Training Manual for my studies?' But DC West responded with a question of his own. 'Does the name Khaled Khaliq mean anything to you?' I had never heard of any such person. 'Who is Khalid Khaliq?,' I asked. 'Khalid Khaliq had a copy of the same Al-Qaeda Training Manual as you and he's in prison for fifteen years.'

* * *

Back in my cell, I began frantically pacing around with my hands tightly squeezing my bald head. I was trying to make sense of how a person who was studying International Relations and research-ing terrorism in the morning was, by night fall, being told that they could be facing fifteen years in prison for terrorism. This thought made me very angry as a surge of tears streamed down my face. But I tried to be optimistic. My lecturers, especially Rod Thornton, will explain to the police that my Master's disserta-tion is on al-Qaeda. Rod could also verify that only last month I had been accepted to study for a PhD under his supervision at the University of Nottingham, which was on al-Qaeda and armed Muslim groups. But then, an overwhelming feeling of fear had brought the pessimism and self-questioning back before I had even managed to wipe away my tears. Why would Rod Thornton – a retired and decorated UK army officer, who had been given a medal by the Queen for bravery and who had known me only for a few months – believe I was using the Al-Qaeda Training Manual for my research rather than for terrorism? Would he see past my brown skin, my beard, and my Muslimness? Would he still stand by me once he knew what I was being accused of? Would he not think, just like the police seemed to be thinking, that I'm using my studies as a 'cover' to hide some terrorist motive?

These questions and doubts were driven by nothing more than sheer confusion and fear. The reality, as far as Rod was concerned, was the total opposite. Yet, in that moment of total fear fuelled by

DC West's claim that I may be going to prison for fifteen years for terrorism, I had lost the ability to believe that anybody could see my innocence; that I was simply researching terrorism because I was working towards becoming an academic, not because I was a terrorist. In that moment after the interview had concluded, my trust in the UK, the country where I was born, raised, and educated, its institutions, its criminal justice system, its police service, its courts, and its people had shattered into a thousand tiny pieces. But, in that moment of fear and powerlessness, the dark irony is that there emerged a sense of liberation from the ideological shackles that had been placed on my mind and had made me internalise all sorts of naïve assumptions about the world and who the 'good guys' and 'bad guys' were. The world was not as black and white as I had assumed. The police and judicial system were not there simply to safeguard and protect the innocent from harm. A Muslim did not have to do much wrong to be viewed with suspicion or classified as a terrorist and disappeared into the matrix of counterterrorism. I felt that all my attempts to demonstrate that I was a 'good' British-Pakistani-Muslim citizen, who was dedicated to his education and was working towards becoming an academic no longer seemed to mean anything. The only thing that seemed to matter was my Muslimness, and how that connected me to terrorism in the eyes of the police.

Normally, I am not that religiously devout and only occasionally perform the obligatory five daily prayers known as *salah*. However, when I was in custody, I had wanted to do nothing more than pray *salah*. God is all I had in that moment of powerlessness and fear. But when the police offered me a prayer mat, I refused it. I did not want to do anything that would emphasise my Muslimness and perhaps risk the police interpreting my practice as something suspicious, something they could use to profile me as a 'radical' Muslim. Praying *salah* was too risky and therefore during the entire period I spent in solitary confinement, I prayed silently in my heart, making an active decision to show no sense of outward religiosity in case it was weaponised and used against me.

With DC West's remark – 'fifteen years in prison' – constantly replaying in my mind, the disbelief and crying as I paced around the cell were soon replaced by raw anger. I was livid that the reason I was in custody was connected to me researching terrorism and now being suspected of it. I approached the cell door, which was wide open. The custody sergeant was sat at the table alone. 'You're not going to believe this,' I said to him. 'Do you know why I am here?' He was never very talkative, and only responded when I asked a question or initiated a conversation. 'I have no idea,' he replied. 'I'm here because I downloaded the Al-Qaeda Training Manual for my studies from an American government website,' I angrily explained. But he tried to close the conversation down and would not react. 'Please don't tell me anything else,' he insisted. This added to my anger. This man was responsible for observing and policing my every move constantly from the moment I arrived, yet he was not interested in why I was here or that I was studying terrorism and was now being accused of it. 'I know you're not involved with the investigation,' I said with anger and frustration in my voice, 'but I'm telling you so you can understand that I am going through all this for what? A fucking document that's related to my studies!'

Around a year later, sometime in 2009, I began looking into Khalid Khaliq's case and discovered that DC West had misled me when he invoked the case outside of the interview room, and that he had done so in two important ways. Firstly, Khaliq had been imprisoned for possession of the Al-Qaeda Training Manual for sixteen months, not fifteen years. Why DC West said this I do not know for sure but I strongly believe that it was to sow confusion in my mind and weaken my ability to stay composed. And it worked. Secondly, Khalid Khaliq, who was associated with two of the London bombers, had been arrested by the police for possession of documents but was suspected of, and reportedly interrogated about, being the 'fifth' London suicide bomber.[1] The CPS had in fact claimed in court that they believed Khaliq was the 'fifth' bomber but there was not enough compelling evidence to prove this theory. He was charged and subsequently convicted for possessing the Al-Qaeda Training Manual (alongside two additional documents[2]) under Section 58 of the Terrorism Act 2000. By omitting this very important context, and by constructing both our cases as somehow being one and the same, DC West had, through seemingly deliberate misinformation, sent my mind into a state of terror.

7
Seven Interviews

Hicham and I were being detained in solitary confinement on separate wings of the second floor of Bridewell. The only time we saw one another was on the second day of detention at the Magistrate's Court. We both appeared before a district judge for a short hearing called to legally rubberstamp holding us in detention beyond three days. The walk to the court was interesting and amusing. I walked through a series of corridors and tunnels that ran below the Bridewell and directly into the court. I had two custody officers walking in front of me and two directly behind me. Stationed at every door of the corridors were uniformed custody officers who I had never seen before. They seemed to have been brought in as part of some additional security protocol. I remember muttering to myself: 'This lot think they've caught Bin Laden.'

When we arrived at the Magistrate's Court, we were led directly into a dock that was behind a thick glass wall. Hicham was already sat in the dock wearing a black suit, black shirt, and had his long hair tied into a ponytail. He had obviously been arrested after he had dressed for work. We smiled and briefly exchanged greetings. 'No talking,' one of the custody officers yelled. I remember asking myself how Hicham looked so calm and composed compared to the way I felt and probably looked. Within a few minutes, the hearing got underway and I attentively tried to listen to a superintendent make the case to the district judge that our pre-charge detention period should be extended. The police, he claimed, had seized a large amount of evidence, including twenty-one computers and electronic devices, from various locations that needed to be examined by the hi-tech Forensic Unit to see if we were terrorists. At the time of the hearing, the police were legally authorised to hold us in pre-charge detention for a total of twenty-eight days, though this has to be done incrementally in stages. The way the superintendent was making his pitch made it sound as if he was going to ask for the entire period in one go. But he requested an additional five days on top of the forty-eight hours the police had already authorised our detention for. Hicham and I were going to be detained until 20 May, and by this date, the police either had to charge us or release us from custody.[1]

When the superintendent was making his case to extend our detention, I was expecting the district judge to at least question the grounds for keeping us in custody but she authorised it without so much as a blink. In fact, according to the assistant chief constable who led the Gold Command for Operation Minerva, the strategic decision-making body set up to manage the fallout from the arrests, the district judge was 'complimentary' about the police operation.[2] So much for me naively thinking that the judiciary was there to serve as a 'check' on police power.

My solicitor Danny Hussey was present for the hearing, which was reassuring. Danny had travelled up from London on the morning of the second day of my detention, after being instructed by the lawyer Tayab Ali. Tayab was the lawyer responsible for coordinating the three pro-bono solicitors who were representing me and supporting my family. He had been referred to my family by my friend Waqar, a law graduate with an interest in politics and human rights law. I had asked the police to inform Waqar that I had been arrested since I did not want to alert my family that I was in detention but it later transpired that the police did not inform him. It was only when my older brother asked Waqar for a recommendation for a lawyer after the search of our home that he became aware of my arrest and detention. Based on Waqar's suggestion, my family contacted Tayab Ali late in the evening on day one of my detention. Without these critical family and community networks, my situation would have been far more desperate. Tayab subsequently appointed Danny Hussey to attend the Bridewell Detention Centre to represent me.

When I went into the first interview, I assumed that the more openly and honestly I spoke with the police, the quicker I would be cleared for release. This was a naïve assumption on my part. After listening to a recording of my first interview, which I had given in his absence, Danny instructed the custody officer to bring me into the consultation room. After a brief introduction and exchange, Danny asked me in a very softly spoken tone as if somebody may hear us: 'Rizwaan, can you tell me what the purpose of a police interview is?' I told him that it was to get to the truth of a matter so if somebody was innocent, they could be cleared and released from custody. I now know how incredibly naïve this must have sounded. But Danny was an experienced lawyer and had worked on a number of serious and complex cases, including terrorism cases, and had probably heard it all before. Without saying a word, he pushed a police document that was in front of him across the table towards me and pointed to a written passage. I read it and discovered that the goal of the police inquiry was to collect evidence through interviews and other means, such as searches, to help the police build a case that was strong enough to charge and prosecute in the courts for terrorism. The police, in other words, would use my words in the interview, as well as other pieces of information to build a case *against* me. Now it made sense why DC Shankey, in the first interview, had told me 'we would ask that you do speak in detail'. The belief that 'I have nothing to hide so I have nothing to fear' does not help when you are being interviewed under caution by the police. In fact, the more you speak, the more material you provide for the police to analyse and use *against* you.

The day after the hearing, Danny had a prearranged commitment and had to return to London. He was deeply apologetic and explained that Tayab had already arranged for a replacement solicitor who he assured me was experienced in working on terrorism cases. This new lawyer, Danny explained, would remain with me until the police and Crown Prosecution Service (CPS) had decided whether they would release or charge me. No more chopping and changing solicitors.

* * *

On the morning of my third day, my new lawyer Nadeem Afzal arrived. He was a towering figure, easily over six foot, with a full-head of hair that was starting to whiten in places. He was wearing a dark blue pin-striped suit that had clearly been tailored, thick black spectacles, a crisp white shirt that seemed to have been professionally pressed, and a dark blue tie. He was confident, quick-witted, funny, and very attentive. In our introductory meeting, it became clear that Nadeem had worked on a number of terrorism cases, and had considerable experience in representing people held in pre-charge detention. He also held a very thorough understanding of the suite of terrorism powers and laws the police had access to when it came to dealing with suspects. He also knew some of the police officers from the West Midlands Counter-Terrorism Unit from other cases he had worked on, including DC West. Nadeem was exactly the sort of person I needed by my side. His experience and knowledge were not only reassuring but his presence made me feel like it would put the police and CPS on notice that by having an experienced legal representative by my side, I was no longer taking anything for granted.

Once Nadeem had familiarised himself with the facts of the case and studied what I had told the police in my first interview, his counsel was similar to what Danny had advised. I was told that I should exercise my right to remain silent in all of the interviews from here on. Nadeem explained that I had gone above and beyond in telling the police everything about the Al-Qaeda Training Manual in my first interview and there was nothing really left to add. He also pointed out that I had explained, in detail, my reason for downloading and possessing the document and answered every other question the police had asked me during that first interview. Talking further in the remaining interviews, he felt, could potentially incriminate me in unnecessary ways. If something changed and he felt it was important to clarify a point or explain something to the officers, he would counsel me accordingly.

His legal advice, I discovered very quickly, was sound. Other than academic material on armed Muslim groups, geopolitics and political science, the police really had nothing of any substance that suggested I was anything other than a Muslim student of International Relations who was studying terrorism and armed Muslim groups. Many of their questions seemed to be about building an intelligence profile of me of the 'mosaic'[3] variety or confirming things that the police already knew the answer to and, in other instances, were seemingly asking them to justify the extended detention period that had been authorised by the magistrate.

I was questioned, for example, about my reasons for going to university in Manchester and why I had studied Politics for my undergraduate degree.[4] I was interrogated on whether I had attended any political protests as a student and, in particular, the demonstrations in London against the publication of offensive cartoons of the Prophet Muhammed (peace be upon him) that was organised by Al-Muhajiroun.[5] I was also shown photographs of a number of different items that had been seized during the search of my car and my home, and quizzed about them, including the tents belonging to my hunger-striking friends which, I was told by the officers, had graffiti which read 'Free Tibet', 'Free Palestine', and 'Stop Funding Murder' emblazoned all over them.[6] 'Clearly tents are used for camping,' DC Shankey said, 'but I will ask you, what is the purpose of these tents? Do you go on outward bound camping exercises? Is there a trip planned or have you just been on a trip?'[7] Of course, based on Nadeem's legal advice, I remained silent.

I was also questioned about a satirical pamphlet called 'Picnic at Guantanamo' that I had purchased from Camden market in London in 2006, pop music CDs, posters on my wall of Dr Martin Luther King, and a novelty t-shirt gifted to me by a Lebanese course-mate which read 'Don't panic, I'm Islamic' on the front of it.[8] I was also asked about the subjects I took for my GCSEs at high school, who I spoke with on MSN messenger, and asked to explain how academic referencing techniques worked.[9] The police also wanted to know what my travel record was like, and asked specifically whether I'd been travelling around Europe, Iraq, or Pakistan, particularly the border area with Afghanistan 'where there is trouble at the moment', as DC West put it to me.[10]

What became clear to me from the moment I began exercising my right to silence was that the police began to reinterpret and recycle some of what I had told them in the first interview and, in some instances, were trying to construct me as a liar, perhaps in order to provoke a response or force me to clarify what I had meant in the hope I would break my silence and, by extension, incriminate myself in the process. In the first interview, for example, one of the officers asked whether I still had a copy of the Al-Qaeda Training Manual on my laptop. I told them that I was *unsure*. Recently, I explained, I tried to access the manual for a piece of work I was doing but I could not locate it on my laptop. I was therefore unsure if the manual was still there. However, once the results from the hi-tech forensic analysis of my laptop were in, the interviewing officers gleefully informed me that the Al-Qaeda Training Manual was indeed still on my laptop. 'You said you couldn't find it,' DC Shankey said. 'Now that was clearly a lie, but I would be interested to know why you felt the need to lie about it, not being able to find that document on your laptop.'[11] Of course, I was not lying about being unable to locate the Al-Qaeda Training Manual on my laptop but the mere fact that I had tried to be as honest with the police by saying I was *unsure* whether it was still there was now being used to accuse me of being a liar. During the seven interviews in which I remained silent, I knew that it did not therefore matter whether I had cooperated with the police and told them everything as honestly and as best as I could remember in the first interview. They would still depict me in whichever way suited them and would ask questions and make statements in a provocative manner to compel me into breaking my silence and, by extension, incriminate myself.

In another instance, the police were repeatedly asking me whether I had made copies of the Al-Qaeda Training Manual or shared it with anyone apart from Hicham. In the first interview, I had answered this question with a categoric 'No', but I was now being asked the same question again. This is because the police and the CPS were considering whether a charge of 'disseminating terrorist publications' could potentially be used if charging me for 'collection of information useful to terrorists' proved impossible. On reflection, I was glad to have exercised my right to silence, though there were also several instances where I had to resist the very strong urge to speak and tell the police how ridiculous their entire case and line of questioning was.

*　　*　　*

During their searches, the police had found a business card for a Kurdish academic and an airline ticket receipt from Istanbul to London in the name of a course colleague who I shall refer to through the alias of Mohammed. They also found a student union card and a Kurdish identification card in Mohammed's name. Mohammed was a foreign student from Kurdistan and a coursemate of mine who was also studying International Relations. He had gifted me his laptop bag after upgrading his own and seeing the poor condition mine was in. I had never known that his items and some of his documents remained in a concealed pocket of the laptop bag. I had assumed he had emptied the bag before gifting it to me. When the police searched the bag and discovered his documents, they asked a whole series of questions in one of the interviews. They wanted to know why I was in possession of them and whether I had used the documents to travel to Istanbul or Kurdistan purporting to be Mohammed. 'It shouldn't be difficult to identify Mohammed,' DC Shankey had told me in the interview.[12] 'We'll simply go to the college [University of Nottingham],' he said and 'they'll go through their records, [and] if he's a current student, we should be able to speak to him quite quickly.'[13] I knew that police had either made these inquiries already and wanted me to confirm matters *or* they wanted to see what my account of these documents was in order to see if it was consistent with what they had learnt from their own inquires. But I was not going to tell them anything, since everything I said would probably be manipulated and used against me. Now that I understood what they were trying to do, I had gone from trusting the police wholeheartedly in the first interview to having no trust in them whatsoever. This mistrust would increase as the questions became more irrelevant and the words from my first interview were being recycled, distorted, and read back to me.

Some interviews were spent purely on questioning me on academic documents that had been forensically recovered from my laptop, and which formed part of the list of evidence against me. One such document, which was one of the three documents reported to the police by the university, was a journal article titled 'Killing in the Name of Islam: Al-Qaeda's Justification for 9/11'. 'Rizwaan,' DC Shankey asked, 'do you want to make any comment? If you can be helpful as to the origins of this document, where it has come from, why indeed you had sent it [to Hicham] would be helpful.'[14] I remembered downloading this journal article but I remained silent. Nadeem, however, did not know it was a journal article and was probably curious about it based on its title. He asked the officers who had authored it. 'It's not somebody we are familiar with,' DC West replied.[15] Nadeem immediately put his hand out to receive a printed version of the article whilst the questions continued. 'I am so sorry,' Nadeem interrupted. 'It does actually say here; they are professors of International Studies at Rhodes College, Tennessee.'[16] I was overjoyed. Finally, something had been said to the officers that will have let them know the questions and statements they were making were both meaningless and vacuous.

During the same interview, there was a document called 'Maria's Methods' that caught the curiosity of the police. 'Is this [document] something you have constructed yourself?', DC Shankey asked me. 'Who's Maria?', DC West added. 'Is she a friend of yours?'[17] I did not know this during my time in custody, but by the time I was being asked 'Who's Maria' on day four of my detention, and fighting the urge to tell them that Maria Ryan is an academic at the University of Nottingham who specialises in the study of US foreign policy and the CIA, the police had already interviewed Maria and knew that she was advising me on my research. But, in the moment of the interview, when I was being asked 'Who's Maria', my mind was elsewhere. I was picturing a scene from the movie *In the Name of the Father* that I had serendipitously watched a few years earlier. The movie tells the true story of a miscarriage of justice involving the 'Guildford Four'. In one of the film's most powerful scenes, Special Branch officers are interrogating and physically abusing Gerry Conlon (played by Daniel Day-Lewis), questioning him about his whereabouts on the night of the 1974 Guildford pub bombing. 'Who's Marian?', one of the Special Branch officers asks Conlon in a thick Cockney accent. 'Who's Marian?', he then screams. 'I'm going to keep asking you the question until you give me a fucking answer. Who's Marian?' Though there was none of the physical or verbal abuse of the sort cinematised in the movie, the question 'Who's Maria' reminded me of this scene and, more importantly, signalled how people had found themselves in prison accused of terrorism despite being innocent. Though the officer's question – 'Who's Maria?' – may have seemed trivial, my awareness and understanding of terrorism miscarriages of justice made me realise that I could take nothing for granted, no matter how ridiculous it sounded or felt.

My desire to break my silence was constantly being tested. In one interview, in fact, I had to work extremely hard to remain silent. The entire focus was on my PhD proposal that I had submitted to the Economic and Social Research Council (ESRC) for a scholarship to research global armed Muslim groups. The officers almost spent the entire interview reading the proposal to me aloud, word-for-word, from the very start to the very end. They then made a series of statements dressed as questions, which, again, seemed to be about provoking me into breaking my silence. 'If you were intent on using the Al-Qaeda Training Manual as a reference, why didn't you make reference to it in this paper?,' DC Shankey asked with my PhD proposal in his hand. 'Why isn't that on your list of references?'[18] Despite strongly wanting to tell him that this is not how literature reviews work in academic research, and that reading a document does not automatically lead to it being cited, I had to remain silent. But the officers would answer their own questions followed by another question. 'Because you know, and I know, Rizwaan, that that Al-Qaeda Training Manual is not an appropriate reference source is it? Isn't that the case?'[19]

I did not know this at the time but by day four of my detention, academics Maria Ryan, Rod Thornton, and Bettina Renz had all independently explained the nature of academic and postgraduate research to the officers and highlighted how academic-referencing and sources worked. Yet, somehow, the police wanted to hear my view on the matter too. The desire to break my silence so I could school the officers was extremely strong but I maintained silence. It was more important that I protected myself from having my words used against me than the need to educate them. By therefore acting on sound legal advice and not speaking in the seven interviews that I sat through with Danny and Nadeem, I lessened the chance of incriminating myself and compelled the police to focus their inquiries on the one thing that their investigation rested upon in its entirety: the Al-Qaeda Training Manual.

8

A Convenient Witness

The task of securing witness statements to help support the police narrative that I had the Al-Qaeda Training Manual for terrorist purposes was complicated by the statements of three academics who knew what my research was focused on, and had been supporting my studies since September 2007. They were my mentor Dr Maria Ryan, who is situated in the Department of American and Canadian Studies, Dr Rod Thornton, who was my Master's dissertation and upcoming PhD supervisor at the time, and Dr Bettina Renz, who was my personal tutor. Her role was to provide me with professional and personal support if I ever needed it. Both Rod and Bettina were situated in the School of Politics and International Relations. All three academics had been interviewed by the police whilst I was in custody but neither Nadeem nor I were aware of what they had said. The police withheld their comments and statements from us.

Maria was one of the first academics to be approached by the police whilst I was in custody. This was on the second day of my detention. The police spent around one hour in her office in the Trent Building. They informed her that it was the possession of documents that had triggered Operation Minerva and my arrest. On discovering this, she laughed and explained to the police that 'there had obviously been a big mistake'.[1] She informed the officers that the documents would clearly be related to my research, which she had spent considerable amounts of time discussing with me.[2] In fact, Maria was one of the first academics I had engaged with about my prospective research when I joined the university in September 2007 since her subject specialism is US foreign policy. I had actually asked Maria to supervise my dissertation but since she was in a different department, this would be a near impossibility. She did, however, dedicate significant time and energy to discussing ideas, recommending readings, and giving me guidance on my research methods.

The interviewing officers were sceptical about Maria's explanation. They told her not to be so sure that my possession of the Al-Qaeda Training Manual was so innocent. In a statement she later gave, Maria recalled:

> The officers made a number of comments which appeared to have the purpose of leading me to cast doubt on the legitimacy of Rizwaan's possession of the [Al-Qaeda Training] manual. They said several times that I had to keep an open mind about why Rizwaan would have possession of such material, and that people were often surprised to discover that someone was a terrorist.[3]

The police officers did not mention Hicham by name but they told Maria that another man had been arrested as part of Operation Minerva in the hope that she would tell them who I was mixing with.

> It appeared as though they were trying to elicit from me whether I knew who [the other person] might be. They were asking me to name people who Rizwaan might be involved with. They were trying to probe whether there was anyone I was suspicious of.[4]

The officers also questioned Maria about my 'politics' and what her understanding of my 'views were on US foreign policy and Israeli foreign policy' too.[5] In addition to this, they questioned Maria about my lifestyle:

> They asked me what Rizwaan was like personally, and questions which appeared to concern whether he was religious or not, such as whether he drank alcohol, whether he prayed, and whether he smoked.[6]

The police were also curious about my views on suicide bombings and questioned Maria on this. When Maria told them 'Rizwaan was opposed to the actions of such people,' and that there was not 'an archetypal suicide bomber,' one of the officers told her that suicide bombers 'may appear to be "westernised"'.[7] Given the previous questions they had asked Maria about lifestyle choices, it is obvious that the police were trying to determine whether I could be a suicide bomber.

* * *

Bettina Renz, whose research is focused on international security, was interviewed by the police in her capacity as my personal tutor and the Master's dissertation convenor; a role that consists of appointing students to an appropriate supervisor so they can advise students on their research. When Bettina was informed that I had been arrested for having the Al-Qaeda Training Manual, she knew that I would almost certainly have had it in my possession for research purposes. I had discussed my research with her on a number of occasions. I had also requested for her to appoint Rod to be my supervisor since he was the university's sole expert on the study of terrorism and insurgency. Bettina told the interviewing police officers 'why' I would possess material that I had downloaded from the internet: 'for research, for his dissertation, and PhD'.[8]

By the time Bettina was interviewed by the police, I had been in custody for four days, and the way the police had described the document to Bettina – as 'illegal material' downloaded from the internet – led her to assume that the document was far more serious and dangerous than it was. Would somebody really be in counterterrorism custody for having a document you can buy from the high street or loan from a library? In a statement she gave later, she explained:

> I had made [an assumption] that the manual was considerably more dangerous than I now know it to be. I made that assumption based on the fact that counter terrorism police officers, who I assumed would have a very good understanding of the manual, were telling me that it was 'illegal material' and that it was the reason Rizwaan had been arrested and detained for a number of days.[9]

Despite not knowing how innocuous and easily accessible the document was, Bettina did her best to explain to the police the process of postgraduate research as a way of contextualising why

I would need access to documents they considered suspicious. In her police statement, she said:

> When researching for dissertations, especially PhDs, you have to read anything you can get your hands on, even if, initially, it doesn't appear to be connected to your subject. Students will always be looking for something that no one has ever used or written about before.[10]

When she eventually discovered that it was *one* document alone that had triggered Operation Minerva and the arrests, she told the interviewing officers: 'I am surprised at the reaction. I consider it drastic.'[11]

*   *   *

Two counterterrorism officers arrived to speak with Rod Thornton on 16 May. At this stage, I had been in detention for two days. Before arriving in academia, Rod had served in the Infantry Regiment of the British army for nine years, including a three-year stint in an intelligence role where he worked alongside the police, the Royal Ulster Constabulary. On seeing the officers who arrived to speak with him, it was clear to Rod that rather than being sharp-suited agents from the TV series *Spooks*, these officers seemed to be ordinary ex-army soldiers like him. He felt a mutual bond with them and tried to be as helpful as possible. The police spent three hours with Rod in his office on 16 May, and then a further two hours on 17 May. But, throughout this entire time, something very odd happened. The officers had failed to tell him what documents had triggered my arrest. Based on the account of two counterterrorism officers, the instruction to withhold this information from Rod was given by the senior investigating officer who was running Operation Minerva.[12]

What made Rod's conversation with the police even more peculiar is that the document that *was* mentioned to him was an unrelated bomb-making manual known as the *Encyclopaedia of Afghan Jihad*. This document spans thousands of pages across eleven volumes and contains detailed instructions on a whole host of military and bomb-making techniques, including eight chapters with 'diagrams and formulas to handle manufacture, and detonate explosives'.[13] It had nothing to do with Operation Minerva or Hicham and my arrest in any respect whatsoever. Much later, Rod described how he was misled into believing that this unrelated bomb-making manual had triggered Operation Minerva:

> One of the documents to which the officers referred was the *Encyclopaedia of Afghan Jihad*. The mention of the *Encyclopaedia of Afghan Jihad* gave me great cause for concern. It is a very large document, which contains considerable tactical terrorist information including, I thought, detailed instructions on how to make the hydrogen peroxide explosives used in the 7/7 and 21/7 attacks in London in 2005. I could see no reason why Rizwaan should have this document in connection with his research and told the officers as much. I assumed that Rizwaan has been arrested and was still in detention after all this time, then the police must have had the opportunity to consider the document and assess it as sufficiently dangerous to justify their actions. The mention of the *Encyclopaedia of Afghan Jihad* served only to confirm that assumption, and my understanding at that time was that Rizwaan had been found in possession of that document or a variant of it.
>
> On this basis, I explained, when asked by the officers, that there was no reason for Rizwaan to have that sort of document in connection with his research. As far as I can recall, after some discussion, we agreed that the correct wording was that such a document [the *Encyclopaedia of Afghan Jihad*] would be illegitimate for research.[14]

By mentioning an entirely different and unrelated document to Rod, the police misled him into formally saying that the document I had been arrested for was 'illegitimate for research'. Armed with Rod's statement, the senior investigating officer responsible for running Operation Minerva then went to the Gold Group, the strategic decision-making body made up of senior officers that had been set up to manage the fallout from the arrests, and told them, according to official meeting minutes, that:

[Rod] Thornton did state that, to his belief, the document in question was a tactical document and the area of study relating to detained person No. 2 was in the area of strategic political issues and therefore his [Rod Thornton's] view was that this material was probably not relevant to his [Rizwaan Sabir's] area of study.[15]

Of course, Rod had said no such thing about the Al-Qaeda Training Manual being a 'tactical document'. Neither did he discuss this document's relevance to my studies. How could he when the actual document I had been arrested for was never mentioned either by me or the police to Rod? What Rod *did* say in his official police witness statement is that 'I would only use strategic items on the internet as this is my subject. Anything tactical, I would not look at simply because I don't need to for what I do.'[16] Rod also told the police that 'there are certain things on the internet I would not read because they would not interest me i.e., tactical items or would be inappropriate'.[17]

During the process of conducting postgraduate research, students collect a vast amount of data, often quite useless and irrelevant, to see if they can find something unique in order to demonstrate innovation and originality. I told the police this in my first interview when they asked me to comment on the Al-Qaeda Training Manual.[18] Bettina had told the police the same thing and corroborated what I had already told them. Maria had also tried to explain to the police how academic research functions:

It was clear to me from speaking to the officers that they had very little understanding of postgraduate research. I tried to explain to them that postgraduate students were expected to make an original contribution to knowledge ... and to that end it would be very important that Rizwaan sought to find primary sources in order to inform his research. Strangely, they seem surprised by this information, and they asked me if there was any way that they could prove that this was what postgraduate work involved. I have to say that I found this question somewhat difficult to answer; I could not think of something to which one could point to prove that this is the case; it is the nature of postgraduate work itself. I tried to explain this to officers.[19]

Now, Rod, my dissertation and upcoming PhD supervisor, and the university's sole expert on terrorism and insurgency, was telling the police the same thing in his official police witness statement too:

> Students look for kudos/one-upmanship in their research, trying to find that piece of original research that others have not. Professors like to see how students do in their research, how far and deep they dig for it.[20]

Despite not being told what the actual document I had been arrested for was, Rod understood that it would most likely be connected to my studies and my research, and my desire to be creative in a way that would earn me a scholarship for my upcoming PhD. Though I had been accepted to study for a PhD the month prior to my arrest, in April 2008, I had not been awarded a scholarship and was having to work harder to improve my chances of securing it. Rod told the police this as a way of contextualising *why* I may have accessed materials they considered illegal. 'Rizwaan has not got funding for his PhD this year,' he told them. 'He therefore knows he has to prove himself better than he is.'[21]

Rod had also told the police that my Master's dissertation was focused on al-Qaeda, which should have helped to provide further context to why I may have material the police considered dangerous. He also supplied a copy of my written dissertation proposal to the police that I had titled 'Smoking Out al-Qaeda: America's Response to Iraq's "Jihadis"'. On receiving the proposal, an officer immediately rushed over to the School of Politics and International Relations administration office and used the fax machine to send it to his superiors. But, despite the context, clarity, and evidence that Rod was supplying to the police despite not being told what document I had in my possession, the senior investigating officer told the Gold Group that Rod had confirmed the document I had in my possession and I was being investigated for was 'not relevant' to my studies. In his civil claim statement, Rod describes what would have happened if the police had told him what the *actual* document that had triggered Operation Minerva was:

If, when I was asked initially by the police about the document in connection with which Rizwaan had been arrested, they had given me a copy of the manual, or even told me its proper name, I could have carried out some brief research on the internet and would have been able to explain that it is a commonplace source for research into al-Qaeda.[22]

During the course of this brief research, Rod would have been able to tell the police:

> I do not consider the [Al-Qaeda training] manual to be an 'illegitimate' document ... It has been cited in many authoritative works on Al-Qaeda, and it is a document to which students are referred in standard terrorism textbooks used on undergraduate courses. It is nothing like the *Encyclopaedia of Afghan Jihad*, which is a different sort of document.[23]

All the comments and information Rod was sharing with the police, similar to what Maria and Bettina had independently told them, was corroborating what I had told the police in my first interview too. However, rather than it absolving me of suspicion, it seemingly had the opposite effect. The police set out to search for someone who would outright say that the Al-Qaeda Training Manual was an inappropriate and illegal text for research purposes. After some frantic searching, they found a man for the job.

*   *   *

Bernard McGuirk is a Professor of Romance Literature in the Department of Modern Languages at the University of Nottingham. He had initially come onto the police's radar when Hicham's line-manager had contacted him for advice when she discovered the three documents that triggered our arrests. McGuirk's initial view of the manual was that it was illegal. Now, the police wanted him to repeat that claim in an official police witness statement to help justify the launching of the police operation and support the narrative that my defence for possessing the Al-Qaeda Training Manual was contested by academics to the Gold Group. A statement from a 'Professor' would suffice for this task, irrespective of the fact that Rod, Bettina, and Maria all had research interests and expertise in matters of security, conflict, and terrorism compared to this Professor of Romance Literature. Academic titles and accolades seemed more important for the police than actual subject expertise. In his official police witness statement, which largely comprised comments around Hicham, McGuirk finally said what the police wanted to hear: 'It was clear to me that possession of such a document was in fact illegal.'[24]

I had never heard of Bernard McGuirk when I was in custody. When the pre-interview disclosure arrived, it said that I would be questioned on what McGuirk had told the police. I was confused and angry. I knew McGuirk was not associated with the School of Politics and International Relations. I also knew he did not have anything to do with the study of terrorism. If he did, it would have been a near certainty that I would know him because I had spent some time researching the academics at Nottingham who worked on this area. Nadeem read the pre-interview disclosure aloud to me in the consultation room, which included the following text:

[Your client] will be asked about comments made by Bernard McGuirk, a senior member of the University of Nottingham who has the opinion that all members of the university should be aware of what was and was not legitimate material and that this training manual in question does not fit into the category of normal research documentation.

I was livid. 'Who is this guy, and what qualifies him to comment on the Al-Qaeda Training Manual?,' I angrily shouted at Nadeem. 'And where the fuck is Rod's statement?' Of course, Rod's statement, as well as Bettina's and Maria's statements, were not complementing the police investigation since they had verified what I had already told the police. It therefore comes as no surprise that they were all being withheld from us. Yet, the statement of the academic who was supporting the police line was produced as if it were a rabbit from a magician's hat.

'Earlier today, the police have spoken to a guy called Bernard McGuirk who is employed at the University of Nottingham since September 1978 in the School of Modern Languages,' DC West said in my sixth interview. '[He] has been at various times the Head of Department in Hispanic Studies, Head of School of Critical Theory, and Director of a Research Centre, a centre for the study of post-conflict cultures.' I remember thinking that not even one of these positions were related to my area of research yet McGuirk's titles were being cited to give him a sense of importance. 'He has said, it is clear to him that the possession of such a document was in itself illegal,'[25] DC West continued. 'Sorry,' Nadeem interrupted. 'What was that introduction again?' Nadeem was clearly just as unconvinced as I was that this professor of romance literature was being relied upon to comment on the Al-Qaeda Training Manual, especially its legality. 'What he is saying,' DC West clarified, 'is that the Al-Qaeda Training Manual is not a document which in his opinion should be used to form any part of any research for any studies of students at the University of Nottingham.'[26] 'Mr West,' Nadeem inquired, 'are you putting him forward as an expert?' 'I'm not putting him forward as an expert,' came the reply.

Then, finally, the question that had been running through my mind throughout the entire interview and before it was asked by Nadeem: 'Have you taken a statement from Bettina Renz or Rod Thornton?' Finally, I thought to myself, we can get some clarity on what the people who matter in this case are saying. 'I think there might be statements by those two,' DC West said. 'Those names are familiar to me. I've heard those names mentioned to me.'[27] That is all that was said about Rod and Bettina during the interview and my entire detention period. Nothing else. I was led to believe that the only person who had been formally interviewed by the police, whose statements were informing the inquiry and would form a central part of the police and CPS decision around whether to charge or release me, would be Professor Bernard McGuirk, who had been given prime importance.

The officer who oversaw and managed the police interviews whilst I was in custody was Detective Sergeant Wong. He was a 'Tier 5' interview coordinator, meaning he is trained to the highest level in managing and coordinating suspect and witness interviews on complex police investigations. DS Wong was aware what Rod and Bettina had told the police. During the course of a later inquiry titled 'Operation Carpatus', where the Independent Police Complaints Commission (IPCC) were forced to direct Greater Manchester Police to investigate complaints that had been made by

Rod and me into the handling of the arrests and the issues around police witness statements, DS Wong made a telling remark. He told the inquiry that whilst Rod and Bettina's witness statements 'did sway to support Mr Sabir's account, they were not specific'.[28] Of course, it was impossible for Bettina and Rod to be 'specific' since the police were keeping both of them, especially Rod, in the dark. Had the police not misled Rod about what document I had been arrested for, their statements, especially Rod's, *would* have been specific. 'The statement of Professor McGuirk,' DS Wong told the Carpatus Inquiry, 'was significant because he was experienced in conducting and advising people on research.'[29] This is like saying that a dentist is a suitable person to advice on matters of heart surgery because dentists conduct surgery too.

The police seemed to have had their suspicions and a hypothesis, and were relying only on those people whose statement and sentiments supported both. As the hours and days in detention passed, I was led to believe that nobody was issuing statements that supported or verified what I had told the police. Nadeem kept reminding me that, despite this, the police had nothing other than one document to suggest that I was a terrorist. But, no matter how much I tried to remain optimistic, being a Muslim in the face of sweeping terrorism laws made me very doubtful.

9
The Decision

On the sixth night of detention, 19 May, my levels of anxiety and fear were perhaps at their most intense. Nadeem had gone to his hotel for the night and promised to return earlier than usual the next morning. Sometime late into the night, one of the custody officers came to my cell. I could hear him coming before he had even reached the door because his keys would always rattle. However, rather than peering through the flap for his usual 30-minute check-up, he unlocked and opened the door. 'Your lawyer's here to see you,' he said. Why had Nadeem returned this late into the night to see me? As I stood up and approached the green metal cell-door, in the corridor I could see a young Asian man stood there, wearing a beige suit, spectacles, and a short goatee-beard. I had never seen him before but I knew exactly who he was based on my earlier conversation with Nadeem. It was Tayab Ali.

Recognising the difficulties that Muslim families experienced when their loved ones were detained for extended periods of time, in addition to assigning a dedicated solicitor, Tahir, to support my family, Tayab had travelled from London to meet with them so he could explain how the legal processes in relation to terrorism cases worked and offer any reassurances. This was a critical task since my family, like myself, had no real-life understanding or experience of policing, the courts, or the prison system. We had never needed to know about such things. What made the legal support my family and I were receiving from Tayab and Tahir quite remarkable, other than their legal knowledge and experience, is that their work was not financially covered by legal aid. Only Nadeem, who provided me with representation at Bridewell, was modestly paid for his time through legal aid. Tayab and Tahir were working on my case, and supporting my family, out of their own pocket and for the sake of the public good ('pro-bono').

Their entire work ethic, dedication, and raison d'être stood in stark contrast to the 'fat cat' lawyer stereotype.

On his return to London, he had stopped by to meet with me at Bridewell. Tayab and I went into the consultation room and after a brief introduction, I asked him questions about my family. We then spoke about the merits of the police case against me, Tayab emphasising that he was quietly optimistic that no charges would be brought and that I would be released. However, he could not be completely sure since the UK's counterterrorism laws, especially Section 58 of the Terrorism Act 2000, the offence that Hicham and I were facing being charged with, was disturbingly broad.

The Section 58 offence criminalises the 'collection of information' that is said to be useful to somebody who is preparing or committing terrorism, and has been the second most commonly used offence to charge and convict people for terrorism since 2001.[1] The offence ignores a person's reason or intention for collecting information useful for terrorism.[2] It is the nature of the information that is criminalised by the offence, not the reason why a person collects such information.[3] For example, you could be a university student, an academic, a journalist, a publisher, a librarian, or even a lawyer who collects information considered 'useful to terrorists' for professional or research purposes but find yourself being arrested, detained, and interrogated as a terrorist yourself. It is the sort of information you possess which is criminalised, not what you plan to do with it.

The offence does include a 'defence' clause, meaning that if you are being considered for charges, as Hicham and I were, you can defend your collection of information on the grounds that you have a 'reasonable excuse' for doing so. However, the expectation, or 'burden of proof' as it is called, was on me to prove that my possession of the Al-Qaeda Training Manual was *not* connected to terrorism. In my first police interview, when I explained this to the police, this was my 'defence'. I was using the document for my postgraduate studies, not terrorism.

Due to the existence of this 'defence' clause, the Section 58 offence may be viewed as being a fair and proportionate law, one in which the police and CPS cannot use to throw somebody in jail on a whim. However, in practice, something very critical is overlooked in this respect. I could only mount a defence *after* I had been arrested on suspicion of terrorism and found myself in an interrogation room being quizzed by the police. I was asked nothing about the Al-Qaeda Training Manual until I entered the interview room on the first night of my detention. Yet, before my defence was offered, I had been photographed, fingerprinted, footprinted, was having my home searched after the courts had issued a warrant, my family had been removed from their home, and was having my name added to a whole series of police data-bases and systems for terrorism. I could only offer a defence *after* a whole series of events had been triggered by the police and Oper-ation Minerva was in full swing. And, when I did get a chance to offer my defence in the interview room, I was being questioned whilst a CCTV camera monitored me, a recording device logged my every word and every silence, and the interrogating officers drew an 'adverse inference', that is to say, were judging, inter-preting, and analysing every utterance, silence, and behavioural reaction of mine, to see if I was a terrorist who was feigning inno-cence by claiming to be a student. The defence clause cannot stop a person being arrested, detained, and investigated by the police. Neither can it stop a person from being charged. The police and CPS could charge me, take me to trial, and let a judge and jury decide whether my 'defence' for possessing the Al-Qaeda Training Manual was 'reasonable'.

What increased the fear in my mind that this could and probably would happen is that the police had withheld the statements of Rod, Bettina, and Maria from Nadeem and me so we had no idea that all three had corroborated what I had already told the police. The only statement that was being cited to support the police view that the Al-Qaeda Training Manual was irrelevant for my studies belonged to the Professor of Romance Literature. I was therefore being led to believe that I had no support and that my life was doomed. And it worked. I no longer felt like I had the privilege of being a postgraduate student at a prestigious university and felt, perhaps, what so many other Muslims and people of colour must feel when they do not have the support or backing of people with social standing to corroborate their cries of innocence: angry, lonely, let down, and afraid.

Though Tayab was quietly confident that I would be released, he could take no liberties given the broadness of the law and the broader political context within which counterterrorism policing and policy functions. So, in order to therefore ensure no nasty surprises awaited me, he advised that I should mentally and emotionally prepare in case I was charged. I could feel my tears welling up but I was trying my utmost to remain composed. He explained that if I were charged, I would most likely be taken to a high-security 'category A' prison, either HMP Belmarsh in London or HMP Woodhill in Milton Keynes. He assured me that if this happened, he would work to get me released on bail as soon as possible. He also explained some basic prison etiquette, rules, what I could expect on arrival, and how I should conduct myself if I was to be remanded. At both of these prisons, he explained, Muslims made up a large proportion of the prisoners, especially for terrorism. 'Make sure you attend *Jumma*,' he said, referring to Friday prayers. 'You'll meet people there and you'll make friends.' 'What should I tell people why I'm in prison?,' I asked. 'Tell them the truth. There are a lot of people in prison for terrorism who have not done much wrong.' The conversation was triggering for me and I recall thinking how could somebody go from being a Master's student who was studying terrorism to preparing himself to be charged and remanded in a high-security prison as a terrorist? How was this even allowed to happen? Is this a dream? As Tayab was about to leave, I thanked him for looking out for my family and for coming to visit me, and embraced him. As soon as I did, all the tears and emotions I had been supressing came uncontrollably pouring out.

* * *

The prospect of being charged was something that had always been real, but I had constantly told myself that my arrest was one big mistake. Somehow, that after explaining matters to the police, things would all go back to 'normal'. But, understanding the broadness of counterterrorism laws, and how terrorism cases were political meant that the police and CPS could charge me and let the courts decide whether I was innocent or guilty. I understood that my fate was at the mercy of a system of power that operated according to bureaucratic processes, systems, and laws which viewed Muslim identity as a proxy for terrorism. What frustrated and angered me was the inhumanity of the whole process. The police officers and CPS officials who were going to decide whether I should be charged for terrorism and disappeared into the prison system were people who knew nothing about me other than what they had inferred from the evidence they had secured, the 'adverse inferences' they had drawn, and the statements they had taken from academics, who, I was led to believe, were not speaking out in my defence or corroborating anything I had told the police in my first interview.

In my cell, I reflected on how I had always tried my best to be a kind and hard-working person, a sort of ambassador for British-born Pakistani Muslims, but my efforts, I felt, amounted to nothing in the face of a system that was built on Islamophobic stereotyping and racial profiling; one that was blinded by a deep-rooted suspicion and mistrust of Muslims. I thought about the stories of prisoners caught by the Americans and sent to Guantanamo Bay as part and parcel of the same global 'war on terror'. I reflected on the cases of Irish people and families who had found themselves wrongly convicted for crimes they did not commit and spent decades in prison for. As I thought about these things, laying on the thin blue mattress knowing that my fate and life was now being decided by others, I sobbed and asked God for help.

* * *

The morning of 20 May, I was exhausted from the racing and crippling dread which had stayed with me for the entire night. I did not sleep and was eagerly awaiting Nadeem's arrival. When he arrived, we went into the consultation room. He must have realised how stressed I sounded and how tired I must have looked because he began by reassuring me that other than *one* document – the Al-Qaeda Training Manual – the police had nothing of any substance to demonstrate that my possession of it was connected to terrorism. They had found no propagandistic literature belonging to armed Islamic groups, found no connection between me and other persons who were even remotely involved in 'terrorism' or what can be described as 'extremist' activity, and there was no other evidence that I was involved in planning anything even remotely linked to an act of violence. There was no evidence that I was involved in a terrorist conspiracy of any kind whatsoever. 'You have a totally clear-cut and legitimate defence for having that document in your possession,' Nadeem explained. His constant reassurances were crucial in keeping me calm, but after a short while I would start to feel anxious and stressed again. To keep me distracted, he would initiate games. 'Name two countries beginning with each letter of the alphabet.' We must have played this about three times and then started asking each other the names of capital cities to keep my mind distracted from the looming decision.

Sometime in the late morning, there was a knock at the door. 'Come in,' Nadeem said. It was DC West. For a police officer to enter the consultation room was highly unusual. In fact, it had never happened before except in one instance when I was once in the exercise yard. This was the first time an officer had entered the actual room in my presence. DC West did not speak with me initially. He told Nadeem that the CPS had not yet made their 'decision' and that they were 'upstairs' still deciding. Before leaving, DC West turned to me. 'It was never anything "personal"', he said. On reflection, I know this was his attempt at apologising for what I had been put through, even though he couldn't find the word 'sorry' to express it. However, in that moment, his words filled me with rage. Here I was, racked by uncertainty, feeling anxious, and absolutely terrified at the very *real* prospect of being imminently charged, remanded in a high-security prison, and potentially being convicted for terrorism, yet, he was saying that none of this was 'personal'. In that instant, and every moment since then, what may have felt to DC West as simply a matter of 'doing his job' was for me extremely personal. I felt indifferent towards his half-attempt at an apology and was far too worried to care about what he was trying to say. My mind was more focused on trying to deal with the anxiety and uncertainty in the face of crippling, overwhelming fear of being charged for terrorism.

I had been told that the police and CPS decision would be arriving soon, but it was now the early afternoon and nothing had still been heard. Every time we enquired, we were told there was no news. The waiting was taking its toll on me, and the sense of anxiety I felt as my life hung in the balance is something that I still cannot put into words. But then, at around 2 pm, there was a knock at the door. A custody sergeant entered and informed us that a decision had been reached by the police and the CPS and that we should follow him into the corridor. As my lawyer and I walked towards the familiar table placed outside my cell, my heart was pounding. A smartly dressed female officer with short blonde hair wore black trousers and a dark shirt, who I had not seen until this moment, was standing by the table with a piece of paper in her hand and a completely blank expression on her face. She gave nothing away. Standing beside her were three men – all dressed in suits – who I had also never seen before. Perhaps the arrival of these new officers signalled something grave and new about where the investigation was heading? I was imagining the worst. The female officer raised the sheet of paper and began reading aloud:

> You were arrested on Wednesday 14 May 2008. You had in your possession a copy of a document titled Al Qaeda Training Manual.

> That document contains information of a kind likely to be useful to a person committing or preparing an act of terrorism.

> The University authorities have now made clear that possession of this material is not required for the purpose of your course of study nor do they consider it legitimate for you to possess it for research purposes.

In the split moment before she read the next sentence, and my heart rate hurried, the realisation struck me that my own institution, the University of Nottingham, was not supporting me, and that perhaps having this statement read to me was therefore a part of the process of being charged for terrorism.

> You are warned that if you are found in possession of a further copy of this material in future, you will be the subject of further investigation, which may include arrest and further detention.

She handed the 'notice' over to me, and ordered me to sign it. 'I would strongly advise you not to sign this statement,' Nadeem immediately said. The female officer handed the notice to Nadeem, who signed it, and handed it back to her. Without saying anything further, she turned around and walked away, accompanied closely by the three male officers. At this stage, the whirlwind of emotions that had been raging within me was soon joined by a newfound confusion. What had just happened? Was I free to go or not? Have I been charged or released? But before I could say anything, the custody sergeant spoke. 'I'm not sure if you've worked it out but you're free to leave.'

*   *   *

Though Hicham and I were released without charge, we were not considered to be innocent. The CPS were convinced that the police may not have dug deep enough into our lives and electronic devices. They therefore advised the police that Hicham and I should 'be kept in custody after the decision not to charge [had been made] to establish if there was evidence of further dissemination [of the Al-Qaeda Training Manual} as this could rebut the defence they had put forward'.[4] The suspicion and interest of the authorities, in other words, did not end with our release without charge. Inquiries continued to see 'whether or not there was any other material on the computers that were likely to change the decision of the Crown Prosecution Service' on whether to charge Hicham and me for terrorism.[5] After an entire month of continued investigation and searching through exhibits, nothing was found and the senior investigating officer was compelled to formally shut down Operation Minerva.[6] Still, however, the suspicion and surveillance would continue. Once you are marked as a 'subject of interest', it is difficult to become 'uninteresting'.

From 9/11 to March 2021, 2,418 people have been arrested for suspected terrorism and then released without charge, as I was. All of them will have experienced similar emotions, feelings, and traumas that my family and I experienced when I was in custody, and long after. Black and Asian people are overrepresented in those arrests.[7] Muslims feel the brunt of the damage that emerges when the police take you into custody, accuse you of terrorism, and turn your life upside down. My experiences and what I have described therefore reflect a broader set of struggles, suspicions, and harms that affect thousands of other Muslims and people of colour too. What happened to me is not an exception to the rule. It is the rule.

10
Accountability

A few months after my release without charge from custody, I instructed lawyers at Bhatt Murphy Solicitors, who special-ise in actions against the state, to bring a civil claim against the police on my behalf. If I was to publicly clear my name in order to continue and progress with some semblance of normality in my life as an academic, then I had to hold the police to account through the courts for the treatment they had subjected me to and formally clear my name. In 2011, after three years of tiring legal work in conjunction with two incredibly talented and astute pro-bono solicitors, Raju Bhatt and Michael Oswald, we were pre-paring to go to trial. I was feeling anxious about being questioned and potentially badgered by lawyers representing the police but I was prepared for court. I had spent a considerable amount of time working with Michael and Raju on the case, and was familiar with the particulars and facts of it. But, around two weeks before the case was scheduled to go to trial, police lawyers wanted to settle the case outside of court, and we were forced to go along with this proposal. The reason was simple: I had no money and could not afford to do otherwise. The insurance policy I had con-tained a clause stipulating that if the police requested to settle the case outside of court, and a trial could be avoided, then we had to accommodate any such proposal. If I had chosen to fight the case and lost, I would have been at risk of having to pay the police tens of thousands of pounds in legal costs.

Though one part of me was relieved that settling outside of court would prevent me from the inevitable stress and anxiety that a court setting brings, I had wanted the case to go to trial. It would have been useful for my lawyers to challenge the claims of police officers like DCs West and Shankey, and other senior officers who were responsible for running Operation Minerva, about their conduct, their statements, their claims, what they had done, why they had done it and so forth. A trial would also have led to the creation of a permanent record of submitted evidence and a formal court transcript. However, no matter how much I wanted it, the trial was not going to happen. I did not have the money to take the police to court and take them to task for what they had done to me. Full and open accountability, it became clear to me, was largely reserved for the rich.

Early one morning in September 2011, I met with Raju and Michael at their offices in Hoxton Square in London. We shared a taxi to Doughty Street Chambers a couple of miles away. Raju, Michael, and I, along with the two barristers who had already been instructed to advocate for us in court   Richard Hermer QC and Alison Pickup – all sat on one side of a large conference room table on the first floor. On the other side sat senior police officers and their lawyers. The meeting went on for hours, and various aspects of the arrest, the law, and other legal intricacies were discussed. I had tried to follow as much as I could but a lot of what was discussed went over my head. Eventually, by the late afternoon, the case was 'settled'.

No apology was issued for my arrest and detention for suspected terrorism. I did receive an apology for an unlawful stop and search under Section 43 of the Terrorism Act 2000 in February 2010. They also agreed to correct or delete a number of intelligence entries held on their intelligence system which contained inaccurate information that I had, for example, a 'conviction for terrorism'. It was also agreed that the police would remove a 'flag' on their intelligence system which marked me out as a 'subject of interest' for terrorism. And, the 'notice' which the female police officer read aloud to me and told me to sign as I was being released from custody, the one that said I would be rearrested if I had a copy of the Al-Qaeda Training Manual in the future, was unconditionally withdrawn. It had no legal basis. In the final moments of the meeting, the police agreed to pay all of my legal fees in full and awarded me £20,000 in damages. When my friends, family, and some members of my community discovered that I had won damages, they asked me why I had settled for such a low figure given the experience I had to go through. The financial settlement is something that did not really register with me throughout the entire three years I worked on the case with Raju and Michael. It was never about money. The damages were an acknowledgement that a wrong had been done; a way of signalling formally that I was an innocent person. In the meeting, there was therefore no negotiations for the financial settlement. A sum was requested by my lawyers. The police and their lawyers left the conference room to discuss the figure and, when they returned, they informed us that £20,000 was accepted. It was the first time that a Muslim person of colour who had been arrested and detained in *pre-charge detention* for suspected terrorism had managed to secure some element of accountability and damages for the way he had been treated. It was a huge personal vindication that gave me a sense of empowerment.

Apart from using the legal process, I also began to think about other ways that I could try to hold the police accountable and bring about changes, not just for me but for the Muslim community as a whole. During one of the police interviews while I was in custody, DC Shankey had questioned my motives for researching al-Qaeda and accused me of using my studies as a smokescreen to hide a terrorist intent. 'What use could that document [the Al-Qaeda Training Manual] have been to you in your studies?,' he said. 'It doesn't have a use does it?' As I sat there silent and afraid of the insinuation he was making, he continued in an accusatory tone to imply that I was 'using [my] studies as an excuse for downloading that [document]'.[1] My motive, he was implying, was terrorism. Since then, I have pulled away from researching how and why armed Muslim groups such as al-Qaeda behave the way they do. I am still curious about those questions but ever since I was suspected of being connected to al-Qaeda myself, I knew there were no solid boundaries between how the counterterrorism system viewed ordinary Muslims and how it viewed those suspected of being terrorists. I now wanted to research what the government was doing, how it was doing it, and why. I therefore changed my PhD research focus to the UK's counterterrorism policies and practices. However, I soon discovered that the interest and suspicion of the police and security state would remain.

11
Subject of Interest

One of the most important reliefs of the legal settlement was that I would no longer be a subject of interest for the police and authorities in the same way that I had been from 2008 until 2011. During this period, as I was busy conducting research on counterterrorism for my PhD and working on the civil claim with Raju and Michael, I was being routinely stopped, searched, and detained at the roadside and the UK border whilst travelling. Though harrowing and distressing, these stops and detentions taught me about police surveillance and intelligence collection, the law, and my rights (or a lack of them in many instances) in a very practical way. But it was nothing to do with terrorism that drove my learning around my rights and my ability to resist. It was a far more mundane and an unnecessarily abusive exercise of authority by a policeman that prompted it.

In early 2010, I was parked on a quiet street in central London in my car on double yellow lines with my hazard lights flashing. As I was about to pull off, a police van that was driving through the street pulled up beside me. There were three police officers in the van, all sat in the front. The policeman closest to me was black, had a shaven head, and looked to be in his late thirties. With a hand gesture, he instructed me to lower my window. 'You're not supposed to be parked on double yellow lines, are you?,' he said in sarcastic tone. I explained that I had been parked only for a matter of minutes to pay the congestion charge and that parking on double yellow lines was 'hardly a crime'. But this comment triggered the officer in a way I was not expecting. 'If you don't stop being a twat,' he threatened, 'I am going to seize your car, put you in the cells, and fuck your life.' I was gobsmacked. In all of my encounters with the police until the time of writing, and I have had a fair few of them over the years, especially since I started driving a car at seventeen years of age, I have never been spoken to in this way. This encounter not only made me feel angered but humiliated too. If I had known the law, I thought to myself for weeks after the exchange, I may have been able to deal with the matter in a better way. I could have perhaps challenged the officer's threat to arrest me by citing what my rights were, what the law did and did not authorise police officers to do, and not allow him to make these triggering and abusive threats. My own ignorance, I felt, was to blame.

But, rather than complaining to his superiors, I took the encounter as a lesson; to understand my rights and the law, in particular the Road Traffic Act and the Police and Criminal Evidence Act, which govern police powers in relation to drivers and stop and search. I had physical copies of both legal texts printed, bound, and always at hand in the car in case I needed to verify police officers' claims about the law. I quizzed legal friends on the significance of case law, watched endless videos of members of the public as well as activists dealing with the police, and talked to my friends about their experiences of being stopped and searched too. But it was not just theoretical knowledge that informed my understanding and ability to deal with the police at the roadside. It was also practical knowledge I was developing as I was routinely stopped.[1]

*　*　*

It was mid-afternoon on 26 September 2010, and I was heading back from visiting my aunty, who lives five minutes from our home. As soon as I drove out of her street, I noticed a marked police car coming in my direction. The two cars that were directly behind me turned off into a side road, and the police car was now directly behind me. Just before I turned right into my street, the police car's blue lights started flashing. I immediately stopped my car, exited the vehicle, and locked the doors. The reason for my actions was simple. There had been occasions in the past when officers who had stopped me reached into my car and removed my keys. One time, an officer opened my door for no apparent reason. I therefore decided to always exit the vehicle whenever stopped, to give the officers no reason to suspect that I may drive off. By the time I had stepped onto the pavement, one of the officers, who was armed with a handgun strapped to his leg, exited the police car and walked towards me. The second officer remained seated on the passenger side of the police car, with his door wide open. He was on his radio, and was soon typing on his laptop computer. I had never witnessed this before, but I suspected a more thorough search of the police intelligence system was perhaps taking place.

My knowledge of the law and of police powers, which I had been studying, had given me a sense of confidence when it came to dealing with these sorts of situations. Though always calm, I became much more assertive. I asked the officer to explain the grounds on which I had been followed and subsequently stopped. The officer claimed that a dark Volkswagen similar to my own car had been involved in an 'incident' earlier that day, and though he could not provide me with any further information about it, he needed to carry out some checks to see whether I may have had any involvement. The officer then asked whether I was known to the police. I always answered this question with a simple 'yes, I am known to the police'. This reply almost always was followed up with: 'and what are you known to the police for?' I would then explain in a few words that it was for suspected terrorism, and that this was the result of a big 'mix-up' since I was a postgraduate student researching terrorism and was therefore released without charge a week later.

In my experience, the purpose of asking whether somebody is known to the police can be twofold: to verify information that the police already hold on the person or as a way of profiling them for further questioning at the roadside. In the case of this particular stop, it seemed to be a mix of the two. Usually, the police would have radioed the vehicle registration plate and received some basic details from the police operator before they stop a person. The fact that I had been followed for a few minutes before being stopped by the armed officers suggests this was most likely to have been the case. During the stop, the officer I was speaking with inspected my vehicle from the outside and then peered into my car through the windows, which seemed to conclude his cursory examination. Meanwhile, the second officer continued his checks on his laptop.

Observing the fact both officers were armed, I brought up the topic of 'gun crime' in Nottingham, a city once referred to as 'Shottingham' in the tabloids for its disproportionately high gun crime rates. The police in Nottingham had become more visibly militarised in their everyday policing with routine armed officers patrolling the city. The officer offered very little comment on the matter and seemed reluctant to be drawn into a conversation on this subject. Eventually, his colleague, still in the car, finished his enquiries and both officers were now satisfied I had nothing to do with the mysterious 'incident' they were refusing to tell me about. I was free to go.

One would think this stop, where almost nothing of note had happened, was a non-incident. Yet not only was the encounter logged by the armed officers on their intelligence system, their report included the following remarks:

> Sabir has a previous arrest for a terrorism related offence in 2008 and quickly identified officers as AFO's [Armed Firearm Officers] and was asking questions about the weapons.

What was meant to be a stop to simply verify my identity in the context of an unknown, separate incident from earlier in the day, which had nothing to do with me, had become an opportunity for the police to ascribe to me an interest in 'weapons'.

Especially troubling about the above intelligence entry is that it is completely decontextualised. There was no context provided in the intelligence log with regards to the mentions of terrorism, even though I had deliberately alerted the officer, as I always do, to the dubious circumstances surrounding my arrest, to the fact I was a researcher-academic on the subject, and that the discussion of 'weapons' was connected to my research on policing, military, and counterinsurgency affairs. Instead, a blunt and decontextual- ised parallel was being drawn between the two subjects and me. It was this particular stop that led an 'interest' marker to be added to my name on the police intelligence system for 'previous ter- rorist related offences'. From here on, whenever the police would do a check at the roadside, they would be alerted that I had a 'marker' that listed me as a 'subject of interest' for terrorism. And all based on a routine stop and search at the roadside. But it was not just referencing to guns and weapons that got a mention on the police intelligence system. My knowledge of the law, as well as the exercise of my rights when stopped and questioned by the police, were logged as something noteworthy too.

12
An Unlawful Stop

It was around 1 am on 4 February 2010. I was sat in my car with a friend outside his house, a few doors away from my own family home. It was a cold night and we both wore scarves and hoods to keep our heads warm whilst we chatted, sipped tea, and smoked cigarettes. After a short while of being in the car, we started watching videos on YouTube, mostly involving the policing of political protests. These videos were part of my attempt to learn more about my rights and the law. What happened next was quite ironic.

A marked police car with two officers – a man and a woman – drove directly past us. On seeing us, the driver turned the police car around, and parked directly behind us. My friend and I both knew what was about to happen. The male officer exited the police car and came towards me on the driver side. The female officer approached my friend from the passenger side. 'What are you doing here parked so late into the night?,' the male officer asked me through the open window. I explained that we were parked outside of my friend's home drinking tea and smoking a cigarette since we were not allowed to smoke indoors and it was too cold to stand outside.

While he made his way towards my car, the officer had caught a glimpse of the video we were watching and wanted to know what it was. I explained that it was a video of two political activists who use a megaphone around London to make satirical jokes as a way of protesting and educating members of the public about corporate criminality. In the intelligence log written after the event, the officer had written that 'he had become curious' because he saw 'a uniformed police officer' in the video. The uniformed man in the video was in fact a security guard working at Canary Wharf in London. Since the guard's uniform was fairly similar to that of a police officer, his error was understandable.

'Do you attend many protests yourself?,' the officer asked. This was a profiling question. If I answered 'yes', they would become more curious and would begin asking even more questions. I thus decided the best course of action would simply be to refuse to answer. Of course, a person can refuse to answer a police officer's question by citing their right to privacy, but in practice, rather than quash the curiosity, it is most likely to intensify it. This is what happened on this cold February night.

The officer told me he understood what I was saying and informed me that he would be checking my car for its roadworthiness. I asked him to explain what legal authority he was acting under. 'Section 163 of the Road Traffic Act,' he explained, adding 'is that alright with you?' Having familiarised myself with this legislation, I knew full well that the officer had a series of powers at his disposal, and that in practice there was nothing I could do other than comply with his demands or risk arrest.

As the officer began inspecting my car, his female colleague approached me and began taking a note of my full name, address, and date of birth. As the driver of the vehicle, I was legally obliged to provide these details. However, as I was giving my details, my friend asked me in front of the female officer whether he would have to provide his details too. I told him that under Section 164 of the Road Traffic Act, and as a passenger in the vehicle, he was not under any legal obligation to do so. The female officer was listening to our exchange as she wrote my details down and radioed my name through. She did not ask my friend for his details. In that moment, this felt like a small victory made possible because of a basic understanding of the law and police powers.

During the remainder of the stop, my friend remained silent throughout the entire exchange. The 'rule' amongst friends was always clear. If ever we were to be stopped by the police, only the driver would speak. The passengers would remain silent until and unless it was necessary for them to say something. I had come across numerous instances, both in practice and via studying videos, which showed that too many people speaking at the same time increases confusion, leads to raised voices, and can cause officers to become more aggressive in trying to maintain a sense of order and discipline. It can also quickly lead to reinforcements being called in, and the situation becoming potentially more volatile. It was therefore in the interest of the group to maintain order and speak only if required. After examining the car, the male police officer reappeared and informed me that he was satisfied with its roadworthiness and agreed to provide me with a stop and search form. When I accepted his offer, the female officer filled the form out, handed it to me, and thanked me for my time. Both officers then went back to their car. I wrongly assumed that was the end of it.

As my friend and I began talking about what had just happened, the police car remained parked behind us for a further twenty minutes. This was a little strange and we did not know quite what to make of it. Were they digging a little deeper on their computer system or were they doing something unrelated to us? What was going to happen next? And then, a second police car appeared and parked in front of mine. We were now boxed in between two police cars and four police officers. Two male officers exited the newly arrived police car while the original two officers got out of theirs. All four approached. The officer who had been heading the stop earlier came to my window, which was now fully open, and crouched down by my door. He was making eye contact. 'What can I do for you now, officer?,' I asked.

He started by saying that I had been transparent with him the first time around during the questioning, and he would therefore be transparent with me now. His tone sounded different this time. It was firmer and more intense. He clarified that he had been searching the police computer whilst he was sat in his car for my name and therefore knew that I had been arrested for suspected terrorism in 2008. Since my friend had not provided his personal details to the officers, and we were both watching a video where he thought he saw police officers, he had reasonable grounds to suspect that my friend and I could be terrorists and they would therefore be executing a search of my car, and of my friend and me, to see if we had anything in our possession that would confirm his suspicion.

I immediately recognised the seriousness of the situation that was developing. 'I would like to caution you,' I told the officer, 'that from this moment onwards anything you do or say can and will be used against you in a court of law should this matter be escalated to a court of law in the future.' Cautioning officers in a way that mirrored their own use of the 'caution' was something I did whenever there was a possibility of the situation escalating or when police actions were connected to my 2008 arrest for suspected terrorism. It served as a way of informing them that their actions might be integrated into the ongoing civil claim that I had brought against the police. It was also a way of letting police officers know that they were not the only ones who had the power to draw inferences from the words and actions of members of the public who they spoke with. The public also had the same right. Occasionally officers may themselves end up in court having to defend and account for their words and actions. I was simply reminding them of this simple fact.

I asked the officer to explain the legal powers he was now using to execute his search, and he clarified that he had access to a range of powers under the Terrorism Act 2000, including Section 41, Section 43, and Section 57. I was familiar with all three, and suspected the officer understood them only superficially, since Section 41 is an arrest power, not a power to search or seize items considered useful for terrorism. Section 43 authorised an officer to search someone on the basis of 'reasonable suspicion' of being involved in terrorism, which meant I would have to comply with the search or risk arrest. If I wanted accountability, I would have to let matters run their course and take the matter to court with the help of Raju and Michael.

The search began with the police officer taking my Blackberry phone and replaying the YouTube protest video we had been watching. Refusing his request to see my mobile telephone would have probably led to more problems, and I therefore complied with his order. A few seconds into the clip, he was satisfied that we were being honest with him about the nature of the video, and he returned my Blackberry to me. My friend and I were ordered to exit the vehicle. My friend was then searched by one of the newly arrived officers whilst his colleague started searching the boot of my car. The only thing I had there were folders containing hundreds of email printouts relating to my 2008 arrest, which I had received from the University of Nottingham under the Data Protection Act. I emptied the contents of my pockets onto the roof of the car, and the officer took an interest only in my card holder. He examined the cards, then put them back into the holder and handed it back to me. By this stage, I was quite confused. My car was being searched under the Terrorism Act, and my friend too, yet I was not. 'Do you not want to search me too?,' I asked. 'We don't need to,' came the reply. The officer searching my car had now opened the rear doors, taken a glance inside and moved to the front of the car. He had a quick look under the front seats and then closed all the doors. The glove compartment and central console in my car remained untouched. It seemed that terrorism powers were being used as a way of legally authorising the police to gain access to the protest video we were watching on my Blackberry rather than an attempt to find items in my possession that would evidence involvement in terrorism. Perhaps this is why the search of the car felt more like a tick-box exercise than a search motivated by a genuine concern that my friend and I were involved in terrorism.

As the search was ending, the police officer and I were conversing about the nature of terrorism laws. In many instances, the officer agreed with some of my criticisms of the law, though he defended them by claiming that the nature of the threat was too serious to not have these powers on the books. The officer then asked me directly what it was that I was supposed to have done and why I was arrested. When I responded by saying that I would prefer not to go into the details of it, he began laughing. I asked him why he was laughing, and he explained that he had been involved in a terrorism inquiry in 2008 in Nottingham. I explained to the officer that in my understanding, the only time there had been a counterterrorism inquiry in Nottingham was that of my own arrest, and so his involvement was probably in relation to my case. Perhaps what he found amusing was that I was refusing to give details about an arrest of which he was fully aware. 'May I ask what role you played?,' I said. I was expecting him to refuse to answer but he was surprisingly forthcoming. He explained that he was part of an armed response unit that had been deployed to the University of Nottingham on the day of my arrest.

This was a very interesting admission. In the aftermath of my arrest, a journalist from the *Times Higher Education Supplement* had come under fire from the police for reporting that police officers on campus on the day of the arrest were armed. The police had subsequently complained to her editor and stressed that this was a low-level anti-terror operation where no armed personnel were involved. Yet, here was an officer saying he had been part of an armed response unit deployed to campus on that day. When the exchange ended, I asked for a stop and search form, which I received, and the officers eventually got into their cars and left. The next morning, I alerted Michael and Raju of the stop and search to ensure it could be integrated into my civil claim. As part of the legal settlement in 2011, I received an unconditional apology for this stop and search which was deemed 'unlawful'. It took a while, but accountability for what happened on that cold February night did come in the end.

The fact that I had asserted my rights at the roadside and challenged the police's questions was itself logged and stored by the police on their criminal intelligence system. The entry written and logged by the officer who headed the stop and search noted that I was 'asking the officers what powers and sections they have to stop and speak with [my friend and I] and to ascertain [police officer] details'. It also noted that 'Sabir seemed to know about the law' and 'has many academic qualifications in Terrorism research and is very involved in redressing what he believes is an oppressive police state with powers that breach Human Rights'. Even though my questioning of police powers at the roadside was entirely legal and legitimate, it was not only logged as criminal intelligence but increased the risk of escalation at the hands of the police in future encounters.

13
Flashing Screens

Around a month after I was released from custody, I was driving a large white van to Germany via the Channel Tunnel at Folkstone, accompanied by my aunty Sofia's husband and my cousin Aamer, who is a German citizen. We were travelling to Germany to buy stock for my uncle's online retail company. When I approached the police checkpoint at Folkstone, there was a queue ahead of us but it was moving quite quickly. The police officer at the booth was waving the cars through without checking papers or passports. As I slowly approached the booth, unsure whether to stop or roll through, the officer instructed me to stop by raising his hand. 'Passports, please,' he said. I handed him all the passports and he began checking them. 'Can you please park the van into that lay-by?' he instructed after a couple of minutes checking the passports. This was my first attempt at international travel since I had been released and I anticipated that there was a very high chance that my name would now be marked. The officer's instruction was therefore unsurprising.

I pulled up into the lay-by and two uniformed police officers arrived. They opened the doors to the van and glanced inside. Except for three bags and a large box containing food and drinks, the van was empty. They asked us which bag belonged to whom. When we each claimed our respective bags, we were led into separate spaces for questioning. I was escorted into the passport booth by the officer. From inside the booth, I could see lots of paperwork, a window that gave a 180-degree view of the port, as well a second police officer who was waiting in the booth. Even though cars were still approaching the checkpoint, I was very annoyed to note they were all being waved through without having any of their papers or passports checked. 'What's the purpose of this stop?,' I asked in an irritated tone. 'You have been stopped under Schedule 7 of the Terrorism Act 2000,' the officer replied.

I had not heard of Schedule 7 at this moment and did not understand what authority it granted the police and what rights it awarded me. When I informed the officer of this, he explained that this power, which was only applicable at the UK border, authorised him to stop and detain any person for questioning and a search for up to a maximum period of nine hours (the limit has now been reduced to six hours), to assess whether they appeared to be involved in terrorism. I was legally obliged to answer all of his questions, he added, and if I refused or failed to answer them, I would risk arrest and prosecution for terrorism. The fact that I did not have a right to remain silent immediately signalled that the Schedule 7 power was designed to allow the police and security services to collect intelligence with maximum ease on any person who was crossing the UK border. The officer explained that a lawyer could be informed that I had been stopped and was going to be questioned, but they were under no obligation to wait for the lawyer to arrive to begin questioning me or searching my property. This right, it seemed, was more about creating an appearance of fairness than actually protecting the person who was stopped under the power. Whilst the officer explained the remarkable powers he had access to, the second officer, who was stood near the door, was searching my bag. Other than clothes, there was nothing in my bag, and in less than a few minutes, the search was over. Then the questions began.

The officer wanted to know my relationship to my fellow passengers and my reasons for travelling to Europe. He then asked whether I was known to the police. I explained that I had become known to the police only since last month because I had been wrongly arrested on suspicion of terrorism. When the officer inquired about the actual grounds for the arrest, I explained that it was connected to having a document in my possession that I was using for my postgraduate studies but that it was all one big misunderstanding and that I was released without charge.

Then the questions shifted to my religion and my local community. Do you pray? Do you visit a local mosque? What is the name of the local mosque you visit? Who is the imam that heads the congregation at your mosque? Throughout the whole period, I had been as forthright as I could be, thanks to the not-so-thinly veiled threat of being arrested and prosecuted if I refused or failed to sufficiently answer. But these questions made me feel deeply uncomfortable in a way that I had not felt before. I knew that I was being used as a source of intelligence on my community. Powerless to really do anything unless I wanted to be arrested, I explained that my local mosque and imam were both apolitical and would not dare to speak about political issues since they were fearful of being investigated by the police for terrorism.

And then, my frustration at the increasing stupidity of the questions began to get the better of me. I was asked by the officer what the name of the 'black cube' in Saudi Arabia was that the Muslims visited. 'Police officers,' I replied, 'who are tasked with counter-terrorism policing should really know the name of the "black cube" that over a billion Muslims visit and pray in the direction of, should they not?' By this stage, I had not even attempted to hide the contempt I now felt for the stop as well as the line of questioning the officer had gone down. 'I know the black cube is called the "Kaaba", which is in Mecca,' he defensively replied. 'So why are you asking me questions that you already know the answers to?' The officer explained that he was trying to work out what my level of understanding of my faith and religion was. His answer, on reflection, was revealing. A great deal of the detention and questioning was based on his desire to build an intelligence profile of me, which included both my political views as well as my religious outlook. This stop was seemingly more about building and enlarging the police's intelligence assessment of me than it was about trying to apparently determine if I was a terrorist. In a broader sense, it showed how the police regard Muslims' political and religious opinions as proxies for assessing terrorist risk. Islamic beliefs, ideas, and practices are treated as suspicious by the security state.

Once the questions ended, over an hour had passed. I was given a Schedule 7 form by the police officer and took the badge numbers of both officers for my records. I was then escorted back to the van, where my uncle and cousin were waiting for me. The officer who had questioned me was stood close by, and I was struggling to control the urge to ask whether my arrest for suspected terrorism in May was the reason he decided to stop the van and detain us under Schedule 7. I felt that a direct question was not going to work. I therefore asked him: 'Did the screen start flashing when you scanned my passport into the system?' He chuckled, clearly seeing through my attempt to be subtle in gathering my own information. 'Our screens don't flash,' he explained, 'but your name was flagged on the computer.' To some people, including the officer himself, this may have been a very trivial piece of information to impart, but its significance cannot be overestimated for me. The dread and anxiety that I felt long before I had even booked my travels for Germany were not driven by 'paranoia' or a sense of 'victimhood' but a marker that was purposefully placed next to my name because I was wrongfully arrested and detained for suspected terrorism. Once you are 'marked' and become a person of interest, it becomes difficult to become uninteresting, as I categorically rediscovered two years later.

14
Travelling While Muslim

As I was stood in the queue at East Midlands Airport on Sunday 8 July 2010, looking at the immigration officers check passports, my eyes fell to two middle-aged white men dressed in dark suits standing at a podium that said 'police'. I had been researching counterterrorism for around two years by now, and I had expanded my understanding of both policing and terrorism quite considerably. I knew these men were Special Branch officers, with powers under Schedule 7 to stop and search.

I patiently waited and tried to hide my nerves, which I experience whenever I travel through airports. But there were anxious thoughts running through my mind. Was my body language okay? What would somebody trained to spot a terrorist infer from it? Would they see something suspicious in the way I stood? Did I look guilty? How would an actual terrorist behave in such a situation? Are these two men stood at the podium part of a routine patrol or are they here to question me? As the thoughts and endless questions continued, I observed that my friend Waqar, with whom I was travelling, had gone towards the self-service immigration machines and used his biometric passport to clear immigration. He then walked past the officers without being stopped. Seeing this made me feel slightly better, though I also noticed one of the police officers staring at me. I looked away and tried not to make eye contact but the way he was fixated on me made me feel it may already have been too late.

As I approached the immigration counter, there was a male border guard stationed at the desk. I handed my passport over and stood in silence, observing that he was taking a lot longer looking at my picture and the pages of my passport, especially the Pakistani visa from my previous visit in 2003. 'That's fine,' he eventually said, returning my passport. Ahead was the police podium.

As I approached it, the officer took a step in my direction. He put his hand out. 'Can I see your passport, please?,' he asked. Without saying a word but thinking in my mind 'here we go again',

I handed it over. 'And where are you travelling from today?', he asked, whilst he brought the passport closer to his eyes to examine the page that contained the Pakistani visa. I had been on vacation in the Spanish city of Granada, I explained, but my return flight was from Malaga. 'And are you travelling alone today?' The truthful answer to this question was 'No' but in that moment, the mix of nerves, fear, and adrenaline, especially around implicating Waqar, led me to answer in the affirmative. However, I quickly realised my mistake in not being open and went into recovery mode; though I knew it was most probably too late. 'Sorry, I'm not travelling alone,' I explained. 'I'm actually travelling with a friend,' and pointed towards Waqar as he looked on. 'Why did you just say you were travelling alone when you are not then?' It was better to just be honest with him. 'Because I don't want to get my friend involved in this or get him into any trouble,' I said. 'Okay. Well, let's move from here because there's a lot of people.' I had noticed from the moment I was stopped that every other person who had crossed the podium would glance over at me and the officer as I was being questioned. It was humiliating; as if everybody was probably thinking I had been stopped because I was brown and therefore probably guilty rather than viewing this as an unfair exercise of police power. The officer's suggestion to go elsewhere therefore came as a relief, though it also was a sign that the matter was being escalated.

As we walked out of the immigration area, through a set of doors, Waqar approached and asked if everything was okay. Trying to hide the nerves and fear for what may come next, I told him not to worry and to wait for me in the arrivals lounge. The officer escorted me to the back of the terminal building; a silent and short walk of around two to three minutes. Eventually, he opened a large door that led into a dimly lit corridor surrounded by several rooms and offices. It seemed to be serving as a police station where, I guessed, Special Branch were based. I was then shown into an interview room, where a second Special Branch officer joined us. The room was small, and had a table with a telephone and two seats on each side. The size, the lighting, and the layout reminded me of the interview room where I was interrogated. Like that room, it was soundproofed, creating an unnatural acoustic. However, this time felt a little different. I felt a little better informed and knowledgeable about the law and my rights, even if they were limited under Schedule 7. I reflected that I was known to academic colleagues, lawyers, and journalists a lot more now, so would perhaps be more protected than somebody who did not have this type of social capital.

'Please take a seat,' the officer said. 'At this moment in time,' I replied, 'I would like to inform the both of you that anything you do or anything you say can and will be used against you in a court of law if this matter is escalated to a court.' The second officer who joined us once I had taken a seat replied with a simple nod and said, 'We understand.' With my passport lying before them on the table, one of the officers began writing down some details. The officer then explained that both my luggage and person would be searched. As the second officer searched me in the interview room, the first one took my bag outside of the room. In less than ten minutes, the officer returned with my luggage, and the interrogation began.

The questions started with the purpose of my travelling to Spain, who I met there, who Waqar was, and whether I had spent any time alone in Spain. Then the questions broadened towards my arrest in 2008 and what my PhD research was focused on. Questions were also asked about my educational background and who awarded me my PhD scholarship. Realising that not answering the questions could lead me to being charged for a terrorism offence akin to obstruction, the only thing I could do was answer truthfully. Soon the questions became more overtly political. What is my opinion of the 9/11 attacks? What is my view of Osama bin Laden and al-Qaeda? What are their goals and what do they want? The police also wanted to know whether I gave to charity, and to whom, and also how much money I was receiving as part of my scholarship. The most memorable question, however, was when the officer asked if I thought terrorists had human rights.

During the questioning, the first officer kept leaving the room for reasons unknown to me. On about three separate occasions, the door swung open and I witnessed at least three different Special Branch officers hanging around outside the interview room. When the officer would then return and take his seat, he would repeat the questions that had already been asked and which I had already answered. The first couple of times this happened, I ignored it and re-answered the question but on the third occasion, I frustratingly told the officer to stop wasting my time and dragging the detention out.

More than an hour had passed when the second officer produced a form called a TACT 1. He filled out the details and told me to sign it. Before doing so, I read the whole form, from top to bottom, and asked the officers to clarify certain points I was unclear on. The first officer who had executed the stop at the police podium explained that under Schedule 7, he was authorised to seize any item in my possession for further examination for a maximum period of seven days. He would exercise this power, he told me, and seize my Blackberry phone and my digital camera.

This angered me. The police had arrested and investigated me only two years ago, searched my family home, and turned my life inside-out in their quest to find evidence to support their suspicion that I may be a terrorist. They were also stopping and searching me on the roadside and were aware that I was researching and studying counterterrorism for my doctorate as well as writing on the subject in the public domain, including op-eds in newspapers like *The Guardian*. Yet, they still wanted to know more. What made the situation even more enraging at the airport was that I was in the midst of my civil claim against the police and in the process of conducting fieldwork, which meant I held confidential information acquired through interviews and meetings with various people, including police officers, who were speaking to me in confidence. I knew that by seizing my Blackberry, all of my communications and conversations with my lawyers and research participants would now be compromised. But I was helpless to do anything. There was no protest or comment that could prevent my smartphone and camera from being seized. If I wanted to do something, it would have to be with the help of my lawyers.

That Sunday evening when I arrived home, I wrote to my lawyers Michael and Raju and explained what had happened. The next morning, they informed me that they had written to the Chief Constable of Leicestershire Police as a matter of urgency and put him on notice that the contents of my Blackberry were connected to an ongoing civil claim and were subject to 'legal-professional privilege'. In other words, the contents of the phone should neither be read nor examined by the police. However, by the time the police received this communication, my Blackberry had been in their possession for almost twenty-four hours and is very likely (though I do not know for certain) to have been forensically examined during this time. Within two hours of my lawyers' letter being delivered to the police, one of the Special Branch officers who I had seen in the corridor the previous day but had no inter-action with, arrived at my home to return my smartphone and camera.

*   *   *

Two years later in 2012, I submitted a series of requests for personal information under the Data Protection Act to various govern-ment departments and police forces. One of these forces was West Midlands Police. In the batch of documents that were disclosed to me, there was one document titled: 'Operation Minerva: Schedule 7 Port Stops for Rizwan Shabir' (*sic*). This document noted the two stops and detentions I had been subjected to at the Channel Tunnel on my way to Germany in 2008 and on my return to East Midlands Airport in July 2010 from Spain. It also indicated that Special Branch had planned to detain me on my return from Spain in an 'intelligence-led' stop. It was either before or during my time in that country that a 'port-circulation' had been issued to Special Branch officers by the National Border Targeting Centre (NBTC) instructing them to intercept me on arrival. This organisation, which is affiliated to the UK Border Agency (UKBA), is respon-sible for collecting and analysing intelligence on people travelling in and out of the UK who are deemed to be of 'interest' to police and security agencies using advanced passenger information and other pieces of intelligence.[1] The Schedule 7 detention at East Midlands Airport was therefore neither random nor the result of some vulgar racial profiling exercise. Neither was it based on my body language as I stood in the queue or on the initial questions in which I changed my answer about travelling alone. Rather, the stop and detention were pre-planned. I was going to be inter-cepted, detained, and questioned irrespective of anything I said or did in that moment.

The use of intelligence-led stops may create an impression that the police are moving towards more focused and appropriate policing rather than using racial-profiling like a person's skin colour or length of beard to determine if they are suspicious. However, it is important to emphasise that 'intelligence-led' policing is based on a form of racial and religious profiling too. Think of it this way: when a person emerges on the radar of the police and security agencies, depending on their ethnic, religious, and racial identity, certain evidence will be collected and, often stereotypical, assumptions made about them. This knowledge ('intelligence') will help the police to create a 'profile' of them; who they are, what they believe, what religion and political groups and campaigns they follow or associate with, who their family and friends are, who they give charity to and so forth. The assumptions and stereotyping used to create the profile will subsequently influence how the police act. If and when the police act, new knowledge will emerge, which the police will then use to inform a new course of action. Intelligence informs police activity, in other words, and police activity produces intelligence, and so the intelligence-cycle goes around. I had experienced exactly this process playing out since my initial arrest as a terrorism suspect. My detention at East Midlands Airport was influenced by pre-existing police intelligence that portrayed me as somebody publicly critical of the police, government, and security state, and as potentially involved in terrorism. Markers and flags of 'interest' were added to my name, and subsequently informed a whole series of stops and searches at the roadside, port detentions under Schedule 7, as well as other forms of surveillance too. Pre-existing intelligence about a person is not based on some neutral and objective policing and knowledge process. It is rooted in stereotypical assumptions that can lead innocent people to experience continued surveillance and violence.

In my case, I was viewed with suspicion despite being a doctoral researcher who was meeting with police and government departments for my research. My academic work and public advocacy, it seemed, sustained their interest. Alarmingly, despite being in the midst of my civil claim against the police in 2010, the police were not dissuaded or deterred from detaining me at East Midlands Airport and seizing my electronic devices, which they knew would contain legally privileged communications with my solicitors. Being 'lawyered-up', knowing my rights, or having a public profile, I had thought, would be a way to protect myself from the police. I now realised this was a naïve assumption. The ever-expanding suite of legal powers given to the police in the name of countering terrorism has given them an extraordinary power over Muslim lives.

15
Spies in Our Midst

During the course of conducting my research on counterterror-ism, I always suspected that the police kept intelligence records on me, especially since I was being routinely stopped, searched, and detained at the roadside and ports. Thus, when I received a printout of all intelligence entries held on me by Nottinghamshire Police on their official criminal intelligence system, everything began to make much more sense. The police had tried to prevent the release of these intelligence files to my lawyers for well over a year by using a gagging order, or what is legally known as 'Public Interest Immunity' (PII). Its purpose is to prevent the release of information the state feels would be damaging to the 'public interest'. My lawyers had been trying to challenge the police's use of this exemption to no avail. Then, one afternoon, completely unexpectedly and somewhat mystifyingly, an unknown man walked into the reception of Bhatt Murphy's offices in London and handed over a large sealed brown envelope that had nothing written on it. He instructed the receptionist to make sure it was handed to my lawyers Michael or Raju. Was this a 'leak' or was this person under official instruction to supply us with the intelli-gence files? Was it a way for the police to end the formal rigmarole of denying us these files over such a long period of time? Neither my lawyers nor I have an answer. The intelligence files con-tained numerous entries, some of which relate to stop and search. However, there is one intelligence entry I will examine in some detail. This entry will remain on my intelligence file indefinitely and it signals how I am viewed by the police, and how Prevent relationships with members of the Muslim community are used to collect intelligence. The intelligence entry states:

> Rizwan SABIR has been accessing the MSN live chat facility on the internet and Facebook pages and stirring up emotions and feelings among other uses by posting comments that are anti

West and anti-Prevent. SABIR is accused of fuelling propaganda with negative comments about police and the government.

Sabir has also been entering into arguments with local people face to face with much of the same and has accused the chair of [the] Muslim Community Organisation – no further details – as having blood on his hands and that he should be ashamed of himself. This is believed to be [because] the chair is affiliated to the Labour Party and [Sabir] is referring to the war in Iraq.[1]

There are two things to emphasise about this entry. First, my criticisms of government policy, especially the Prevent strategy, are recorded on a criminal intelligence system. Based on the intelligence 'code' assigned to it ('E41'), this entry can be accessed by all UK police forces and disseminated to law enforcement and prosecuting agencies in the European Union and European Economic Area.[2] This raises all sorts of questions about how certain types of legitimate and lawful activities as well as political views critical of government can be used to inform law enforcement actions whenever the need arises, not only in the UK but overseas too.

Secondly, the log contains several inaccuracies. The claim that I had been 'accessing and using Facebook' is untrue. I did not use Facebook at the time the intelligence log was created in 2010. The claim I had been 'entering into arguments with local people face to face' implies there were various people and multiple arguments. There was *one* argument, on a single occasion and with a single person, the chair of a group called the Muslim Community Organisation.

Intelligence can be incomplete, inaccurate, and can fail to reflect the full facts. It may also be constructed and recorded in a way that is biased against the subject of the entry, encouraging the police to treat them in an unfavourable way in practice. This is partially why a significant part of my legal claim against the police involved deleting or correcting intelligence entries. Whilst the police agreed to do this in relation to some of the intelligence they held, the entry quoted above was neither deleted nor amended. At the settlement meeting in London, the police refused to amend or delete the entry on the ground it was 'important'. It therefore remains a 'live' piece of intelligence on my file that is indefinitely held. The entry shows how the police use pejorative and sweeping language to misrepresent their targets, which in turn influences the kind of treatment they are subjected to.

One might assume the police had accessed my computer files and chat-logs in order to acquire information about my use of platforms such as MSN Messenger. But the information was actually obtained through a relationship between Nottinghamshire Police and the 'Muslim Community Organisation' (MCO), which had received funding through the Prevent policy. A Prevent relationship, in other words, was used by the police to surveil a critic of government policy. Officially, the policy is described as not operating as a mechanism for conducting surveillance and intelligence collection on political views and opinions. But the Nottinghamshire Police intelligence entry demonstrated that this claim is not always true and that Prevent serves, amongst other things, as a mechanism for surveilling Britain's Muslim communities, especially Prevent's critics.

The moment I came across this intelligence entry, I guessed who was its 'source'. The incidents described in the intelligence entry relate to two people who worked for the MCO, an organisation that was in very frequent contact with Nottinghamshire Police both before and after the entry was created and logged on the police's intelligence system.

The incident described in the first paragraph of the entry relates to a single conversation between a person called Adam and myself that took place in late 2009 on the MSN Messenger service.[3] At the time, Adam had been hired by a Mr Khan to carry out work on counter-extremism in the local community. In the financial year 2008/9, the MCO had been awarded £60,000 in Prevent funds to deliver counter-extremism projects in an inner-city area of Nottingham.[4] I had known of Adam since he was a member of my local community for a number of years, but we had never actually spoken until this one online interaction on MSN. I was asked by a trusted friend of mine from high school who knew Adam to educate him on Prevent and counterterrorism more broadly because of my lived experiences and also my subsequent research. I asked my friend to introduce me to Adam on the MSN Messenger service and to remain in the chat as an observer.

The general gist of the conversation[5] was that Adam was as excited as he was boastful that MCO had received thousands of pounds from the government to carry out Prevent work. He did not divulge the amount of the grant, despite my repeated questions about it, only that they had 'a lot more than I could imagine'. He also spent a considerable amount of time defending Prevent and talking about the positive work MCO could do with government money, and how critics of government such as myself had it all wrong about Prevent and were not doing anything to help the situation on the ground. When I challenged his points, explaining how Prevent was being used to collate mass intelligence on entire communities, he remained unmoved. To support my points, I sent him a copy of the newly released 'Spooked' report, written by Arun Kundnani, which offered in my view a compelling argument that Prevent was a programme of mass surveillance targeted at Muslim communities.[6] Adam remained dismissive and, against my persistence, seemed to have lost interest and exited the conversation.

The second part of the police intelligence entry relates to an incident involving a political argument (not 'arguments') with Mr Khan sometime in 2006 at my father's workshop in an industrial estate in Nottingham. Mr Khan was a very senior figure in the MCO and, at that time, also a Labour councillor. The argument in 2006 centred around my questioning of Mr Khan's anti-war credentials. He was dismissive of the idea of resigning from Labour in response to Tony Blair's key role in the Iraq War. At the time, I argued that not resigning made him part of a political party that had 'blood on its hands', and that his membership was a cause of shame. On reflection now, this feels like a harsh argument to make, but it is one I made as a naïve twenty-year-old anti-war politics student. It was not the substance of our conversation that embedded the encounter in my mind, but the fact that Mr Khan grabbed me by the collar and threatened to 'sort me out' if I continued arguing with him. My father, on seeing what had happened, was angry with me for being disrespectful to my elders, and ordered me to leave his workshop, which I did. Sometime after this, I saw Mr Khan at my father's workshop again, and used the opportunity to apologise to him. He apologised in return for his conduct, and the matter, as far as I was concerned, was resolved.

Sometime after coming across the intelligence entry in 2011, I saw Mr Khan outside my local mosque having just completed Eid prayers. I asked him whether he had given any information to the police about me but he flat out refused the claim. When I revealed I had evidence showing our argument from 2006 had somehow appeared on a police intelligence system, he threatened to sue me for slander. This is the full context of the so-called 'argument' mentioned in the second paragraph of the intelligence entry.

The intelligence entry is dated 22 February 2010, which significantly falls right in the middle of a five-month period during which the police were routinely meeting with the MCO.[7] From January to May 2010, the police met with the MCO on eight separate occasions. 22 February 2010 is the date the information contained in the intelligence entry was uploaded to the police computer. Incidentally, out of the four meetings before the 22 February, two were 'informal meetings' for which 'no minutes were taken' and for the other two meetings, 'no minutes were received' by the police.[8]

All this suggests that relationships nurtured through Prevent were employed to collect 'criminal intelligence' on my entirely lawful activities and on my critique of Prevent and government policy. During the course of my research, people such as the deputy director of Prevent and government policy, who I spoke with at the Home Office, claimed that the word 'intelligence' should not be used in the context of Prevent since it conjures up images of secret surveillance. This was the remit of MI5, he claimed, not Prevent. However, *all* intelligence is logged on the same intelligence system, regardless of its source.[9] Prevent may not exclusively be a surveillance programme but it works to complement a secret surveillance infrastructure of which it is therefore an extension.[10]

16
The Trace

Intelligence on lawful political opinions and engagements may be collected by the police, but it is of interest to other security agencies too. I discovered this when information from the Crown Prosecution Service (CPS) was released to me under the Data Protection Act. A document titled 'File note re: [redacted] and Rizwaan Sabir (Operation Minerva)' contained the following text:

> Sabir is a postgraduate student in the Politics department (not a mathematics student as originally briefed). He is British-born with a Pakistani background and has been heavily involved in the University [of Nottingham] with Pro-Palestine issues. He was arrested on one occasion because of an incident between the University Palestinian society and the University Jewish Society. There is only one minor trace of him at Thames House.[1]

Thames House is the name of the building which houses the UK security service, MI5. The 'trace' at Thames House refers to an entry in MI5's databases that, according to correspondence I had with the CPS, was held on MI5 computers and was shared with the police whilst I was being investigated for suspected terrorism.[2] It is impossible to know for sure what events led to MI5 recording me on their system. I can think of two possibilities. The first involves a brief association with one person and the second is an involvement in student political protest.

In August 2006, I was working as a travelling fundraiser for Oxfam in Birmingham city centre when I bumped into Moazzam Begg on the high street. Begg had been held in US military custody without charge or trial in Afghanistan and Guantanamo Bay for a total of three years, where he was tortured, and then released without charge in January 2005. I was aware of his story from the media and having read his autobiography but this was the first time I had ever met him in person. I introduced myself to him as an undergraduate student who was studying politics, and expressed an interest in arranging for him to come and share his story with fellow students at my university. He provided me with his email address and asked that I arrange matters via email. On 4 September 2006, I sent him an invite via email but, for an unknown reason, he did not reply to me and did not attend my university. This encounter with Begg is one event that may be a possible basis for why I became of interest to MI5 prior to my arrest in 2008.

The second possibility is that I appeared on MI5's radar in connection to my involvement in a pro-Palestinian student protest at the University of Nottingham whilst I was a Master's student. The protest was organised by the student Palestinian Society to take place on 30 November 2007. A mock 8 x 10ft plasterboard 'wall' was erected by members of the Palestinian Society to obstruct one of three pathways leading to the entrance of the university's main Hallward Library. The inconvenience of a blocked path was intended to symbolise the daily challenges and struggles faced by Palestinians in the occupied West Bank as a result of the separation wall that Israel had built on and around Palestinian land.

On the day of the protest, I happened to be walking to the Hallward Library to collect a book when I witnessed the protest. Although I was not a member of the Palestinian Society, or even aware that a student protest was planned, I decided to stand in solidarity with the small number of student protestors. Shortly afterward, representatives from the university's student Jewish Society appeared and began voicing their anger. Palestinian Society members and I pointed out the protest was peaceful and it was our democratic right to assemble and raise awareness of the plight of the Palestinians and the realities of Israeli occupation. Though voices were raised, and fingers were pointed, the exchanges remained civil. No threats were made by either side and there was no use of inappropriate or abusive language. This was, ultimately, a political debate concerning two sets of students.

Within a few minutes, university security officers arrived, who demanded that the wall be dismantled. When the protestors refused and continued with their protest, the university reported the matter to the police. Two police cars with around four police officers subsequently arrived onto campus with their sirens blaring. They ordered that the wall be dismantled on the legal ground that it was 'obstructing the highway'. The Palestinian Society, though frustrated and angered by what they believed to be unfair treatment, complied with the order and began dismantling the wall.

I expressed my discomfort to the police sergeant at the closing down of a peaceful student protest and raised questions around the police response, which I felt was unfair. Again, there was no raised voice, no threat of violence, and no bad language. I remained calm throughout. On hearing my objections, the police sergeant ordered that I remain quiet or 'You're coming in.' Slightly afraid but also angered by the fact that he was threatening to arrest me, I muttered 'law-trip' under my breath. The officer heard me. 'What's a law-trip?,' he asked. 'What you lot are on,' I replied. To my complete surprise, and true to his words, the officer replied: 'That's it. Breach of the peace. Take him in.'

Though I was being told that the legal grounds for my arrest was a 'breach of the peace', my offence in reality seemed to have more to do with 'answering back'. I was bundled into the back of a police car, driven to the police station, and held in a cell. A few minutes later, the police sergeant who arrested me arrived and handed me a cup of coffee. He instructed me to follow him to the custody desk. There, he explained the legal grounds for my arrest to the custody sergeant and asked me to provide him with my personal details, including my name, address, and date of birth, which I did. I was then told that I was free to leave. On being escorted to the exit, the police sergeant gave me a 'talking to' and explained how I was wrong to have challenged his authority. I left the police station and returned to campus to continue my day as normal. The entire process from the moment of my arrest until my release lasted for around an hour. No fingerprints, photographs, or DNA swabs were taken. The police made a note of the protest and my arrest in the following way on their intelligence system:

At 1125 hours on the 30/09/2007 officers attended the Nottingham University due to a demonstration getting out of hand. On arrival the officers found that a large plasterboard wall had been constructed and was blocking a highway. This wall had been constructed by the student Palestinian Society in protest to a wall that is being built by the Israeli government in the West Bank. Also at the demonstration were members of the Student Jewish Society. A member of the student Palestinian Society became quite excited with his comments towards the student Jewish society and was arrested to prevent a breach of the peace. This male was Rizwaan Sabir dob [redacted] of [address redacted]. SABIR is no trace PNC details confirmed by DVLA. SABIR is an Asian male 5ft 06" tall of medium build. He has short black hair and a short black beard.[3]

This intelligence entry notes that there was 'no trace' of me on the Police National Computer (PNC) and that the police therefore had to confirm my details through records maintained by the Driver Vehicle Licensing Agency (DVLA). This was unsurprising because until this arrest, I had never had any involvement with the police.

Other intelligence files reveal how intelligence on pro-Palestinian activists had already been collected by the police, and then merged with new intelligence that was collected during my time in custody, in order to assess whether I should be charged and prosecuted as a terrorist. A second police intelligence report, dated 30 January 2008, contains the following text:

Further to memex entries CIRR00970346 and CIRR00972009 that refers to the demonstration outside the Hallward Library on Nottingham University Campus on 30/11/2007. The demonstration involved the student Palestinian Society building a wall in protest to the events involving the Israeli government in the West Bank.

The following people were present:

[Name Redacted]
[Name Redacted]
[Name Redacted]
[Name Redacted]

OFFICER COMMENTS

[Name redacted] is believed to be [name redacted] date of birth [redacted] at Nottingham University [redacted] not in halls of residence
[Name redacted] is believed to be [name redacted] date of birth [redacted]
[Name redacted] is believed to be [name redacted] date of birth [redacted]
[Name redacted] is believed to be [name redacted] date of birth [redacted].[4]

The names of pro-Palestinian students who attended the protest outside the library in which I was arrested for a breach of the peace were being logged by the police two months after the event.[5] Attending a peaceful pro-Palestinian protest, in other words, is enough for a person's name to appear on the security state's radar. The third police intelligence report is dated 24 April 2008 and contains the following text:

During Wednesday 23/04/2008 there was a protest outside the Hallward Library Notts University by a Palestinian faction protesting Israel's occupation of Gaza. It was relatively low level and passed without incident. However, there have been tensions between the two communities on campus during this educational year so it should be borne in mind that matters have not yet run their course.[6]

Members of the Palestinian Society were later included in an intelligence report that was produced whilst I was in custody for suspected terrorism. The document – which is titled 'Nottinghamshire University Palestinian Society' – opens with the following text:

The Palestinian Society is a registered society at the University. It is not believed to have a website (unable to locate through internet research) but has an email address of [redacted]. Current members are believed to be...[7]

The report then goes on to name each of the ten members of the society, including myself despite the fact that I was never a member of the Palestinian Society, and logs key pieces of information next to their names, including full name, date of birth, address, telephone number(s), email address(es), social media account(s), information taken from the Police National Computer, nationality, and family members.[8] Next to the names of four of these ten people, it includes the following text:

> involved in demonstration at University of Nottingham 30/11/07 during which Rizwaan Sabir was arrested.[9]

As the report continues, there is an eleventh and twelfth person being logged with the following text next to their name:

> The two persons below are not confirmed as members but have been seen at a Palestine demonstration.[10]

The entry then notes the following about them:

> [This person was] photographed with [the President of the Palestinian Society] in an article regarding the Palestinian wall demonstration during which Rizwaan Sabir was arrested. Seen in company of [name redacted].[11]

What the inclusion of these two people shows is that the police were not only surveilling those who were thought to be members of the student Palestinian Society but also those who were seen to be associating with them or were seen at a pro-Palestine student protest. *Association* with a person who is a pro-Palestinian activist, in other words, is enough for a person's name to appear on the security state's radar.

Such speculative overreach can also be seen in another intelligence report which was also created whilst I was in custody. This time, the intelligence report makes note of my 'associates'. What is revealing about this list of 'associates' is that out of the thirteen people who are listed, eleven have 'member' or 'possible member of Palestinian Society' written next to their name. It seems the only 'associates' the police were interested in were those who were members of, or associated with, the Palestinian Society.

During the course of my detention for suspected terrorism, the police and CPS had collected all of the above intelligence entries in relation to pro-Palestinian activism at the University of Nottingham – in addition to other pieces of intelligence – in order to assess whether to charge and prosecute me for terrorism.[12] Whilst campaigning in defence of Palestine may be an entirely legitimate, legal, and democratic form of political activity, it is the kind that does not go unnoticed by the security state and its surveillance infrastructure.

It is almost impossible to be sure what the exact reason was for my having an entry on MI5's files. The broader and more important point is that there is such a lack of transparency surrounding MI5's activities that it is impossible to hold them to account for their actions and behaviours. As such, they constitute a permanent danger to democratic principles.

17
Suspicious Scholarship

When I started my PhD research on counterterrorism, I thought I would no longer be viewed as a suspect or as somebody who was worthy of surveillance because I was no longer examining terrorist documents and propaganda for my research. But I was wrong. After having conducted my fieldwork and interviews with police officers and Westminster civil servants, I obtained emails through the Data Protection Act which showed how I continued to be suspected of being part of some terrorist syndicate.

In one email exchange with a civil servant at the Home Office, for example, I had requested a copy of a classified document – 'Counter-Terrorism Local Profiles' (CTLP) – used by police to inform the creation of localised risk assessments of terrorism. After various email exchanges, I was invited down to the Home Office and issued with a copy of the CTLP on the strict condition I would not disseminate it any further. The exchange was polite and pleasant but on reviewing the emails I secured, I discovered that a month before the meeting, the Home Office were talking with the Association of Chief Police Officers (ACPO) on whether to release this CTLP document to me. '[Home Office officials] will discuss it with the relevant stakeholders in ACPO [who will in turn] provide us with comments,' reads the first part of an email.[1] A couple of paragraphs down, after a Home Office official explains to a colleague that I am a 'frequent applicant of the Freedom of Information Act', they go onto say: 'if you weren't already aware, Mr Sabir was one of the "Nottingham Two" who were arrested in May 2008 for suspected involvement in Islamic terrorism.'[2] Though my objective in requesting this document was to inform my understanding of how risk was being assessed by the police, my motivations were implied to be driven by perhaps something more sinister.

Not only were police officers suspicious of my PhD research, officials at the Home Office were also apparently concerned.

This became evident from partially redacted emails I was able to obtain. I was able to triangulate these redacted emails by comparing and matching their content and the dates with my own correspondence.

One email was sent by a detective inspector situated at the ACPO who was working on Prevent. One day before my scheduled interview with him at the ACPO headquarters in Westminster, he sent an email to the Home Office informing them of our proposed meeting and my 'controversial' background:

> Rizwaan Sabir has contacted me several times over the last few weeks. He has attracted controversy as you will see if you google his name. He was the student detained for 6 days in 2008 whilst a student at the University of Nottingham under Operation Minerva. Mr Sabir has already posed the attached questions in an e-mail which I did not answer but I have agreed to meet him tomorrow.[3]

The day after the interview, the detective inspector sent another email to the Home Office, briefing them about some of the questions and points I had raised. This is not a full summary of the interview but perhaps these are the points the detective inspector felt were the most important for the Home Office to be aware of:

> I said I would update you after my meeting with PhD student Rizwaan Sabir. Rizwaan contacted me several weeks ago, seeking information to assist with his PhD studies. I agreed to meet rather than exchange emails. I knew his name and was aware that he has been controversial in the recent past. Rizwaan asked me a series of questions which he had asked others employed in the sphere of Prevent. He asked if I knew about informal briefings which took place between Special Branch officers and university staff. Rizwaan was quite persistent and asked many questions about police interaction with Muslim students and about the number of universities where radicalisation towards AQ [Al-Qaeda] is taking place. He has quite an anti-police stance (his blog on the Ceasefire website demonstrates this). He clearly has a grievance due to his days in custody under TACT

[the Terrorism Act 2000], which undoubtedly fuels his percep-
tion of the police.[4]

This same detective inspector had done his due-diligence in
preparation for my interview with him. In my interview, I asked
him whether involvement in a peaceful political protest on a university campus, say in support of Palestine, could prompt the
police to create an intelligence report on a protestor. He replied
with the following:

> It might be that, for example, a PC [Police Constable] at Not-
> tingham [Police] knows about a wall being erected. That
> information might be put onto an intelligence log but not nec-
> essarily that Rizwaan Sabir was involved in it.

The purpose for asking this question was to determine whether
political protest was being logged on intelligence systems because
of the time I had been arrested to 'prevent a breach of the peace'
for my involvement in a pro-Palestine student demonstration in
2007 at the University of Nottingham.

What is important to note is that the detective inspector knew
about this student demonstration and my arrest when I posed
the question to him. Since it was quite a low-profile protest that
happened four years earlier, it was likely the detective inspector
had accessed police intelligence files, which contained a record
of my pro-Palestinian student activism at the University of
Nottingham.

In other documents that were disclosed to me, there was correspondence between Nottinghamshire Police and the ACPO in
London. In one piece of correspondence, my use of the Freedom
of Information Act (FOI) to secure information on Prevent was
being questioned by Nottinghamshire Police. By way of context,
I had submitted two FOI requests and asked for Nottinghamshire Police to disclose the engagement and meetings they had
with two local Muslim organisations – the Karimia Institute and
the Muslim Community Organisation. On receipt of my requests,
Nottinghamshire Police had contacted the ACPO strongly urging
them to reject my request, invoking three grounds: that I was
being 'vexatious' by 'making repeated [FOI] requests'; that I was

trying to 'annoy and disrupt' the police; and that I was 'attempting to discredit the work the [police] force carries out as part of Prevent with Muslim organisations'.[5]

Nottinghamshire Police, like the ACPO and the Home Office, seemed to think my researcher profile was perhaps a 'cover' for some 'ulterior' purpose. This, incidentally, may help explain why a significant number of FOI requests I had sent to government departments were all being sent to the ACPO and logged centrally by the Central Referral Unit.[6] I may have been released without charge from custody but, just like the officers during my time in detention had suspected my possession of information was being used for a suspicious purpose, government departments, civil servants, and police officers were still viewing my research on counterterrorism through a similar lens of suspicion. But this suspicion and subsequent surveillance did not emerge out of nowhere. It was aligned with intelligence entries about me on Nottinghamshire Police's own criminal intelligence system.

18
A Safe House

Around a year after my legal case concluded in September 2011, my energy and attention fully shifted towards completing my PhD. However, my sense of anxiety and fear that I was being surveilled remained intact. This was especially the case since I now had more time to reflect on the previous few years I had spent fighting the legal case, collecting information on my own case, and analysing counterterrorism more broadly for my PhD research. Based on the materials I had collected, I knew that I was of 'interest' to the police and MI5, both before my arrest for suspected terrorism and most certainly after it. My anxiety was not therefore some figment of a traumatised imagination but was based on observable evidence that I had in my possession. Despite this, I tried to reassure myself that there was no real reason to be fearful. I had done nothing 'wrong'.

But this reasoning was not able to calm my anxiety no matter how many times I repeated this line to myself. I knew that I had done nothing 'wrong' when a trace appeared on MI5's radar prior to my arrest in 2008. Neither had I done anything 'wrong' when I was arrested and detained in 2008 for suspected terrorism. Yet, I was still subjected to detention, investigation, inquiry, and subsequent stops and searches. I therefore knew in my mind that a person did not have to do 'wrong' to become of interest to the security state or be treated as 'suspicious'.

What increased this sense of anxiety is that through my research, I had come to understand that the police and MI5 were not only interested in violent individuals who were planning and executing armed attacks. They were also interested in peaceful, lawful dissent and political activism more broadly, as well as the wider Muslim community whom they suspected of harbouring and ideologically supporting armed and political Islamic groups. During that time, I also discovered and reported on how counterterrorism police were monitoring peaceful anti-capitalist groups using the same framework and approaches meant to be reserved for dealing with terrorist organisations.[1] I therefore knew that even though I was innocent and not engaged in violence, this did not guarantee protection from the police and security services, and their surveillance machine.

For surveillance to have an ability to shape and mould behaviour, a person needs to suspect they 'may' be being watched. This suspicion is enough to generally prompt a person to change their behaviour in order to ensure they are not the victim of some sort of direct state action, especially violence. I, however, already knew that even before my arrest for suspected terrorism I was already known to the police and MI5, and then appeared on the radar of government departments whilst I was doing PhD fieldwork. There was, therefore, no uncertainty around whether I was of interest or a 'marked' person. *I knew* I was. No matter how much I tried to reassure myself that I was innocent and 'not important enough to be surveilled', the other part of my mind refused to accept this idea wholeheartedly. Whilst I tried to reason with myself, it felt as if my mind was being torn into two opposing directions. My mind and my life started to feel like I had entered a strange Kafkaesque state where I was accused and surveilled for something but was never quite sure what this 'something' was.

* * *

After my legal case concluded, I lived alone in an apartment in Manchester and constantly felt like somebody may have been entering my home when I was away. I thought they were moving small items around in order to 'gaslight' me, to make me feel as if I was losing my mind. In order to help determine whether this was happening, I began placing a small wooden chip into the gap between my front door and the door frame when I left the apartment. If the wood chip was disturbed on my return, I would know somebody had entered in my absence. But I felt that this was not good enough. I wanted whoever may be entering to *know* that I was aware of their presence. I thus began placing a glass of brightly coloured juice behind my front door. If somebody opened the door in my absence, they would knock the glass over and stain the carpet. Then I would be sure. Needless to say, the wood chip and the fruit juice were both unmoved; and whilst I felt better knowing that nobody had entered my apartment the few times I did this, I felt quite depressed at my act, and stopped doing it.

In early 2013, I decided to move back into my parents' home in Nottingham for the write up of my doctorate but my sense of hypervigilance and paranoia started to intensify. Whilst I had been suspicious of strangers for a considerable period of time, this suspicion now started to impact my understanding of my own family and friends. When I spoke about my research and told them about the things I was studying – about how this had helped me understand the world better but had also depressed me – their advice was often that I should not be so personally invested in the subject, and that I should take things easy. However, rather than viewing this as well-intentioned advice from people who cared for me and my welfare, I began to suspect that my own family and friends were actually working for the police and security services, and were tasked with pacifying me. I was being given this advice, I thought, not out of concern for my well-being but as a way of preventing me from researching counterterrorism and advocating for the rights of the Muslim community. In my traumatised mind, I recall questioning whether this was even my *real* family.

I began to feel alone, isolated, and trapped. Soon, I started spending time away from Nottingham, with friends I knew would not ask me about my research and would not speak to me about issues that could 'trigger' me. I also began to sleep rough in my car, usually in a lay-by somewhere in the countryside that was quiet and secluded. If somebody wanted to spy on me, they would have to go out of their way to do so. In a deserted area, I reasoned, somebody's presence would immediately be visible. Being in the car also made me feel as if I had a higher chance of outrunning the security state if I needed to physically escape from them. Of course, the strange irony is that being in a vehicle makes pinpointing your movements with the help of surveillance cameras quite straightforward, but this made no difference to me. The police and security services already knew who I was and could probably pinpoint my movements through my smartphone. The reason for confining myself to the car was to be alone, and to have a safe space that could double up as a tool that would make physically following me more difficult.

But I knew this approach of trying to outrun the security state was in vain, and my attempt to constantly stay mobile was not going to be sustainable in the long run. Under intense pressure, I started wondering whether I should just go and surrender to the police and MI5. I could then ask them why they were spying on me and what they wanted. Maybe if I let them interrogate me, I wondered, they will call off all surveillance and just leave me alone. Anything, I told myself, would be better than this open-air prison I felt I was now living in, where my body was free but my mind felt like it had been placed into a vice that was being tightened by the police and MI5 with every passing minute. Strangely, the thought of being in a physical jail with its thick metal doors and brick walls felt more appealing than this open-air prison that nobody was even willing to acknowledge existed.

* * *

By April 2013, I was pretty much living rough in my car, and was constantly on the move. Again, whilst my memory is fragmented, I recall one evening when I ended up driving for over four hours from Nottingham to stay with my friend in her three-storey home in a leafy suburb of West Glasgow. My friend was studying for her PhD, and another friend, who had already completed his, was already lodging with her. Another one of the rooms was rented to a tenant on a short to medium-term basis. The attic, which had a huge window overlooking large trees, a well-maintained garden, and the rear of other homes, was where I would stay. When I arrived, I did not mention to either of my friends that I was living rough in the car or that I wanted to use the home as a 'hideout'. Over the next two days that I stayed, I spent a considerable amount of time in the attic and pretty much paced back and forth around the large room whilst my mind raced with thoughts quicker than I could process them. Despite the exhaustion from continually being on the road and sleeping rough in the car, the sense of helplessness and the fear that I was being hunted and chased caused me to sob continually. I could hardly sleep. At night, I would be wide awake and restless, trying to do anything to stop my mind from racing, and failing each time.

I was not sure whether my friends could tell I was going through a rough time, but they generally left me alone. The few times my friend came up to see if I was okay, I would put on a brave face and tell her that I was fine. What could I have told her without sounding completely 'crazy'? That I was being hunted by MI5? That I felt invisible forces were trying to entrap me so they could imprison me for a very long time for terrorism? That it felt as if somebody was trying to psychologically destroy me in order to prevent me from finishing my doctorate and advocating for my community? The best thing to do in this situation, I reasoned, was to remain silent and deal with whatever I was going through quietly. The last thing I needed was somebody accusing me of being 'mad'.

At the same time, I was reluctant to share my feelings openly with them because I began to suspect that both my friends were working for the security and intelligence services. In my imagination, the fact that a young woman from Scandinavia was renting one of the rooms made me think this was an intelligence safe house where international spies resided and rested. In another instance, when my friend told me her husband was away in India to attend a family member's funeral, I suspected this was the 'cover' story being given to me to explain his absence whilst he was on an overseas operation. As these incidents reveal, I was seeing everything around me, even the most banal and ordinary, through a gaze of hyper-suspicion. Rather than paying my condolences, I remember saying: 'A funeral. Of course.' This was my way of subtly signalling that I knew what was happening here and that my friend and her husband were both intelligence agents. There were many instances when I made such 'coded' remarks and comments. In fact, most of my conversations during this period of my life seemed to comprise coded language, phrases, and words. It was too risky to just speak openly and freely. I felt that since I was surrounded by intelligence agents, I could end up having my words weaponised and used against me. The best thing was to therefore either remain quiet or speak in a coded manner.

And then, one evening in Glasgow, I could no longer maintain the 'code' and confronted my male friend who was originally from the Swat valley in Pakistan but had now secured his UK citizenship. We were both stood in the kitchen. The radio played at a low volume in the background and the extractor fan roared whilst vegetarian food simmered on the cooker. 'I know,' I said to him. 'I know.' He looked at me intrigued for a second but did not respond to the comment. 'I know this is a safe house for MI6 and I know you are working for MI6.' He momentarily paused and with a blank expression said, 'Yes, but do not tell anybody.' In that moment, I felt euphoric and relieved. Like an entire weight had been lifted off my mind and shoulders. In my mind, I had cracked a deeply complicated puzzle that the vast majority of people neither had the ability nor desire to solve. At the same time, I told myself that I was neither paranoid nor 'mad'. I was a perceptive and emotionally intelligent person who had an ability to see and understand things that were invisible to most people.

Needless to say, my friend's home was neither an MI6 safe house nor were my friends working for MI6 or the security state. I do not know exactly why my friend went along with what I said, but I suspect it may perhaps have had something to do with him realising I was unwell and that it was easier to perhaps agree with me rather than challenge what I was saying. Within a matter of minutes though, the euphoria had been replaced by the realisation that I had travelled to Glasgow to hide from the security state but had in fact driven right into their midst in this intelligence safe house. Everything I seemed be doing to protect myself, I felt, only led me to being further compromised and endangered. Then the self-questioning started. What does this realisation mean in practice? Do I have to work for the intelligence services now? And since I will refuse to do so, what will be the consequences? Will I be set-up? Imprisoned? Killed? Feeling the security state's vice tightening once again around my mind, I decided I needed to get out of Glasgow and get back on the road. But I could not just get up and leave without raising suspicion. I had to wait until the morning. That night, I arranged my belongings and packed my backpack but when the morning came, my car keys had gone missing. As I frantically searched for them, my friend eventually told me she had them and would not give them to me because I was in no condition to be alone and absolutely in no condition to drive. It was clear by this stage that my friends had realised I was unwell and were doing well-intentioned things to try and protect me from myself. But at that moment, their actions sent my mind into total despair.

My only tool for staying what felt like a step ahead of MI5 and the police was my ability to use my car to escape from them. Now, this tool had been taken away from me too, and I felt like I was being held prisoner. Despite knowing that the police and MI5 work together, in my state of panic, I dialled 999 and reported to the police operator that I was being held prisoner by my friends. I called the police not because I felt they would be able to help me. No. I needed somebody from a state institution to formally note that I had alerted the authorities of being held against my will and that such information, if the need arose, would be critical in the future in case I was disappeared or killed. It was my attempt at creating a record that would be helpful in tracking me down if I mysteriously went missing. At the same time, by alerting the police, I was hoping to pressure my friends, whom I suspected of being intelligence agents, to return my car keys. Both of my friends, who had continuously tried to reassure me they were not my enemies, had discovered that I had called the police on them and realised that I was out of control. I would not listen to anything they were saying. In fact, there was nothing they could have said during this time which would have convinced me to trust them. I could trust nobody.

Within a short space of time, a male police officer arrived at the house. My friends told him that I was researching counterterrorism for my doctorate and was experiencing some sort of mental breakdown as a result of the subject matter. I was in the same room but I was reluctant to speak to the officer in front of these 'intelligence agents' who were claiming to be my friends. I therefore remained silent and asked the officer to go into the dining room if he wished to speak with me. When we did, I could not express what was actually going on in my mind. Not only was my mind racing with multiple and often contradictory thoughts faster than I could even make sense of them, but I also felt that the officer was under a duty to collect intelligence on me and to communicate whatever I told him to MI5, who I knew work directly with the police. So, despite having called the police in order to record what I was experiencing, I was unable to actually *say* what I was feeling or thinking out of fear that it would endanger me more. I felt helpless and completely alone by this stage. There was nobody who could seemingly understand or protect me; it was a terrifying and lonely place to be.

I do not actually remember anything I said to the police officer in the dining room but I do remember him jotting down some notes in his pocket notebook. We then went back into the front room where my friends were sat. Based on the earlier conversation the officer had with them, he decided to call my family and spoke directly to my elder brother. My brother reassured the officer that he would drive to Glasgow and take me back to the family home in Nottingham. Despite my repeated cries to want to drive my own car, I was not able to and was instead made to wait for my brother to arrive who then took me home. Leaving my car in Glasgow, however, was causing me considerable anxiety. I kept thinking that since I had figured out my friends were intelligence agents running a safe house, there would be consequences. And then my mind got lost in a whole array of 'potential' things the police and MI5 may do, including rigging my unattended car with explosives that they would park at Glasgow airport and then later 'discover'. They would then have their 'evidence' to prosecute me in the courts.

19
Sensing a Set Up

On my return to Nottingham, the sense that I was going to be set up by the security services continued to overpower my mind. Whilst I do not recall the exact timeframe since my memory of that time is quite fragmented, I recall thinking that the Leeds Marathon was going to be bombed. This thought was prompted by a recent visit to the city to see my younger brother Hamaad, and two cousins Haaris and Zirwa, who were all studying in the city at the same time. During my time in Leeds, in my state of hyper-vigilance, a few things stood out to me: vehicle number plates, road signs, and the workers on a building site that overlooked my brother's apartment. The road signs, and in particular a mobile sign on wheels with digital writing informing the public about the Leeds Marathon and subsequent road closures, was interpreted by me as a sign that the Leeds Marathon was going to be targeted. The police, obviously could not tell the public this fact but in order to minimise disruption and casualties, they were trying to make people avoid the area. Thus, the workers too were undercover police and MI5 personnel who were on the lookout for suspicious people and behaviours. The fact that they were positioned so close to Hamaad and Haaris's apartment was interpreted by me as a sign that they suspected not only me but my family too.

I rang Hamaad and told him to leave Leeds and come back to Nottingham immediately. When he asked what had happened and why I wanted him home, I refused to tell him over the phone since I was convinced my phone was bugged. Without asking any further questions, he caught the train and within a few hours, he was home. I told him not to tell anybody but I suspected that the Leeds Marathon was going to be bombed. Hamaad looked at me with a mix of anger and confusion and asked why I was saying such things. I did not know with any certainty that the marathon was going to be bombed, I told him, nor did I have any evidence to really support my belief. It was just a feeling that the marathon was going to be hit and I therefore needed him to be away from the city. My brother, by this stage, was beyond annoyed with me for making him travel for two hours to share my paranoia, and returned to Leeds the same day.

As the days passed, the sense of panic and feeling that something 'bad' was going to happen started intensifying. I felt compelled to do 'something' in order to protect myself rather than waiting for something to happen and for the police to come rushing through my door to take me away; either because they suspected I was involved in an attack or because I refused to share information with them to prevent an attack. I therefore decided to telephone a contact whom I had met during my fieldwork in Birmingham. She worked in a civilian role at the West Midlands Counter-Terrorism Unit. I explained to her that I was probably going to sound 'crazy' but I had a feeling that an attack was going to take place in the UK, and that I was going to be blamed for it. I told her that I did not know what was going to happen and that I had no evidence to support my feeling. I just needed her to know I am neither involved nor responsible for anything that may happen. She explained that she would seek advice on what I was saying and call me back. When she called back, she informed me that she had discussed what I had said with the assistant chief constable of West Midlands Police, who was in charge of counterterrorism activity. The officer, she said, wanted me to call and speak with him directly.

I felt angry and scared at the same time, and was thinking contradictory things. Should I call the officer or not? What will happen if I do? What will happen if I don't? If an attack does happen, and it emerges that I did not say something, will I be accused of being involved or complicit? Was this a 'test' of some sort being orchestrated by the police and MI5 to determine if I will allow people to die by not saying something? As my mind raced with these sorts of questions, calling the officer, I felt, seemed like the only option available to me. If something did happen, my reporting the issue to the police would be my defence in court.

I dialled the officer's number and explained that I had a strong suspicion that somebody was going to orchestrate a terrorist attack in the UK and was going to try to implicate me. The reason I was calling him, I said, was so he knew that I had nothing to do with it and that I was an innocent person. As I professed my innocence, I sobbed like a helpless child. The only thing I recall the officer saying is that he knew I had done nothing wrong and that he was going to dispatch two officers from the West Midlands Counter-Terrorism Unit.

The thought of being believed, of my innocence being acknowledged, made me feel better for that moment, as did being in the custody of police officers. Being in police custody would at least mean nobody could blame me for not reporting my suspicions, or accuse me of being involved in the terrorist attack. But within a matter of minutes, knowing counterterrorism officers were on their way to meet with me sent my mind into a frenzy of fear and panic. All the rationalisations I had made to myself before calling the police now all seemed to be stupid and short-sighted, especially since the police would be in a position to expand their intelligence files on me and perhaps exploit my state of weakness and vulnerability for their own ends. But it was too late now.

I went downstairs, and in order to ensure my family was not alarmed when the officers arrived, I told my mum that I had rung the police and told them there was going to be a terrorist attack. I explained that I did not want to call the police but I had no choice in the matter and returned to my bedroom awaiting the police's arrival. Around thirty minutes later, there was a knock on my door but it was not the police. It was my aunty Sofia. Sofia, who is a sharp-minded entrepreneur and mother of three, is the youngest of my dad's three sisters. Whilst I was in custody, it was Sofia who served as a family representative to my lawyers and was aware of the legal processes and powers that were at play. It was therefore natural for my mum to contact her about what I had told her, revealing the importance of pro-active family support networks in moments of crisis such as this. On her short drive to my home, she had the foresight to speak with Tayab Ali, the lawyer who led the team of pro-bono solicitors during my time in custody, over the telephone. Tayab told Sofia that they would deal with the police and in the meantime should pass a message onto me: 'Rizwaan needs to see a doctor. Not a police officer.'

20
Seeing Spies

It was mid-afternoon when we arrived at Nottingham's main hospital, the Queen's Medical Centre. The Accident and Emergency Department was quite busy and we had to wait for around thirty or so minutes to be seen. I was taken into a room and assessed by a psychiatric nurse who had white hair, was quite old, and spoke with a thick Scottish accent. I do not really remember much from this encounter or the exact sequence of events; only that I kept thinking the psychiatric nurse was working for MI5. Having returned from Scotland only a few days earlier, the fact that this nurse was Scottish made me feel as if this was a coded attempt by the MI5 to inform me that what had happened in Glasgow was not going to stop just because I had pre-emptively called the police on them, left Scotland or was seeking medical support. The security state, I felt, were telling me that there was no escaping them now that I had 'found' their safe house, and that they would therefore be watching and observing everything I said and did. There would be a 'price' to pay.

After the initial assessment by the psychiatric nurse was over, I was discharged and told to return in two days, when another team of psychiatric practitioners would meet with me. But I did not want to go back since I did not feel safe there. No institution, in fact, could be trusted. As my research had informed me, every public body is involved in counterterrorism and surveillance activity in one way or another through the Prevent policy. Prevent surveillance, in fact, became a legal duty for all public bodies to conduct with the introduction of the Counter-Terrorism and Security Act of 2015 but the policy was already in place informally in education and health services before this time, including the time when I was taken there.

When I got home, I discovered that the psychiatric nurse had prescribed me sleeping pills. When my family told me to take the pills, which were coloured blue, I refused to take them. The pills, in my mind, symbolically represented the security state's desire for me to 'sleep' so I could neither be a researcher of counterterrorism nor advocate in defence of Muslims. It felt like an active attempt at pacification. But, by the late evening, I had caved in to the endless pressure my mum and Sofia had placed on me, and after reciting the name of Allah, I took the sleeping pill. I awoke at sunrise, and even though I had managed to sleep the longest for quite some time, I woke up in a state of extreme anxiety. I felt something 'bad' had happened. But before I did or said anything, I felt the need to make ablution and perform *salah*. I then went downstairs, reached for the television control and put the news on. Every channel that I flicked through was breaking the same story: the Boston Marathon bombing. 'I told you something was going to happen,' I said to my mum. She looked at me as if she had seen a ghost.

*   *   *

Later that day, I had to go back to the hospital to meet with two psychiatric doctors and one psychiatric nurse. The purpose of the appointment was for my mental state to be assessed in order for a diagnosis to be made. I remember on arrival undergoing a pre-assessment in a small room which had either one or two medical practitioners sat on chairs. One of the doctors, dressed in a lilac shirt and a tie, introduced himself and added: 'I am from Yorkshire.' I do not know what the purpose of this comment was, but I was immediately triggered by it. I thought the doctor was working for MI5 and signalling that my belief that the Leeds marathon, which is in Yorkshire, was going to be bombed was good but not quite good enough since I had gotten the country wrong. I recall thinking, are the security services trying to determine how I had managed to figure out a marathon was going to be bombed? Are they trying to recruit me or are they trying to undermine me? The only other thing I remember from this entire pre-assessment was the same doctor at some point telling me to drink a shot of a clear liquid in a small glass. I refused to take it but Sofia, who was with me in the room, gave me a hard stare and sternly told me to drink it. My feeling was that if this was an MI5 agent who was moonlighting as a doctor, and I did not comply with his command, then I would find myself in even more danger than I was presently in. Feeling that there was no choice, I drank the shot.

I was taken into another room which had two male doctors and one male nurse. All were sitting and holding papers in their hands. This encounter reminded me of the interrogation room during detention, where police officers also sat with papers in their hands. Only now, I told myself, these were not police officers; they were intelligence agents, whose jobs here in the hospital were simply a cover for their true identities as spies. The chief doctor who led the assessment sat to my right. He introduced himself and, based on his name, I knew he was Muslim and a non-native English speaker. 'Where are you from?', I asked him. 'I am from Egypt,' he replied. With news of the Boston marathon bombing running at the forefront of my mind, I felt that the Egyptian doctor's presence was the UK intelligence agencies' coded way of informing me that what I had predicted was not just a domestic UK matter any more, but one that had an international dimension to it. This is why the panel of three men included this Egyptian man, who I suspected was working for the CIA. The psychiatric nurse, who occupied the middle seat and sat immediately in front of me, was a white male, roughly in his late thirties or early forties. He had a physique which one would typically associate with a rugby player or, as I thought at the time, the military. Out of all three of the men, it was this nurse who I found to be the most intimidating. Throughout the entire assessment, he did not say a word and his eyes were fixated on me. He observed me throughout non-stop. Even when I looked at him, he would not break his eye contact and stared at me throughout the assessment. At the end of the assessment, the Egyptian doctor asked him if he wanted to say anything. This is the only time he looked away from me, turning to tell the Egyptian doctor: 'No. I have nothing to add.' I remember nothing about the third person, another doctor, who sat to my left.

I do not remember much of what was discussed in this assessment but I do remember being extremely vague and ambiguous in my answers. All I was thinking of is that these men were all intelligence officers representing UK and US intelligence; but I could not determine what their goal was. Did they want to recruit me? Interrogate me? Undermine me? The notion they may actually be medical professionals doing their jobs is something I simply could not accept at that time.

A few days later, the findings of this initial assessment were sent to me and my GP in a formal letter written by the Egyptian doctor. His conclusion was that I was 'experiencing an acute psychotic episode, the exact nature of which would be hard to determine at this stage'. In his view, I needed time away from my PhD for a total of six months and needed to start a programme of anti-psychotic medication which, I later found out, is used for people with schizophrenia and bipolar disorders. Years later, a psychiatrist and psychologist informed me that the assessment made in 2013 by the Egyptian doctor was incorrect. There was, they concluded, something far more complex at play and they therefore referred me to the 'complex trauma' team in the NHS. After the initial diagnosis of 'acute psychosis' had been made in 2013, in addition to medicines I was prescribed, the Egyptian doctor also advised meeting with a mental health worker whose role was to engage in some form of talk-therapy.

The case worker was in her late twenties and had a strong sense of empathy and understanding. Her presence and our conversations did help me talk through some of the things I was feeling, but I could not be fully open with her since I did not completely trust her. In fact, I suspected she may have been providing summaries of our conversations to the police and MI5. Thus, whenever I spoke to her, I felt quite restricted in what I could say. In total, I met with her for around six months and was on medication over roughly the same period before being discharged. As my life moved forward over the following years, I was actively controlling my thoughts and self-disciplining my behaviour. I also refused to really speak about the psychiatric problems I had been experiencing.

For all of my adult life, I have been aware of countless examples of people who have suffered under counterterrorism practices in ways that cannot be imagined, even in our darkest nightmares. Individuals have been indefinitely detained without charge, trial, or rights in internment camps such as Guantanamo Bay. People were kidnapped and disappeared to secret CIA-run prisons that nobody even knew existed, where they were tortured, beaten, and raped. I had no right to complain about what I was feeling, considering people in the UK in the immediate aftermath of 9/11 had been thrown into high-security prisons such as Belmarsh, without charge or trial, or house-arrested, based on secret evidence neither they nor their lawyers could see or challenge in open court. Compared to these people, I had no right to complain. After all, I was given access to a lawyer, the due process of law, and the right to remain silent without facing the threat of physical torture, abuse, and rape. Of course, whilst I was livid that my life had been turned upside down because of the arrest and detention, and that some things had become more challenging, especially at the roadside and whenever I travelled overseas, I kept telling myself I was not physically harmed or abused in the same way and therefore I had no right to talk about or complain about what I went through. In fact, as time went on, if somebody asked questions about the arrest and detention, I downplayed the whole thing. What was a life-changing experience had over time become *only* six days.

21
Coming to America

Whenever I travelled in and out of Britain, I was at risk of being stopped, forced to answer questions, and required to allow the data on my mobile devices to be extracted. Each time it happened, it had a corrosive impact on my psychological well-being. Airports were particularly triggering. When I travelled to Paris in 2013 and to Brussels in early 2015 to give academic presentations, I refused to fly. I took the Eurostar to Paris and drove to Brussels. In October 2015, I was invited by the Brennan Center for Justice at New York University to talk about my academic work in Washington, DC. I had to decide whether I was ready to fly again.

On receiving the request, I had wanted to accept it without any question. I was an early career academic and needed international speaking opportunities. I had also never travelled to the US so this was a good opportunity to tick it off my bucket list. But, the thought of flying to America of all places triggered all sorts of questions, anxieties, and doubts in my mind. Was it wise to travel to the US alone knowing I would almost certainly be stopped? Was it worth the hassle? Was it worth reigniting the trauma that every word I utter, when I will, no doubt, be detained, will be scrutinised by the police and border guards? Is it right to deny these professional opportunities to myself because I felt afraid of the security state? My anxieties were especially strongly felt because of the mental health problems I had had two years earlier. I was aware that flying to the US could be quite triggering. I was unable to decide, and thought it through for a few days. I also sought counsel from two trusted friends. In the end, I decided to confront my fears and travel.

I emailed the organiser and asked her to send me a more formal invite that included her contact details and the hotel I would be staying at. 'I want to be able to hand over the invite and relevant details all in one email to the Department for Homeland Security on arrival at JFK,' I told her in an email. 'I suspect there is a high chance I will be questioned about my travels and so forth on arrival. Sorry for being paranoid, and appreciate the understanding.'

On the morning of my flight, the nerves and panic were overshadowing my mind and I had wanted to cancel the whole trip. I had been unable to sleep the entire night, and I was now reaching what felt like a tipping point. However, the *'fight'* element soon kicked in and I knew that cancelling the trip would mean having to forever live with the feeling that I had internalised the threats of the security state to such an extent that I was doing their job for them by self-policing and self-disciplining myself, by not flying. If I wanted to break the shackles they had placed on my mind, and which I was now keeping in place, I had to fly and confront this fear head on. And so, I set off for Manchester Airport and began mentally preparing myself for the detention that would inevitably happen when I arrived at JFK Airport to catch my connection to Washington, DC.

*   *   *

I cleared security at Manchester Airport and made my way to the aircraft gate. I waited until the queue had significantly lessened before trying to board. I was sat close to the gate and observed the Delta Airlines staff member scanning boarding cards into a silver machine that had a barcode reader built into it. Every time she scanned a boarding card, the light flashed green, she smiled and wished the passengers a pleasant flight. When the queue had lessened, I approached the gate and handed my boarding pass to her. She scanned it but the screen did not flash green. It flashed red and the words 'security' appeared on a small digital screen. The woman returned my boarding card and within a matter of seconds, a large-framed man, easily over 6ft tall with short dark hair, an ungroomed beard, and wearing a grey suit, appeared. 'Excuse me, sir,' he said in an American accent. 'I need to ask you some questions. Please follow me.'

We stopped a short distance away from the gate in a vacant area. We could both be seen but not heard. The man asked to see my passport and boarding card. After looking through them closely, he noted down my details on a piece of paper that was attached to a clipboard and asked what my purpose for travelling to the US

was. When I explained that I had been invited to brief policymakers around counterterrorism, he wanted to know who had invited
me, why they had invited me, what line of work I was involved
in, where I would be staying, what my personal and work email
address was, what my home and work address was, and what my
mobile number and office telephone number was. In this situation, the 'choice' was simple: answer the questions being put to
me or refuse to answer them on the basis of protecting my privacy
and most probably be denied boarding. He made a note of everything I said and returned my passport and boarding card. 'Thank
you for your time,' he said. 'You may go back to the gate.'

I returned to the gate and handed my boarding card to the same
airline staff member for the second time. She scanned it, and the
light, once again, flashed red. The words 'security' reappeared. The
airline staff member was about as surprised as I was. 'I'm sorry,
sir. You may not make this flight,' she said. 'Please go over to that
desk and speak with the woman sat there.' I walked a few yards
away from the gate to a counter, where a smartly dressed older
British woman was sat wearing an identification badge belonging
to the British Airport Authority (BAA). During the short walk,
I observed the large American man who had questioned me in
the first instance was copying information from his handwritten
form into a Blackberry smartphone. 'Hello,' I said to the woman.
'The Delta Airlines staff member at the gate has sent me to you,'
I explained. 'Your boarding card and passport, please,' she replied
in a cold tone. I handed it over and watched her scan my boarding
pass into her computer. As soon as she did, her computer monitor,
which I could see, showed a red banner across the top of her screen
with the word 'security' in large white letters appearing.

When I left my home, I knew I would certainly be stopped
when I arrived at JFK to catch my connection to Washington, DC
but what I was completely unprepared for was the level of scrutiny
I would encounter *before* I had even boarded the plane to the US.
From all the conversations I had had with family and friends who
had travelled to the US, none had been subjected to pre-flight
stops and questions at the point of departure in the UK. To this
day, I have asked numerous people who have travelled to the US
and none have experienced being stopped before boarding the
plane, let alone twice. There seemed to be a different set of rules

COMING TO AMERICA · 119

at play for those who were marked on the security state's radar as being involved in 'offences against the state'. When I therefore saw the word 'security' appear on the BAA woman's computer, I was convinced in that moment that there was a high probability that I may be denied boarding. The woman asked me similar questions to the American man but did not ask for my contact details. The whole question-and-answer process lasted around four minutes or so, and eventually she returned my passport and boarding card to me and followed up with a 'thank you'.

I went back to the gate for the third time now and handed my boarding pass to the same airline staff member. She scanned the barcode on the boarding pass, and this time the light flashed green. 'You are catching this flight after all,' she said in a light-hearted tone. 'Third time lucky,' I replied. If this is the level of scrutiny *before* I had boarded the flight, what was going to happen on arrival at JFK?

*　*　*

The immigration counter at JFK Airport was manned by a middle-aged black man sporting a Department for Homeland Security (DHS) uniform. I handed my passport over and was asked the same questions I had now been asked twice already. What was the purpose for travelling to the US and how long would I be staying? Where would I be staying? When would I be leaving? After answering all his questions, the DHS agent ordered me to look into a biometric computer so a picture of my eyes could be taken. I was then instructed to go to a room where I would receive instructions on what would come next. Some of my Muslim friends who had travelled to the US – Mohsin the office-worker, Shazad the insolvency practitioner, Harry the dentist, and Zeeshan the religious philosophy PhD student – had forewarned me about this room. I once heard somebody refer to it as 'the Muslim Suite' on social media. Each one of them had been pulled aside and taken into this room for questioning, demonstrating just how routine it is for entirely ordinary, law-abiding Muslims who travel to the US to be stopped and questioned on arrival for no seemingly obvious reason other than their Muslimness.

The large room was brightly lit and had a considerable amount of fixed seating. A large counter ran from one end to the other. Walking into the room, I noticed that the DHS agents were almost exclusively black or Hispanic. The security infrastructure of the US is fundamentally suspicious of racialised people. Yet, ironically, it was only workable on a day-to-day basis because of the contributions of racialised people themselves. The agent behind the counter was black, had dreadlocks, and wore a creased short-sleeve white shirt. I introduced myself and he asked for my passport, which he placed into a plastic tray with an accompanying sheet of paper and instructed me to take a seat until I was called.

When I first entered the room, there were around five men there – all people of colour – who sat in silence. There was no overt feeling of anger or outrage discernible in the room; no complaints; no sense of entitlement or confusion as to why we had been pulled out of line and placed in this room. It was as if we all knew *why* we had been selected. For the next thirty or so minutes, as I sat waiting, I observed that the only people who were being sent into this room, except for one young white woman, were all varying shades of non-white. They would enter the room, report to the desk, and within five to ten minutes, be asked a few cursory questions at the counter, and then be returned their passport and permitted to continue with their travels. With the clock counting down to my connection to Washington, DC, I went back to the counter to inquire when I would be seen. 'Somebody will be coming for you soon, sir,' the biracial woman who was now stationed at the desk told me. 'Please take a seat and wait to be seen.' I realised there was very little I could say or do, so I went back to my seat. Around ten further minutes had now passed until I heard my name being shouted loudly in a thick American accent 'Sabir?' I raised my hand, collected my red rucksack, and approached the counter. 'I am Rizwaan Sabir,' I told the young, white, male DHS agent with broad shoulders who had emerged from a room behind the counter. 'Please follow me, sir. I need to ask you some questions.' We walked through the reception area into a corridor and then a small room that had a white table and one seat on each side. There was a large glass wall that was smoked so nobody could see in nor out of the room. I was told to take a seat whilst the agent arranged his paperwork.

And then the questions started. What is your purpose for visiting the US? Who invited you? Why has an invite been extended to you? Where are you staying during the course of your stay? Do you use the WhatsApp chat service? Are you a Twitter and Facebook user? What is your username to both social media accounts? What is your mobile and office telephone number? Who is in your family and what are their ages? Which country was your father born in? Have you ever visited Pakistan? Where in Pakistan did you stay when you visited? Where do your family live in Pakistan? Then, the question I had been dreading: 'Are you known to British police for anything?' I did not know whether the DHS agent was asking me this question because he did not know the answer, or because he *did* know and wanted me to give my reading of events so he could log it on the DHS intelligence systems accordingly. After I explained why I was known to the UK police, how it was all one big 'misunderstanding', and answered his follow-up questions about the arrest and detention, the line of questioning became much broader and more political.

What is your opinion of al-Qaeda and ISIS? Why did al-Qaeda attack the US on 9/11? How does the US government and law enforcement agencies counter both groups at home, and also in Syria and Iraq? I was asked questions on what I thought were the most effective methods for conducting surveillance on terror suspects, and what use drone warfare served, especially in terms of their surveillance worth. Finally, the agent asked what the content of my paper was and whether I would be talking about anything that I had mentioned today. I explained that there would be some broad discussion of the issues I had explained to him but I would ultimately decide on the structure and content of my paper once I reached my hotel. 'But this depends on whether you will allow me to enter the country,' I said to him as a way of bringing his questioning, which had been running for around an hour at this stage, to an end. 'Oh yes,' he said. 'You are allowed to enter.' He stamped a blank page in my passport and returned it to me. I breathed a sigh of relief, something which he picked up on. 'I am Italian,' he explained 'and I am sometimes stereotyped as being part of the Mafia so I know how you must be feeling.'

Though the agent did not have to share this sentiment with me, I did appreciate him doing so. Then, in this spirit of mutual understanding and empathy, I asked him whether he could tell me whether other US security agencies would have access to the intelligence he had collected in our interview. During the answering of his questions, I had used national security terminology – for example, 'ops' for operations, 'intel' for intelligence, 'UAVs' instead of drones and so forth. Perhaps this helped build a rapport and suggested that I understood the work he was involved in. So, when I asked him which agencies would have access to the transcript of my interrogation, he replied that *all* US agencies involved in national security work would have access to it. 'Does this include the FBI and the CIA?,' I asked. Slightly more hesitant this time, he said, 'Yes, they will.' Becoming known to these agencies is a lot easier than one may think.

I thanked the agent for granting me entry to the US and asked for directions to my connecting flight. 'I know a shortcut,' he said. 'I'll take you.' We walked through a series of doors and open areas that were unpopulated and then into an area which housed baggage belts. The agent wished me well, shook my hand, and we parted ways. I would re-experience this same sentiment – the 'friendly cop' who apologises for any undue stress after subjecting you to coercive intelligence gathering – two years later when travelling to the Middle East.

*   *   *

As my friend Kashaan and I cleared the security gates at Stansted Airport in London and made our way to the gate of the aircraft in August 2017, I noticed two men wearing suits who were observing passengers. They were Special Branch officers. Kashaan and I were travelling to the United Arab Emirates (UAE) but our connection was in Istanbul, a city that was used as a transit point for foreign fighters wishing to travel to Syria during the Syrian civil war. With the subject of foreign fighters therefore high on the news and security radar, I suspected there was a high probability that we were going to be stopped. Despite travelling for a holiday, I was still feeling quite nervous and anxious. These feelings increased when I noticed that one of the officers, who had ginger hair and wore a beard, kept looking at me. Every time I looked at him though, he would look away, and then after a few seconds, would stare at me again. I knew from my previous experience at East Midlands Airport what this meant. I wondered if a port-circular had been issued instructing Special Branch to stop and detain us for questioning on this occasion too. My friend Kashaan is a bearded middle-aged man and a very frequent flyer to the US and the UAE for his work in the tech sector. He is somebody who has been stopped and interrogated countless times by police and airport security. He knew what was going to happen too.

As our turn arrived in the queue, we handed our boarding cards to the Pegasus airline staff member at the same time. She scanned them and wished us a safe flight. As soon as we took a couple of steps towards the aircraft though, both Special Branch officers immediately approached us and separately. The ginger-haired officer approached me. 'Excuse me, sir,' he said in an Irish accent. 'Can I see your passport, please?' Unsurprised by the order and without offering any resistance, I handed it over, knowing a series of 'vetting questions' were now imminent. These questions are asked by officers to assess whether a passenger should be allowed to continue on their journey, or whether they should be detained for further questioning under Schedule 7. 'Have I seen you before?,' he asked. 'Have you been on any aid convoys to Syria?' I was unable to contain my amusement at the question, which had racial stereotyping and profiling built into it. 'I have an extremely common face that is often mistaken for somebody else,' I said. He asked where I was flying to and I explained that our connecting flight was from Istanbul but we were actually going on vacation to the UAE and then onto Oman. As he looked through the passport, in the most non-confrontational tone I could find, I asked the officer what the reason for stopping me was. 'Because you couldn't look more nervous even if you were trying to,' he explained. Despite my best attempts at containing my sense of fear and anxiety that I feel when I fly, I was an open book. Then more questions were asked. What was the purpose for my travel to the UAE and Oman? What did we plan to do once we had reached the two countries? When would we be returning to the UK? Not wanting to be detained under Schedule 7 nor wanting to miss the flight, I answered all his questions and emphasised that we would most certainly be returning, implying that we were not 'foreign fighters' on a one-way journey. 'Thank you,' he said. The official vetting questions were over, and I was free to travel. Kashaan had also been cleared.

The officer who had been questioning Kashaan joined his colleague and whilst both of them stood together, I asked them if stopping us was the result of pre-planned intelligence in the form of a 'port-circular' or whether it was completely random? 'No,' the officer who questioned Kashan replied. 'It's not the result of a port-circular. How do you know about port-circulars?' I explained that I was an academic and my research area was counterterrorism and armed Muslim groups. On hearing this, the officer's tone shifted. He sounded almost more relaxed because, I assumed, he probably felt like I would understand why we were being subjected to these screening questions at the gate. 'What is the impression of counterterrorism policing amongst the Muslim community, and especially toward the Schedule 7 power?,' he asked me. Though I knew this was a background intelligence collection question, I obliged the officer and explained how and why Schedule 7 was viewed as a heavy-handed law that was leading to a sense of exclusion and anger amongst many Muslims who I had spoken with over the years. The officer nodded along as if to acknowledge what I was saying and thanked my friend and me for our time.

22
A Tap on the Shoulder

In late 2015, I was at a conference at the School of African and Oriental Studies (SOAS) in London, where I was delivering a paper on how counterinsurgency theory, and especially psychological operations (Psy-Ops) and strategic communication can help us understand how state-manufactured counter-extremism think-tanks such as the now defunct Quilliam Foundation were being used to ideologically challenge political Islamic groups. On completion of my presentation, a man approached me. He was from the '77th Brigade', which is known colloquially in the media and on the blogsphere as the 'Twitter Brigades'.

The 77th Brigade is a newly established unit of the UK military that merges all military units formerly used to conduct communications, propaganda, media, and psy-ops work. The name of the unit is a tribute to the '77th Infantry Brigade', a British-Indian guerrilla unit that operated clandestinely behind enemy lines during the war against the Japanese in Burma and sought to spread confusion and destruction amongst enemies.[1] I had heard of this unit from media reports but had never met anybody who worked there. Until my encounter with this man – let's call him Major Hussein – the Ministry of Defence had mostly ignored my formal requests for meetings, interviews, and information. When Major Hussein introduced himself as from the military, I therefore showed a keen interest in him and the work he was involved in. Major Hussein informed me that he had approached me because he wanted to solicit my advice. Both perplexed and curious at what an officer from the UK military, whose unit was involved in the very things I had been examining and critiquing at length only minutes earlier, needed my advice on, I agreed to advise him and proposed a meeting.

Four months later, we finally met in a café in Nottingham in March 2016. Major Hussein had driven for around two hours to make the meeting and was already at the café when I arrived at the agreed time. He was sat on a table in one corner of the café, away from most of the other tables and customers. He was casually dressed and was softly spoken. He gave the impression of a calm and composed character. We exchanged pleasantries and I asked him what he needed my advice on. For around fifteen minutes, Major Hussein explained that he and his neighbour, who was a serving police officer with the Metropolitan Police Service, had been having an on-going dispute. Major Hussein therefore needed my advice on how to 'effectively complain' about the officer. On hearing this, my first thought was Major Hussein had put in a considerable amount of time and effort into meeting with me for a matter which could have been discussed over the telephone or even email. I nevertheless decided to accept what he was telling me at face value and offered him advice I felt could be useful to him: seek legal advice, be patient, and contact the Independent Police Complaints Commission if the need arose.

Major Hussein asked me about my experiences of dealing with the police and my involvement in Operation Minerva. Though quite open about my experiences with law enforcement and the surveillance machine, I tend to get apprehensive about sharing information when others initiate a conversation on these subjects. And thus, I answered the Major's questions but kept my answers quite brief and relatively broad. The conversation then started to shift. Major Hussein asked where my interest in counterinsurgency had arisen from. I explained that using counterinsurgency and military doctrine helped me analyse and contextualise counterterrorism more broadly and helped me connect what the UK security state was doing domestically with its operations in active war theatres such as Iraq and Afghanistan.

On hearing this, Major Hussein informed me that one of the reasons he wanted to meet me was to talk about some of my ideas and theories featured in my conference paper. My paper, he asserted, referenced ideas, theorists, and arguments, that were outdated, too theoretical, and inaccurate. The UK military, he claimed, was not conducting 'Psy-Ops', a concept I had mentioned in my paper. The military unit I had published a chapter on in an academic book – the '15 PSYOPS group' – had recently been disbanded, which indicated, in his view, that the UK military was no longer engaging in Psy-Ops. As I listened patiently to his arguments, I began to realise that this meeting seemed to be, at least in part, an attempt at trying to 'influence' me and my ideas, especially since his unit – the 77th Brigade – is involved in precisely such activity. I kept quiet and listened attentively. Major Hussein claimed that the military's role in 'kinetic' (i.e. violent) operations was very minimal and that the military was 90 per cent about undertaking 'non-kinetic' (i.e. non-violent) and 'non-lethal' activities. The creation of the 77th Brigade, he explained, was evidence of this shift in military culture and strategy. 'You should go and see for yourself,' he said.

The prospect of going into the UK military's official Influence unit to do interviews and ethnography excited me, and I finally felt like the meeting with Major Hussein was heading in the right direction. However, I also knew the military had been resistant to my attempts at trying to get them to engage with my research. I therefore asked Major Hussein whether the military would even allow me – a researcher and academic with a history of public advocacy against the security state's overreach – to simply go and conduct fieldwork with them. He immediately clarified that he was not proposing I visit the 77th Brigade as a researcher or an academic but rather that I join the 77th Brigade as a soldier. The purpose behind approaching me at the conference, agreeing to meet with me, and then travelling for two hours was now clear: recruitment.

When I therefore asked him outright whether he had met with me for the purpose of recruitment, he denied it and said the military did not go around 'tapping people on their shoulder'. Such things were a myth, he insisted. He went on to criticise MI5 for their underhand and coercive attempts at recruiting informants, especially young Muslim men. MI5's methods, Major Hussein argued, were not just ineffective but counterproductive. I agreed with his assessment and told him so. But I knew that his comments were intended to differentiate the military from MI5 and thus to cast his organisation in a more positive light.

Driven by nothing more than sheer curiosity to help me assess what would be happening next, I asked Major Hussein why he felt I was suited to join the military. In response, he explained that the 77th Brigade was focused on adopting new approaches to warfare and conflict-prevention, and that they were therefore seeking people who could bring new ideas and critical thinking to the table. If you have the same people saying the same things, he explained, the 77th Brigade would simply amount to 'business as usual' for the military. To be effective, therefore, they needed different people from all walks of life, who could bring unique skill sets to the military. Rather than taking another person's word, he insisted, I should 'go and see' for myself, and offered to connect me to the person heading recruitment for the 77th Brigade.

Until this moment, I had refrained from challenging anything Major Hussein had said, nor did I ask as many questions as I would have liked. I was trying to build a rapport that would give him the confidence to speak with me in the context of a formal and on-the-record academic interview that I could subsequently use in my scholarly work and publications. My desire to therefore remain open, attentive, and uncritical of the military and the practices it engaged in were perhaps being interpreted as a sign that I may be seriously open to this offer. The suggestion to 'go and see for yourself' had now moved towards talk of an introduction to the head of recruitment.

I started to feel a sense of anxiety and, in order to demonstrate some resistance to his proposal and to start drawing this attempt at recruitment to an end, I questioned him on the UK military's record on racism. Unsurprised by my question, he explained that he was often asked such questions and that his answer was pretty much always the same: that the military is no more racist than the rest of UK society. I agreed with this assessment. I then asked him about cases of abuse and torture, in places like Iraq, involving UK military personnel. Unmoved by the question, he said that such events were the result of individuals behaving improperly. The screening and vetting process during the recruitment stage of the military, he explained, tried to prevent such people from joining but they sometimes got through. However, since they were problematic people before they joined the military, they continued being problematic after they had joined. By arguing that it was individuals who were responsible for the negative publicity the military received, Major Hussein had erased the role of military cultures and structures that have historically constructed people of colour and Muslims as dangerous peoples who need to be watched, controlled, and killed. Perhaps this is why Major

Hussein was so insistent that individuals could make a difference and why I should join the ranks.

What this attempt at recruitment demonstrated to me was that whilst institutions may monitor, surveil, and collect intelligence on what somebody does and says as a way of pre-empting and preventing the emergence of resistance, the security state also pro-actively works to influence, recruit, and co-opt critics into their ranks. The purpose is to appropriate for their own purposes the critics' ideas, networks, and knowledge to influence the behaviour of people viewed as enemies. When Major Hussein messaged me the day after our meeting and asked, again, whether I would like details of the 'recruiting guys at 77', I knew what was happening and refused to engage. But the effects of this encounter, and the meaning of it, had a negative effect on my mental health, which had been suffering consistently since 2013.

23
Counterinsurgency

On being arrested, detained, and investigated for suspected terrorism and then subsequently surveilled at the roadside and at air and land ports, and whilst I was conducting my research and fieldwork, I was doing nothing 'criminal'. However, I still found myself subjected to police interest, surveillance, and the interest of the military who attempted to recruit me into their psychological warfare unit. In order to understand the reasons for such action and interest, we have to understand 'counterinsurgency' and the way it views and instrumentalises individuals and entire communities.

Historically, counterinsurgency warfare was created and used by Western states such as the US, UK, Italy, and France in the early twentieth century to defeat native resistance to imperial domination in colonies such as Algeria, Malaya, Vietnam, Libya, Northern Ireland, and, more recently, Afghanistan and Iraq. Whilst each of these conflicts were different in their own right, there were some overarching similarities in the way these conflicts were fought, especially the integration of violent and non-violent methods, targeted not only at suspected insurgents but also at *potential* insurgents and entire civilian communities – the 'water' in which insurgent 'fish' swim. Communities are therefore divided into a 'good' camp, which comprises native people who can be partnered and allied with in order to fight on the side of the government, and a 'bad' camp, which comprises individuals who are to be either 'turned' in favour of the state, and if this fails, imprisoned or killed.

This British approach to fighting counterinsurgency warfare, especially since the 1960s has largely consisted of using a combination of violent and non-violent practices in what has been termed 'hearts-and-minds' counterinsurgency. This approach of fighting war comprises four main areas of practice. The first is undertaking limited acts of pre-emptive violence in accordance with specially designed laws that work to legally sanction what the security state does. The second is conducting ongoing surveillance of suspects, potential suspects, and broader civilian communities in order to generate knowledge that informs state violence and the creation of propaganda (or what is increasingly called 'influence' in contemporary military parlance). The third is focused on increasing cooperation between civilian and security institutions, especially in terms of conducting surveillance and delivering social welfare programmes that will allow the government to influence civilian communities and thereby socially and politically control them. And the fourth is about using propaganda to manipulate and persuade civilian communities to either support or become indifferent to what the government does at home and abroad.

The overwhelming majority of counterinsurgency activity is driven by the desire to use violent and non-violent actions on a 'pre-emptive' and 'preventive' basis in order to quash resistance or challenge from expressing itself before it has surfaced. The use of pre-emptive killing in this respect through, for example, drone strikes is perhaps one of the most obvious ways in which preventive and pre-emptive violence is undertaken in the present day. The use of internment, including in the North of Ireland during the so-called 'Troubles',[1] Guantanamo Bay,[2] and British prisons in the immediate aftermath of the 9/11 attacks, are also clear-cut examples of pre-emptive and preventive violence. The same pre-emptive logic also applies to a whole series of contemporary counterterrorism laws in the UK that deal with 'preparatory' offences that permit the security state to target people before their violent plans have materialised into actual violence based on 'circumstantial evidence' that is more akin to *intelligence*.[3] The same applies to offences which allow the UK government to imprison a person for terrorism without necessarily having to prove that they actually *intended* to commit or incite terrorism. These sorts of offences, alongside non-terrorism offences, are used to 'disrupt' suspects for terrorist crimes that are predicted to happen in the future but for which there is no actual evidence that can be used to secure a terrorism prosecution today. The same pre-emptive and preventive logic goes to the heart of 'counter-radicalisation' policies such as Prevent too. Here, individuals are targeted by the state based on a set of loosely defined 'indicators' that seemingly suggest a person is going to become a terrorist in the future and therefore needs to be targeted with surveillance and then an individualised 'de-radicalisation' package long before they have done so.

The merger between militarised approaches, ideas, and practices related to *pre-emption* and *prevention* of resistance have been central to counterinsurgency warfare throughout history, especially when the military was encouraged to adopt more of a 'policing' role in the maintenance of British rule abroad.[4] But, despite the policing role the military adopted, there was still a distinction between the institutions of the police and the military. The police were used against citizens to ensure the law was upheld and the military was used to deal with external enemies of the state.[5] From the 1970s onwards, and especially with the war in the North of Ireland raging, the split between both institutions became increasingly blurred. The Republican enemy in the North of Ireland was operational 'overseas' but was also 'at home', leading to a fusion between policing and the military that would eventually be extended to dealing with other left-wing and racialised groups, and eventually be applied to the 'Muslim threat' too from 9/11 onwards.

The commitment to undertaking pre-emptive and preventive action that draws inspiration from counterinsurgency warfare, in other words, did not start with the so-called 'war on terror'. History is littered with examples showing how racialised communities have been controlled through militarised processes of 'internal colonisation',[6] especially in the US, where programmes such as COINTELPRO were used against the civil rights movement and the Black Panther Party.[7] More recently, similar processes are being used against black civil rights activists and anti-racist movements in cities such as Ferguson[8] as well as Muslim communities in Minnesota too.[9] In the UK context, counterinsurgency was used to fight the war against Irish Republican groups in the North of Ireland[10] and then applied in the policing, surveilling, and disruption of anti-war, anti-capitalist, and trade union activists too.[11] More recently, counterinsurgency is being used to police, discipline, and regulate Muslims, 'gangs', and those with 'alternative' politics more broadly.[12]

Until very recently, those on the 'far right' of the political spectrum have not been subjected to blanket counterinsurgency and counterterrorism policies in the same way as racialised and left-wing movements. But around 2011, a shift started to happen when the 'far right' was formally integrated into the Prevent de-radicalisation programme, leading to self-congratulatory cheers by Prevent practitioners that the programme was no longer exclusively focused on Muslims and could no longer be accused of Islamophobia. Counterterrorism was now supposedly blind to skin colour and ideology.[13] The apparently 'colour-blind' nature of counterterrorism was reinforced in late 2016, when the white nationalist group 'National Action' became the first fascist organisation to be proscribed under terrorism laws since the Second World War; two more proscriptions of far-right groups followed. Then, in 2018, MI5 took charge of surveilling and mapping white nationalist groups rather than leaving it to the police, who had historically dealt with the matter through a 'public order' framework. However, the latest data-set from the Home Office shows that the people impacted by terrorism laws are still disproportionately racialised.[14] The same disproportionality can be seen in the way racialised people are sentenced, subjected to state intervention, surveilled, and sanctioned more broadly too.[15] The coercive apparatus may be made up of people and processes that do not *intend* to be racist, but racism should be measured by the *outcomes* and *consequences* of institutional culture, policies, and practices, not just an individual person's *intentions*.[16]

Though counterinsurgency-infused counterterrorism may claim to operate in a 'colour-blind' and racially neutral way, this does not tally with the way it is implemented both historically and at present.[17] When Rod was being interviewed by the police and I was in custody, one of the police officers made a passing comment to him that 'this [police operation] would not be happening if the student had been blonde, Swedish and at Oxford University'. This tells us that even some of those engaged in policing recognise the racism and class bias of counterterrorism.

By laying claim to colour-blindness, the state is able to assert that Britain is a multicultural society that seeks to protect *all* people in an equal way. This not only helps blunt anti-racist critique of counterterrorism by allowing the government to claim that they

are targeting the violent and witless racism of white nationalist groups, it also helps them keep the structurally racist and
Islamophobic institutions, systems, and practices in place which
construct and treat Muslims as inherently dangerous and threatening 'outsiders' worthy of coercive control and intervention.[18]
Most importantly, though, it permits the government to claim that
anti-Muslim racism is an unfortunate 'side effect' of counterterrorism and counterinsurgency rather than being a key organising
principle of both.

* * *

What has changed since 9/11 is that the impetus to use violence
on a *pre-emptive* and *preventive* basis has become stronger due
to the historically situated orientalist and racist readings of the
danger that racialised people, and especially Islam, poses to the
Western world. The suggestion to use pre-emptive state violence
is rampant amongst policymakers and 'terrorologists' who claim
that armed Muslim groups such as al-Qaeda and ISIS are 'new'
terrorists who pose a far more lethal threat compared to the 'old'
terrorists of the past[19] such as the Irish Republican Army (IRA).
New terrorists, the theory goes, want to maximise the number of
deaths and casualties, perhaps using chemical, biological, radio-
logical, and nuclear (CBRN) weapons, whilst also wanting to die
in an attack themselves on apparently religious grounds; meaning
the security state cannot wait for an attack-plan to get close to
fruition before acting. The risk is considered to be too high.
Also, due to globalisation, the information technology revolution, and ease of international travel and financial and knowledge
exchange, terrorism is claimed to have become far more likely an
option than it has perhaps ever been in the past. The 'new terrorism' theory therefore views the danger from armed Muslim
groups to be far more severe than the 'old' secular terrorism of
groups like the PLO, IRA, and MK,[20] and therefore encourages the
use of an expanded web of pre-emptive surveillance technologies
and state violence.

Thus, the entire policing, military, and legal architecture used to
deal with armed Muslim groups since 9/11 has been designed on
the principles of pre-emption, prevention, and pre-crime. There

is a difference between the concept of *pre-crime* and *crime pre-vention* which is worth highlighting since pre-crime can often be conflated with crime prevention to excuse and justify the security state's highly draconian pre-crime counterterrorism legal and policy infrastructure. Jude McCulloch and Sharon Pickering succinctly explain the difference between both of these approaches. Pre-crime is said to be focused on 'rooting out future terrorists rather than what might be thought of as root causes'. *Crime pre-vention*, on the other hand, is said to be centred around using 'non-punitive measures that reduce opportunities to commit crime or address the broader context in which people commit crimes'. *Pre-crime*, in respect to counterinsurgency and counterterrorism, is about predicting and pre-emptively neutralising those who *may* engage in armed struggle in the future in more technically efficient and sophisticated ways. *Crime prevention*, however, is about addressing the social and political causes of a conflict in order to minimise the need for people to engage in armed struggle in the first place. The great paradox of counterinsurgency warfare is that it claims to be about using political means to prevent the use of military violence but its notion of the pre-criminal hides the political drivers of violent revolt. This makes counterinsurgency a form of warfare that is focused on fighting a *tactically* better, more innovative, and savvier war than it is about *politics* and related political solutions.[21] 'In simply tinkering with the tactics,' argues Laleh Khalili, 'counterinsurgency produces its own defeat again and again, with no memory of prior losses, thus repeating the same fundamental mistakes'.[22]

Pre-emptive and preventive measures express themselves in the context of contemporary counterinsurgency and counterterrorism in two main ways: firstly, through violence and threats of violence that are targeted at individual suspects but which, when communicated, can have a disciplinary and coercive influence on the broader Muslim community. Such coercive action can often prompt the 'suspect community' to change their behaviour, for example, by not resisting or challenging unjust state practices, for fear of the consequences. Though acts of violence may be used sparingly or in a limited manner, they can still discipline and pacify entire communities. Secondly, through manipulative and persuasive practices, including propaganda and social welfare activity, an attempt is made to co-opt and pacify Muslims so they do not engage or support resistance to the government in the future. Counterinsurgency, in this respect, is a struggle between the government and insurgents for the loyalty, support, or indifference of Muslim communities, a so-called battle for their 'hearts and minds', in which violence and non-violence are used in conjunction with one another.

24
A Different Way of War

The 'hearts and minds' variant of counterinsurgency warfare is considered to be a more humane and just form of fighting war compared to the so-called 'enemy-centric' approach which relies on overwhelming levels of violence to destroy an insurgency. The hearts and minds approach prioritises working in conjunction with civilian institutions to provide security, governance, and welfare for individuals and communities as a way of securing their acquiescence and consent, which will in turn, it is understood, weaken the insurgency and eventually lead to its demise. But this does not mean that violence remains unused in the 'hearts and minds' approach to fighting war. 'Make no mistake', writes David Kilcullen, the influential liberal soldier-scholar who strongly advocates for the 'hearts and minds' approach to dealing with armed Muslim groups, that 'counterinsurgency is war, and war is inherently violent. Killing the enemy is, and always will be a key part of guerrilla warfare.'[1]

The killing and violence undertaken in this form of counterinsurgency warfare is referred to through the title of 'minimum force'. This is a term used to describe the process in which the security state uses no more violence than is absolutely necessary to secure its key objectives and goals.[2] The use of extreme violence is discouraged because it has a high potential of giving rise to perceptions that the government and military are arbitrary and disproportionate in their conduct. This could, in turn, deter Muslim communities from partnering with the state and supplying intelligence to them on suspects, their hideouts, and plans. Too much force being employed by the state is also said to have the potential to drive Muslims into embracing the insurgents and actively supporting them.[3] However, not using force and violence whatsoever has the potential to construct the government as weak and timid, and may prompt resistance to become stronger. This point is summarised well by UK military officer Major-General

Charles Gwynn, who, writing in his 1930s counterinsurgency handbook *Imperial Policing*, says:

> Excessive severity may antagonise [the loyal] element, add to the number of the rebels, and leave a lasting feeling of resentment and bitterness. On the other hand, the power and resolution of the Government forces must be displayed. Anything which can be interpreted as weakness encourages those who are sitting on the fence to keep on good terms with the rebels.[4]

The philosophy of minimum force is therefore about finding a 'balance' between communicating the government's capacity and willingness to use violence but working to ensure that its use is not viewed as being excessive or arbitrary in case it 'radicalises' people. During the later days of the British empire, the use of the minimum force philosophy was believed to have helped prevent the emergence of mass rebellions in the colonies and enabled the British to maintain control and dominance over the natives for a considerable period of time.[5] The government through the idea of minimum force was therefore able to construct itself as using violence only as a last resort, and usually in accordance with spe-cially designed laws that helped portray its violence as fair and justified. This principle around using violence in accordance with the law is central to the 'hearts and minds' variant of counterin-surgency warfare, and has an important place in contemporary military doctrine. The UK's most recent counterinsurgency field manual, for example, notes that operating within the law is central to 'maintaining legitimacy' and 'a crucial factor in gaining consent'.[6] Law, in this respect, works to legitimise what the state does and therefore becomes a *weapon* in its own right.

Acting in accordance with the law does not mean that the state's actions are subject to the same judicial accountability that govern non-terrorism offences. As a whole series of offences in the UK's counterterrorism legal armoury show, laws have been created which weaken legal safeguards and procedures, and allow the gov-ernment to secure military and security objectives without the law acting as a barrier. There are, of course, instances in which the law can be used by powerless people and communities to resist the security state but these instances are an exception to the rule, *not* the rule itself.[7] Most of the time, the law serves as an 'instrument of legitimation' for the state and its military and works to justify what both do.[8] One leading British soldier-scholar who encouraged the use of law as a *weapon* and a legitimiser of state violence was General Sir Frank Kitson. Kitson built his military expertise in colonial counterinsurgency wars fought in Kenya, Malaya, Cyprus, Oman, and the North of Ireland, and then later, encouraged the use of counterinsurgency warfare methods for the management and pacification of left-wing movements in the UK too.[9] Many of his central ideas, innovations, and experiences have been fully embedded into contemporary counterinsurgency theory and doctrine in multiple ways.[10] On law and its usefulness as a weapon, Kitson writes:

> the law should be used as just another weapon in the government's arsenal, and in this case, it becomes little more than a propaganda cover for the disposal of unwanted members of the public.[11]

History is awash with examples of exceptional laws authorising the use of violent and coercive practices by the security state to deal with insurgents, especially in the colonies and, then later, in the North of Ireland too. Though the post-9/11 legal architecture has continued in a similar tradition, the law has, in some respects, become even more draconian. During the conflict in the North of Ireland, for example, the police could legally detain a suspect for a maximum period of seven days before having to either charge or release them from custody. In contrast, under present-day terrorism laws, a person can be detained without charge or trial for a total period of fourteen days.[12] In another instance, when the Prevention of Terrorism Act was introduced in the 1970s it was a 'temporary provision', meaning it had to be kept under constant review by Parliament due to the exceptional powers it authorised. However, in contrast, the foundational law that was written and introduced with a view to dealing mostly with armed Muslim groups, the Terrorism Act 2000, is a permanent law. It is, in other words, not subject to even elementary levels of Parliamentary scrutiny or checks in the same way that the Prevention of Terrorism Act in the 1970s and onwards was. Though the

concepts of pre-emption and prevention were both central practices of colonial counterinsurgency and the war against armed
Irish groups, it seems that both 'risk and threat anticipation' practices when it comes to dealing with armed Muslim groups has
expanded since the 9/11 attacks.[13]

But, other than a small band of human rights organisations
and critics, for the broader UK public, there was and remains a
seeming acceptance for what the security state does, perhaps
because its activities are 'lawful'. The law, in this respect, is not
and should not be viewed as a neutral arbiter between right and
wrong. Instead, it should be understood as the avenue through
which state exercises its violence, making it a weapon within
and of itself. And regardless of whether state violence is justified
through law, it still has a corrosive and disciplinary impact. Take
my own arrest for suspected terrorism as just one example. Though
entirely lawful, it not only had a negative effect on me but also
on other students and academics, especially Muslims and people
of colour, who were studying or researching terrorism. On more
than one occasion, people told me that based on their knowledge
of my arrest and detention, and the circumstances surrounding
it, they have either not accessed primary material on the internet,
'thought twice' about accessing it for fear of the consequences, or
informed their line managers, professors, or 'ethics committees'
in order to minimise the risk of falling foul of anti-terror laws.
Despite not being subjected to violence themselves, people, and
especially racialised Muslims, have been coercively influenced
and have changed their behaviour on the basis of an overarching
threat of violence looming over them. Regardless of whether the
security state exercises its violence through 'lawful' or 'unlawful'
means does not lessen the coercive and disciplinary effect on a
broader set of people. All lawful violence does is give the act a
veneer of legal legitimacy.

A hearts and minds approach also necessitates that military and
policing goals be integrated into civilian institutions to ensure that
all instruments of state power are brought to bear on the enemy
as well as potential enemies. In the UK today, this requirement,
especially around passing intelligence to the authorities under
the Prevent 'de-radicalisation' policy, is enshrined within law. The
Counterterrorism and Security Act 2015 stipulates that all public

sector institutions must work to 'prevent people from being drawn into terrorism' and also police 'non-violent extremism'. The latter is claimed by the government to 'create an atmosphere conducive to terrorism and can popularise views which terrorists exploit'.[14] Put another way, public sector workers within schools, colleges, universities, health, and local government are legally compelled to look out for who potential terrorists are by policing and monitoring ideas that neither support nor promote terrorism. There are two noteworthy points worth emphasising about this.

Firstly, since state violence is generally viewed as an action that causes physical pain as opposed to psychological harm, the use of civilian institutions to police and surveil ideas and views that are claimed to be 'conducive to terrorism', with the backing of the law, minimises and even erases the violent and traumatic effects that such activity creates in the minds of those classified as *potential* terrorists. Using civilian institutions in this regard therefore allows the state to behave violently in a way where the effects and harm of it are erased. Secondly, since reporting and referring suspected and potential terrorists to the authorities is a 'legal duty', public sector workers, even those who may be sceptical of the government counterterrorism agenda, are forced to go along with Prevent because it is 'law'.[15] The law in this sense not only enables and justifies the security state's exercise of coercion but also forces civilians to participate in using violence in its name. 'Hearts and minds', with its talk of minimum force, legally justified violence, and civilian 'buy-in' may construct this variant of counterinsurgency warfare as being 'non-violent' compared to the more militarised 'enemy-centric' variant of counterinsurgency, but, in practice, it simply fights war *differently*.[16]

25
Global Insurgency

Integrating counterinsurgency theories and methods that seek to win Muslim 'hearts and minds' into UK counterterrorism seem to have been influenced by a discourse put forward by a number of influential soldier-scholars that view armed Muslim groups, led by al-Qaeda, as constituting a 'global Islamic insurgency'.[1] One such person is Dr David Kilcullen, who has comprehensively written about counterinsurgency warfare and held noted politico-military positions within the US military, notably under General David Petraeus, as 'Senior Counterinsurgency Adviser, Multi-National Force – Iraq'.[2] He has been influential in the UK too and has been cited by the UK Prime Minister and Foreign Secretary[3] as well as within the UK's counterinsurgency field manual in the chapter on 'Information Operations'.[4] Kilcullen's ideas, in other words, are not just theoretical and are therefore worth exploring in more depth.

In Kilcullen's reading, al-Qaeda is not simply a terrorist group. It is a 'global Islamic insurgency' akin to a 'virtual state' that draws on the benefits of globalisation and technology to fight what he calls 'global Jihad'.[5] Whilst al-Qaeda may not control territory or Muslim communities, Kilcullen argues, it 'represents many elements of traditional state power'.[6] He sees it as a type of 'supra-state' but one which has neither legal nor political legitimacy in world affairs.[7] In this respect, al-Qaeda is viewed as not only posing a violent threat to nation-states but also an ideological and subversive threat to the Western-led world order.[8]

Al-Qaeda, in this respect, is not simply engaged in violence because they 'hate' or 'resent' the West or they have a religious duty to cleanse the world of its moral decadence, as the *new terrorism* theory claims. The violence of al-Qaeda, like all insurgent violence, is at its heart 'political'. It is difficult to see al-Qaeda in this light because insurgency generally aims at the liberation of a nation or a people but al-Qaeda has 'ended up fighting a foco type insurgency on a global scale, in which acts of armed struggle are

geared towards the formation of a people rather than the liberation of a people'.[9] Al-Qaeda's own outputs seem to show that its
use of violence is undertaken with an eye to political, media, and
public opinion.[10] For example, in July 2005, Ayman al-Zawahiri,
al-Qaeda's then deputy leader, wrote a letter to the al-Qaeda leader
in Iraq, Abu-Musab al-Zarqawi, and tried to persuade him not to
kill Western hostages he had taken captive by citing the effect this
would create in media and on public opinion:

> We are in a battle, and that more than half of this battle is taking
> place in the battlefield of the media. We are in a media battle in
> a race for the hearts and minds of our Umma.[11]

Whilst politicians and some experts often claim that al-Qaeda is
an apolitical entity, its violence and thinking seems to be based
on the calculated use of violence to challenge the modern world
order and pave the way for the creation of a 'Caliphate', an inherently *political* goal.

The merger between armed Muslim groups from around the
globe under its leadership to form the global Islamic insurgency
was not the result of a masterplan by al-Qaeda alone. It was
also, in part, a reaction to the indiscriminate ways in which the
US executed its global 'war on terror'. In response to 9/11, the
US targeted a whole host of locations around the world beyond
Afghanistan and Iraq, including the Philippines, sub-Saharan
Africa, and Georgia.[12] By 2008, the US military was engaged in over
sixty countries worldwide as part and parcel of the global 'war on
terror'.[13] This overreach is considered to have led many locals who
were neither involved nor interested in furthering the cause of the
'global Jihad' to align with al-Qaeda. Not only did this amplify the
threat but led to the so-called birth of a whole host of 'accidental
guerrillas'[14] as well as the exploitation and development of existing
and new links between local, regional, and international groups.[15]
US actions, in other words, helped disparate and different armed
Muslim groups consolidate under al-Qaeda's leadership to form a
so-called 'global Islamic insurgency'.

In order to fight it, breaking its links with local and regional
armed Muslim groups is deemed critical by Kilcullen through
a strategy he calls 'disaggregation'. '[A] disaggregation strategy

means different things in different theaters', Kilcullen argues, 'but it provides a unifying strategic conception for the war.'[16] To put it another way, the security state keeps the strategic enemy – the global Islamic insurgency led by al-Qaeda – in the forefront of its mind but it employs methods and tactics that are tailored to local, national, and regional circumstances to weaken the overall global Islamic insurgency al-Qaeda leads. Under Kilcullen's strategy though, for the West to find 'victory', not every geographical location or 'theatre' needs to be militarily pacified. A strategy of disaggregation, he writes, 'only demands that we identify, and neutralise, those elements in each theatre that link to the global jihad'.[17]

* * *

European countries such as the UK are claimed to be 'a transit area for extremists, a source of intellectual capital, exploitable grievances, and [a] legislative safe haven' for armed Muslim groups and their advocates.[18] It is, Kilcullen argues, 'an actual battle ground in the War on Terrorism'.[19] This 'battle ground', however, does not just concern individuals and cells who engage in armed attacks. Rather, it concerns so-called 'Muslim subversives' who seek to non-violently and lawfully advocate for Islam to be used as a political framework in the governance of Muslim lives. 'Bad Muslims' who promote such an idea are often said to be 'non-violent extremists' in policy discourse and are constructed as 'terror apologists' in the media. At the same time, European countries such as the UK are said to host a broader Muslim community that is deemed to be vulnerable to ideological indoctrination by these 'bad Muslims'.

In the UK today, dealing with them takes place less through overt acts of violence due to negative media effects that such activity can prompt. Instead, it takes place through Prevent for two broad reasons. Firstly, bad Muslims are viewed to be engaged in spreading an 'extremist' ideology that often does not promote or incite violence and are therefore targeted through counter-ideological methods too. Secondly, counter-ideological activity through Prevent, with the compliance of civilian institutions, operates through structural processes and bureaucracy which largely conceals what is happening from the broader public. This lessens the potential for criticism being directed at the security state than if they were to arrest and detain Muslims for making arguments that insurgents and other critics of the government also make.

The military equivalent of Prevent, from which it seems to draw its inspiration, is 'counter-subversion'.[20] Under a counter-subversion approach, it is not those who engage in planning or executing violence that are the prime targets of security state activity. Instead, it is those people and groups who engage in non-violent resistance to state and governmental power through often legal and legitimate means. Subversive acts, according to soldier-scholar Frank Kitson, are said to include 'the use of political and economic pressure, strikes, protest marches and propaganda'.[21] Groups that have been engaged in such activities, including trade unions, environmental activists, anti-war protestors, and Labour politicians have all been treated as subversives and subsequently surveilled by the intelligence services.[22] More recently, Muslims have also been placed into this 'subversive' category for two broad reasons.

Firstly, and broadly, it is based on the fact that the opponent has been diagnosed as a global Islamic insurgency, which, like all insurgent movements, Kilcullen says, 'ride and manipulate a social wave of grievances, often legitimate ones, and … draw[s] [its] fighting power' from [its] connection to a mass base.' 'This mass base', Kilcullen writes, 'is largely undetectable to counterinsurgents since it lies below the surface and engages in no armed activity.'[23] The second reason is connected to the fact that the UK has served as a place of sanctuary for political refugees and ideologues of various persuasion. Karl Marx and Sigmund Freud both fled political persecution and were given refuge in the UK. In the 1980s and 1990s, a number of Muslim dissidents also escaped political repression at the hands of autocratic regimes in the Arab and Islamic world and settled in the UK. Whilst this period witnessed some armed Muslim attacks in Europe,[24] it was generally associated with ideologues organising against foreign regimes rather than Europe. Whilst Europe during this period is claimed to have become 'a nerve centre for the global jihad' – where major cities were dubbed 'Londonistan', 'Milanistan', and 'Hamburgistan'[25] – security agencies remained largely indifferent to their activities since they were not organising against European governments.[26]

With the 9/11 attack, the mood radically transformed. Europe could no longer remain indifferent or complacent when it came to Muslim ideologues and propagandists who were claimed to have 'radicalised' Muslims to commit armed attacks, including suicide bombings in Madrid, London, Paris, Brussels, and Manchester. In immediate response to a number of these attacks, an exceptional series of laws were quickly passed in the UK, often without much scrutiny, that authorised these ideologues and Muslim suspects on the intelligence service's radar to be pre-emptively arrested, investigated, and interned in British prisons.

As the threat diversified to so-called 'lone-wolf' attacks executed by unsophisticated individuals said to 'radicalise' on the internet,[27] a firmer commitment was made by the UK government to challenge any person who held an 'extremist ideology' (even if it was not encouraging or promoting violence) since it was claimed to be the heart of the terrorist threat. 'This government', the UK Home Secretary declared in 2015, 'will challenge those who seek to spread hatred and intolerance by forming a new partnership of every single person and organisation in this country who wants to defeat the extremists.'[28] To accompany the long list of counter-terrorism powers would be an all-of-society effort in which all instruments of state power would be used against those individuals and institutions who may operate within the law but share an ideology and grievances similar to those promoted by al-Qaeda.

The subversive 'enemy', to put it another way, is not the entire Muslim community. It is 'bad Muslims' and their allies who challenge, question, and non-violently resist the UK government, especially their wars in the Muslim world. It is these bad Muslims who are considered to be the enemy and subsequently disrupted and prevented from gaining access to ordinary Muslims; viewed to be susceptible to ideological influence and indoctrination and therefore vulnerable to becoming future terrorists and insurgents. 'It makes more sense to see Europe's Muslim communities', Kilcullen argues, 'as a target of terrorist sponsored subversion than as a source of subversion.'[29] In order to protect these people from being influenced by bad Muslims, the approach that is recommended for European governments by Kilcullen should be focused 'primarily on strengthening, protecting, and building networks of trust with at-risk communities, and only apply active measures to neutralize subversive actors as a secondary task'.[30] But, to build 'networks of trust' and inform the most appropriate course of action against subversives, the security state conducts surveillance of entire communities to map and understand their make-up and behaviour. Entire communities therefore become both agents and objects of state surveillance.[31]

26
Armed Propaganda

The words 'intelligence' and 'surveillance' oftentimes induce ideas and imagery associated with secrets, phone-tapping and the covert monitoring of internet and email traffic of the sort associated with agencies such as GCHQ. Whilst 'signals intelligence' – the practice of covertly intercepting communications – is something that is done with some sophistication, as the US whistleblower Edward Snowden revealed to the world in 2013, not all surveillance is conducted through such methods. For David Omand – who served as the Director-General of GCHQ in the mid-1990s, and who was responsible for overseeing the creation of the UK's CONTEST counterterrorism strategy – 'much of the information that goes into making an intelligence assessment is available openly if you know where to look'.[1] Similarly, Kilcullen says that in fighting modern insurgencies, secret intelligence is less relevant than information which is not classified by any government.[2]

In seeking to understand and respond to the broader Muslim community, the security state also relies on the police to collect intelligence as part of their routine and daily engagements. Muslims are treated as both agents and objects of surveillance. The purpose in this sense is less about finding terrorists to prosecute and imprison and more about developing a 'rich picture' understanding of who potential government partners are, who can be 'turned' in favour of the state, who is indifferent to what is happening, who are the potential political opponents, who needs to be disrupted, fought, and so forth. Surveillance and mapping, to put it another way, becomes a central and ongoing task for the security state. It goes to the heart of everything the security state does.

Some of this surveillance is undertaken to collect what soldier-scholar Richard Clutterbuck calls 'contact information'. This is information which helps the security state find its enemies and informs its use of state violence against them.[3] At the same time though, the police are also involved in collecting what Clutterbuck calls 'background information'.[4] This is information that is often open-source and collected during the course of ordinary policing duties and engagements.[5]

The police in this sense become important to intelligence gathering since they are 'more familiar with the terrain, culture and population [and are therefore] more adept at gathering intelligence whether on or off duty'.[6] They also have 'permanent roots in the country and stronger local knowledge', which makes the process of collecting intelligence simpler for them.[7]

In my case, intelligence collected by the police may well have been passed to them by the Muslim Community Organisation in Nottingham in 2010, where I was claimed to be 'anti-West' and 'anti-Prevent'. This is a good example of 'background information' collected by the police not necessarily to inform an arrest or prosecution but to guide the police and security state's broader conduct and practices towards the subject of the intelligence entry. On at least one occasion, this entry was used by the police to try to deny me access to information on Prevent. In another instance, after ten or so days of my release from police custody, a unit in the Home Office – the RICU – had collated a detailed list of all the academics and students who either criticised the arrest and operation in the media or challenged its reasoning. The accounts of journalists, who wrote with a critical tone, were also logged.[8] Again, this is another example of background intelligence being collected to inform action and messaging, which, in the case of the Home Office unit, included 'lines to take' when answering media questions.[9]

A diagram contained in a leaked classified police document on Prevent, shown in Figure 1,[10] shows that the targets of police surveillance are not just suspected and future terrorists who are classed as being 'vulnerable to radicalisation' but are 'all Members of the Community'. Muslims, in this sense, are treated as both agents and objects of surveillance through the airport stop and search power of Schedule 7 and other intelligence gathering and analysis protocols.

The purpose of Schedule 7 is not only to find terrorists but also to collect background intelligence on a person's political, religious, and ideological views, as my own experiences have illustrated.[11]

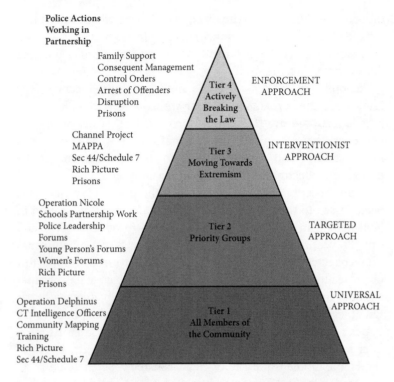

Police Actions
Working in
Partnership

Family Support
Consequent Management
Control Orders
Arrest of Offenders
Disruption
Prisons

Tier 4
Actively
Breaking
the Law

ENFORCEMENT
APPROACH

Channel Project
MAPPA
Sec 44/Schedule 7
Rich Picture
Prisons

Tier 3
Moving Towards
Extremism

INTERVENTIONIST
APPROACH

Operation Nicole
Schools Partnership Work
Police Leadership
Forums
Young Person's Forums
Women's Forums
Rich Picture
Prisons

Tier 2
Priority Groups

TARGETED
APPROACH

Operation Delphinus
CT Intelligence Officers
Community Mapping
Training
Rich Picture
Sec 44/Schedule 7

Tier 1
All Members of
the Community

UNIVERSAL
APPROACH

Figure 1   Pyramid diagram taken from a leaked classified document authored by the Association of Chief Police Officers showing the types of surveillance methods used to determine which types of Prevent activity should be directed at different individuals/groups.

Source: Association of Chief Police Officers (Terrorism and Allied Matters), 2008, p. 11.

Because a person who is stopped does not have a right to remain silent under Schedule 7, the police and security services are able to freely and easily collect intelligence on individuals and the entire Muslim community.

The second method of surveillance is 'Rich Picture', the codename given to a joint police and MI5 intelligence collection and analysis programme that is used to identify 'investigative opportunities' for the police[12] and, according to my correspondence with the current Metropolitan Police Commissioner Cressida Dick, works to 'help identify individuals and areas within local communities which may present a risk or threat [to national security]'.[13] As Figure 1 shows, Rich Picture collects intelligence not only on suspected terrorists or those who are deemed 'vulnerable to radicalisation' but rather on 'all members of the community'. Whether overt or covert methods of intelligence collection are used, whether background or contact information is collected, it is all fed into the system.[14]

The influence of counterinsurgency theory on this model of surveillance is starkly visible from Figure 2, which is taken from Kilcullen's work. The figure shows how surveillance and intelligence networks operate across all levels of society to collect information, including the 'population base'. It also shows that the 'audience for propaganda' is not just insurgents, terrorists, and those claimed to be 'sympathetic' to insurgents, but ordinary people who make up the 'population base' or rather 'all members of the community' too.

Though one may ask why collecting vast swathes of background intelligence on the entire Muslim community is worthwhile, the soldier-scholar Frank Kitson helps us understand the purpose of this practice. Kitson argues that whilst all intelligence may not be reliable and may not permit the security state to take immediate action, background information is important but only if there is enough of it to be exploited.[15] A piece of information that may be considered irrelevant in isolation, in other words, has the potential to become useful when it is correlated with other information. The security state therefore becomes committed to collecting intelligence on a routine and a continuous basis. When the police stopped, searched, and detained me for questioning and then subsequently wrote intelligence entries that were stored on their Criminal Intelligence System, they were putting this reasoning into practice. The same was true when the student Palestinian Society at the University of Nottingham was under routine and continuous surveillance by the police. Kitson, for example, writes:

One of the main factors involved [in information collection] is continuity, and a platoon or company which can stay in the same region for a long time is worth several times as many men who are constantly moved from one place to another, because of the contacts and background knowledge which the stationary troops can build up in a particular area.[16]

Whilst Kitson is referring to intelligence in the context of the counterinsurgency war in the North of Ireland, we can see his idea around surveillance continuity at play in the regional network of Counter-Terrorism Units (CTUs) and their smaller counterparts Counter-Terrorism Intelligence Units (CTIUs) that were created in 2008. Both are involved in ongoing and routine surveillance activity, especially in conjunction with civilians and local communities. A senior police officer told a Parliamentary Select Committee hearing shortly after the network's creation:

> The real power and value of the current network is that it is embedded at the local level, where it picks up local intelligence [since] it is closely engaged with the communities.[17]

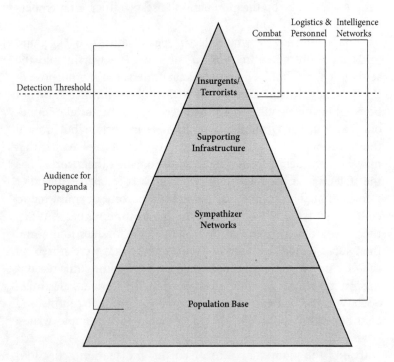

Figure 2   Diagram created by the author and using Figure 1.1 from David Kilcullen's writings, specifying where surveillance and intelligence networks operate and who constitutes an 'audience for propaganda'.
Source: Kilcullen (2010, p. 8).

The role of police officers who engage with the community in this respect is to collect and exchange 'key bits of intelligence' on individuals as well as physical and online spaces thought to be used for 'radicalisation' and terrorism.[18]

∗   ∗   ∗

Historically, states have also sought to collaborate with social scientists, in order to collect information on 'adversary culture' as part of counterinsurgency strategies. During colonialism, for example, European nation-states employed anthropological methods and techniques to understand the culture and politics of the natives in order to control, dominate, and influence them to support their own subjugation and domination. Anthropology, observes Warren Chin, was 'at the intellectual heart of the imperial project'.[19] It has been described as a 'war fighting discipline'.[20] The relationship between the academy and the security state was blurred during the rivalry between the US and Soviet Union in the Cold War, too.[21] During this conflict though, it has been claimed that there was no real reason to study the culture of the Soviet Union. 'In a conflict between symmetric adversaries, where both are evenly matched and using similar technology, understanding the adversary's culture is largely irrelevant', argues military anthropologist Montgomery McFate, one of the leading advocates of studying 'adversary culture' in the war against armed Muslim groups and insurgency. 'The Cold War, for all its complexity pitted two powers of European heritage against each other', she claims. 'In a counterinsurgency operation against a non-Western adversary', she declares, 'culture matters.'[22] To put it more simply, studying adversary culture is important in counterinsurgency warfare but critical when the enemy is non-European.

Kilcullen similarly places value on studying Muslim and Islamic culture. 'Cultural competence', he argues, is 'a critical combat capability' in the fight against the global Islamic insurgency.[23] Without it, he declares, 'it may be impossible for counterinsurgent forces to perceive the true meaning of insurgent actions, or influence populations and their perceptions'.[24] Cultural knowledge, in other words, is critical in producing and targeting 'propaganda' for the sake of influencing the Muslim community. Kilcullen also places a significant amount of importance on developing a detailed cultural awareness of communities through what he calls 'basic intelligence' rather than secret intelligence:

> In modern counterinsurgency, where there is no single insurgent network to be penetrated but rather a cultural and demographic jungle of population groups to be navigated, 'basic intelligence' – detailed knowledge of physical, human, cultural and informational terrain, based on a combination of open source research and 'denied area ethnography' – will be even more critical.[25]

The US-led wars that were fought in both Afghanistan and Iraq were embedded with social scientists in what became known as 'Human Terrain Systems' (HTS). The remit of HTSs was to embed academics with the military to study culture, communities, and people (the 'human terrain') to help create a situation whereby they could eventually be influenced to change their behaviour in favour of the occupation forces and its goals. Though criticism of HTSs has been strong, especially around the ethics of the research findings being weaponised,[26] this has not stopped social scientific methods being used to study adversary culture, including domestically in the UK.

The task of studying Muslim communities and their cultural and religious practices as a way of targeting them with propaganda and influence for counterterrorism purposes falls to the Research, Information and Communications Unit (the RICU). The RICU, based in the Home Office in London, was established in 2007.[27] This is the unit that logged critical commentary on my arrest and detention. The inspiration for the unit was the Political Warfare Executive (PWE) that was created during the Second World War. The PWE has been described by two influential former British military officers as 'a shadowy yet hugely successful information warfare unit' that was responsible for taking 'the propaganda war to the enemy – and to neutrals – via disinformation, covert radio stations, leaflets, and what became known as "sibs" – false rumors'.[28] One civil servant involved in the creation of the RICU recalled that 'the Home Secretary understood that we needed a PWE if we were serious about strategy making, and engaging in the battle of ideas, seamlessly from operational theaters abroad to the home front'.[29] This is similar to what Charles Farr, the former Director-General of the Office for Security and Counterterrorism (OSCT) that is situated within the Home Office and oversees the RICU, told a Parliamentary Select Committee hearing:

[The RICU advises] not just government [but] officialdom, from a brigade commander in Helmand province through to the Chief Constable in Yorkshire, about how they may wish to characterize the threat we face and describe the response that we are making.[30]

In relation to my own arrest and detention in 2008, RICU's 'lines to take' consisted of, amongst others, the following 'key' messages:

- I am unable to comment on the specifics of an individual operation
- Terrorism is a **real and serious threat to us all**
- UK counterterrorism legislation is not aimed at a particular race, religion, or any other group. They are aimed at terrorists, whatever background or section of society they may come from.[31]

RICU's task is to ensure consistency in UK messaging all the way from the local to the global level; demonstrating that the underlying ideas driving the strategy and methods overseas are connected to what is happening here in the UK too. Since the unit's creation, it has undertaken a series of research projects – some of which are classified – as well as having commissioned external 'public relations' agencies and academics, to undertake research on Muslims.[32] The targets of their propaganda and influence campaigns have been those deemed 'vulnerable' to becoming terrorists in the future. Some of these campaigns, however, have not been declared as being funded or created by the UK government, showcasing how 'deception' and 'manipulation' – both of which are forms of violence – are intrinsic to propaganda and behavioural change.[33]

The methods of collecting information on entire communities as well as their culture are therefore not only informed by police intelligence but also social scientific research methods that seek to understand 'adversary culture'. Commander Steve Tatham, a retired British military officer and a strong advocate of influence and 'strategic communication', advocates the use of 'Target Audience Analysis' to research and understand the target of propaganda messages. 'Target Audience Analysis', Tatham and Rowland remark, 'may necessitate desk-based research, expert interviews, simple polling if available, field-based structured depth interviews, and remote monitoring of current behaviour (perhaps using Intelligence).'[34] The person or institution doing the influencing, they declare, 'needs to use anything ... that is available to build up a picture of the problem space and the relationships and behaviours between groups in that space'.[35] According to the UK's counterinsurgency manual, 'target audience analysis is a continuous process conducted on groups and individuals, with priorities informed by mission needs'.[36] To put it another way, background and open-source intelligence is used in combination with social scientific research on a continuous basis to understand and target Muslims with propaganda to influence a shift in their behaviour in favour of the government.

* * *

The term 'propaganda' is not a word that is used in British military doctrine when it comes to describing its own actions and ideas around communicative activity. It is used only when describing what insurgents do. To describe their own activity, the umbrella term 'influence' is used. 'Counterinsurgency is about gaining and securing the support of the people both in the theatre of operations and at home', the UK's counterinsurgency manual notes. 'Influence activity therefore underpins everything which British forces undertake because counterinsurgency is as much about the battle of perceptions as it is about military operations targeted against insurgents.' But 'influence' is not undertaken through messages that explain an action. Instead, influence is about undertaking actions that will communicate a message and prompt a change in behaviour of Muslims in favour of the government.

Communicative practices that seek to 'influence' have been referred to in the past through a whole host of names, including propaganda of the deed, 'hearts and minds', psychological operations (Psy-Ops), political warfare, and more recently, 'strategic communication'. The UK Ministry of Defence define strategic communication as 'primarily a philosophy' that is based on 'the alignment of words, images and actions' for the purpose of realising influence and inducing behavioural change.[37] An example would be useful here to show how 'strategic communication' operates. When occupying forces engage in development work such as building a health centre or a school that offers free services to the natives, the primary driver is not primarily to help those who are suffering from ill health or to assist those who desire an education. The purpose is to demonstrate to the natives that the occupation forces are concerned for their welfare and well-being in order to 'influence' their behaviour in a way that will benefit the occupation forces. The effects of building a health centre or the school could result in a whole host of outcomes. It could, for example, generate indifference to what is happening, it may generate compliance, maybe even consent. In order to best understand how the message will be received, studying and analysing the natives is critical. When information is communicated, it is not only important to consider the means through which information is transferred. 'Of greater importance', Mackay and Tatham point out, 'is the culture, history, and traditions of its intended audiences, for it is these that will determine if the message will succeed or fail.'[38]

Whilst every action will communicate a message, what is distinct about 'strategic communication' is that the outcome or end result is considered before an action is executed. Whether it is an armed drone-strike in Somalia, a student who is arrested and detained in the UK, or whether it is a health centre in Kabul or Kirkuk that is built, the effects of such actions are assessed before the action is undertaken in order to maximise influence. 'Traditionally in the course of conventional operations', declares Kilcullen in the chapter on Information Operations in the UK's counterinsurgency manual, 'we use information operations to explain what we are doing but in counterinsurgency we should design operations to enact our influence campaign.'[39] So, an act such as opening a health centre or arresting somebody should not be done only to help the natives to be healthy or to apprehend a suspect. Rather, the influence an act will have on a broader community should be factored into the equation before it is executed.

Studying adversary culture and Muslim communities is done to develop information that will inform the security state's propaganda activity that will influence a broader set of people into changing their behaviour. Information, to put it simply, has become a weapon of war in and of itself rather than being a means of supporting weapons of war. Perhaps the term 'armed propaganda', as employed by David Kilcullen, is a more honest term to describe what the security state and military are doing rather than a term like 'strategic communication' which largely conceals the reality of this practice through a bland and innocuous term.[40]

*   *   *

To answer the question of why I was arrested, detained, and investigated by the security state, and then subsequently subjected to routine and ongoing surveillance through stop and search requires understanding the counterinsurgency-infused approach to counterterrorism that the UK security state has employed. The security state not only targets suspected terrorists and insurgents but also seeks to pre-empt and prevent ordinary people from engaging in any activity or ideas that the government claims is indicative of future terrorism. Being a political activist who advocates for Muslim rights, especially in an anti-war context, as well as being in possession of terrorist propaganda, are two ways in which this assessment is made.

In the case of my own arrest and detention for suspected terrorism, the entire investigation rested on my possession of one document that had been downloaded from a US government website and which could, incidentally, be purchased from high street bookshops or loaned from the library. However, cases where students have been arrested and detained on a university campus for studying and researching terrorism has since my arrest and detention become very infrequent. In fact, since 2008, there have been no counterterrorism operations executed on a university campus where somebody has been arrested and detained for possessing primary research material relating to the study of armed Muslim groups and terrorism.

The first reason for this is because the security state has coercively communicated its ability and willingness to use violence through my own case, and, at the same time, created a situation where universities police and monitor their own students and staff who access terrorist propaganda. The methods of exercising control and discipline, in other words, has changed, not the control and policing itself. Secondly, the risk of negative publicity in arresting and detaining a student who is researching armed Muslim groups and terrorism is quite high for the security state, especially when it relies on good old-fashioned state violence through arrest and detention. However, this does not mean that the security state's desire to pre-empt the behaviour of Muslims has stopped. Instead, through the creation and embedding of the Prevent de-radicalisation policy throughout the British public sector, individuals can be 'spoken to' through non-arrest and non-detention avenues. We can see this at play in two noted case studies.

The first case involves postgraduate student Mohammad Umar Farooq. Farooq was undertaking a Master's degree in Terrorism, Crime and Global Security at the University of Staffordshire and was questioned by a university complaints officer after he was spotted reading a textbook on terrorism written by Professor John Horgan and Dr Kurt Braddock in his university library.[41] He was asked by the complaints officer for his views on British values, foreign fighters, homosexuality, ISIL, and al-Qaeda. Not fully satisfied with Farooq's replies – which the media reported 'raised too many red flags' for the complaints officer – she reported her conversation to the university security department, who logged the incident and initiated an internal investigation into the student.[42] Farooq only become aware of this internal referral and investigation after a security guard informally mentioned that a staff member had raised some concerns about an exchange in the library and some of the opinions he held. Farooq subsequently raised an internal complaint regarding his treatment and eventually went on to receive an apology from the university for his treatment.[43]

The second case involves an unnamed final year undergraduate student at the University of East Anglia who was questioned by Special Branch officers at his home for reading extracts from the ISIL magazine, *Dabiq*.[44] This reading formed a part of his module 'Clash of Fundamentalisms'. He and his course-colleagues had been instructed to consult the extracts by their professor.[45] The website the student accessed the extracts from, according to a university spokesperson, was involved in 'analys[ing] and challeng[ing] the publication of extremist ideologies'.[46] What therefore seems like an entirely legitimate source for students to consult as part of their studies had prompted questioning and scrutiny of one student by Special Branch officers.[47]

Though neither of these students were arrested or detained under terrorism laws, the fact they were pre-emptively approached and questioned shows how counterterrorism has evolved to discipline and control people in a more insidious and underhanded way compared to the way I was treated. This subtler and pre-emptive way of exercising state violence relies upon a complex web of surveillance in which public sector workers such as academics and doctors collect and share information internally within their own organisations and externally with the police on those who they think may pose a potential future terrorist threat.

The problem with using a pre-emptive and preventive approach is twofold. Firstly, it requires the state to exponentially expand its surveillance infrastructure in order to predict future risk, which has a deeply corrosive and traumatic effect on the psychological well-being of innocent people from 'suspect communities'. And secondly, the person being subjected to pre-emptive and preventive action has the burden of proof placed on them to demonstrate that they 'mean no harm'. However, since 'enemies', by default, intend to cause harm, proving one's innocence becomes a thankless task. Muslims not only find themselves living under the watchful and pre-emptive eye of the security state. They also have the unenviable task of constantly demonstrating their innocence by condemning terrorist attacks undertaken by their co-religionists the world-over and proactively distancing themselves from anything even remotely resembling 'Islamic-politics' and Muslim community organisation for fear of being branded 'extremists', 'terrorist-sympathisers' and so forth.

And the use of coercive and intrusive actions the security state engages in is made possible because they are often undertaken in accordance with specially designed laws. These laws allow the security state to not only target those who are marked as 'suspects' but also create and construct new suspects out of ordinary people who are classed as potential future terrorists too. However, whilst coercion and threats may lead Muslims to comply with the government out of fear, it can never generate consent for what the security state does. And this is why the security state much prefers to undertake its violence in accordance with the law; to lay claim to the fact that its employment of violence is subject to scrutiny as well as 'checks and balances' as a way of signalling to both the target Muslim community and broader British communities that their actions are appropriate, fair, and legal.

Even though the greatest of liberal critics may not agree with the security state's exercise of violence, they will often understand that the state's actions are lawful and therefore grant it a degree of legitimacy and freedom to operate. This is perhaps why liberalism and counterinsurgency both go hand-in-hand. They both believe there is a better technical and legally legitimate way of fighting this war rather than questioning its racialised application, the violence, coercion, and surveillance it relies upon, the knowledge it uses to justify itself, and the harmful effects this type of warfare has on entire communities. Resistance and criticism for the security state's use of counterinsurgency infused policies and practices should not only revolve around calling out the tactics used to fight this type of war. It should also question counterinsurgency's historical and strategic foundations, its overwhelming use of violence and surveillance against entire communities, and challenge how both knowledge and law are used to legitimise and justify the coercion and control associated with this type of warfare. The purpose of doing this is simple: to understand in whose interests, for whose benefit, and whose name the violence and coercion of the security state is undertaken.

27
A Relapse

When I began writing this book in early 2018, the triggers I had been educated to spot by my mental health caseworker ahead of being discharged – things like paranoia, hypervigilance, feelings of being watched, followed and so forth – were all being pressed. But I told myself that this was all part and parcel of writing a book on this very subject, and I didn't have any right to complain. I had to power through it. These feelings and emotions, I reasoned with myself, were occupational hazards. I told myself that I was mentally stronger, more resilient, and more knowledgeable as a person compared to 2013 and was therefore in control. But as I tried to write, I could feel the hypervigilance and paranoia steadily rising day by day. For example, I began to suspect that my laptop was being remotely monitored. That my apartment was bugged. Everything I was writing was being read by the security services. I felt that my Twitter feed was broadcasting coded messages to me. I therefore decided it was perhaps sensible to take a break from this book and catch a breath. When my friends invited me to join them on the last leg of their European road trip in September 2018 in Barcelona, I jumped at the opportunity, not realising what was about to happen.

Despite the anxiety that invariably follows me whenever I travel, the flight from Manchester to Barcelona was smooth. On arrival, I scanned my passport at the E-Border machine and stood in front of a facial recognition screen. I observed how the machine was taking considerably longer to read my face compared to those who had passed before me. Around fifty seconds must have passed as the machine 'processed' my face, and then a graphic of a policeman appeared accompanied by written English text: 'Wait to be seen by a police officer.' Within a few seconds, a uniformed Spanish police officer appeared. He checked all the pages in my passport, looked me up and down, and waved me through. In total, this lasted no more than a minute and, compared to the other experiences I have had at airports, was minor. But it took place at a time when I was already feeling quite anxious and hypervigilant. It triggered me in a way that I was totally unprepared for. All of a sudden, I felt like this was a coded and coercive warning being issued to me by the UK via the Spaniards: 'You may have left the UK but we are still watching you.'

One part of my mind immediately recognised that interpreting this stop as a 'coded' message indicated that I was perhaps unwell and would need to speak to somebody when I returned to the UK. But the other part of my mind was telling me that I was *not* unwell. Maybe my insights and perceptiveness, I thought to myself, had been labelled as 'psychosis' to delegitimise what I know and feel. Maybe it is a way of constructing me as a 'madman' in order to erase my ability to tune into hidden and coded messages that others simply cannot see or understand. As my mind raced with these sorts of thoughts and questions, I felt like my brain was being torn in two.

When we got to the villa my friends had rented for the three-day stay in Barcelona, my condition began to worsen. With a private swimming pool and CCTV cameras installed both inside and outside the property, I suspected the villa belonged to the intelligence services. I felt that it had been purposefully allocated to us in order to give me a coded message that they somehow knew I would be able to decipher: 'stop critiquing the British security state, stop writing this book, work for the intelligence services and you can live a life of luxury and comfort in a villa with a swimming pool'. The villa felt like it was doubling up as a 'show-home' and a 'psychological laboratory' that was being used to assess how people behaved and reacted to coded offers of recruitment made by the security state.

But everything about this coded offer by the security state could not be taken seriously, and the symbolism of the CCTV cameras helped me reach this conclusion. No matter how much they may have wanted me to work for them, I felt, they would always watch and monitor me. Accepting the offer may lessen the pain and pressure my mind was feeling in that moment, I reflected, but in the long term it would mean spending my life in a position of subjugation and servitude, only in a luxurious prison such as this villa. I would rather have nothing if the alternative was losing the chance to think, speak, and write about what was being done to my community.

The three nights I stayed in this villa were pretty much focused on trying to keep myself calm and ensuring my friends were not aware of what was happening to me or what I felt the security state was trying to do. There was no way of proving to them what I felt and suspected, and if I started explaining how these coded messages were being targeted at me, there was a possibility they would worry and this would perhaps spoil the last leg of their holiday. I therefore tried to stay quiet most of the time and not say anything that would reveal what I was experiencing.

We spent the day exploring the streets and sights of Barcelona and at night, while my friends slept, I sat alone in the warm weather of the outdoors veranda, and paced restlessly around the garden staring at the swimming pool until they would eventually wake up and start their day. On the first night, I managed to sleep for around two hours but the remaining two days in this apartment I could not get any sleep and did not even attempt to. I was afraid that if I slept, something 'bad' may happen, similar to that night when I took sleeping pills in 2013 and awoke to news of the Boston Marathon having been bombed.

When the three days were finally up, it was time to leave Barcelona. I was catching a ride with my friends to the German city of Bochum to spend the next three days there with my cousin Aamer and his family, before catching my return flight to the UK. This part of the trip had been planned before I left the UK, and although I was desperate to return home to the UK, I felt I should not deviate from my original plan. I did not want to alert the security state that I felt afraid or vulnerable and I had to remain strong despite the coercive pressure I felt was being placed on me.

Upon arrival at Aamer's home in Germany, and despite the fact my mind and body were both exhausted, I lay in bed for most of that night. I could not sleep for more than a couple of hours though. My mind was racing and seemed unstoppable. I got out of bed around sunrise, headed into the garden, and paced back and forth endlessly trying to make sense of what was happening to me and what I needed to do. The contradictory and opposing thoughts were relentless, unstoppable.

One afternoon, Aamer asked why I was spending all my time alone in the garden and if I was okay. But I did not want to tell him what I was going through. I felt that there was very little point in saying anything to anybody at this stage. They would not understand and may even think I was 'mad'. 'I am in the midst of writing a book and need time to reflect and think,' I said to him. 'Since the weather is so beautiful, there is no better place to be than the garden.'

Aamer offered me the keys to a small studio apartment he owned nearby, and said I was welcome to use it as a writing space to complete the book if I needed to be alone. 'Nobody will disturb you,' he said. He also offered me his son's car since he had not yet passed his driving test. Both of these offers were extraordinarily generous and summed up Amar's selfless nature. But, at that moment in time, I could not stop my mind from being triggered by his offer, and I began to believe Aamar was working for the German intelligence services. His offer of material possessions – a home and a car – was being extended to recruit me either to work for the Germans or to recruit me on behalf of the British. There was, however, no difference between these two countries in my mind at the time since I considered they all had an interest in dealing with the 'Muslim threat' in one way or another. Trying not to sound alarmed or triggered, I thanked Aamer and refused his offer.

As I continued pacing around the garden, a few hours had passed and a 'breaking news' alert appeared on my smartphone. The chief of the domestic intelligence agency of Germany, the news report stated, had been unexpectedly dismissed from his post. As soon as I saw the headline, two thoughts rushed through my mind. Firstly, this breaking news was in response to the German intelligence services' failure to recruit me via Aamer. Somebody had to pay the price for this botched recruitment attempt and it was the chief of German intelligence. Secondly, I felt that refusing Aamer's offer whilst my smartphone was close to me suggested it, and I, were both being listened to on a 'live' basis.

With one day left until my return flight to the UK, I needed the time to pass quickly and I needed to also get away from Aamer, whom I now strongly suspected of being an agent. I rented a car and began aimlessly driving around Germany. Then, as evening approached, I drove to the city of Prague in the Czech Republic. Within twenty-four hours, I had ended up driving the car for a total of 1,200 miles, sleeping in the car for an hour at a secluded lay-by, and stopping only to refuel the car or for food. As I drove, I was convinced that my smartphone was being monitored. I had considered leaving it at Aamer's home, but I could not muster the courage to do so. I feared that if I did anything to make it harder for the security state to monitor me, they may resort to physical violence or imprisonment. By having my phone on me, I could maybe avoid a worse fate. But there were moments when the sense of being actively surveilled and followed were heightened beyond expectation. I recall one particular instance of this happening that sent my mind into a state of terror.

I stopped at a service station in Germany to get a coffee and was speedily writing out some rough thoughts on the uncertainty of being under surveillance, using the 'notes' app on my Apple iPhone 8. I felt this was perhaps the best way to help myself; write it all out and get it off my chest. I typed the following text:

Where surveillance exists there's always half a chance that you are under surveillance and therefore being monitored through more intensive and intrusive measures but are unable to verify or know. In this situation, you can try and take precautions but you will never be able to be 100 per cent sure. And this is the whole point of the method of attack. To never fully let the adversary or enemy know that they are under attack. To make them feel like they are going crazy. JTRIG, baby. GCHQ. Explain how JTRIG tactics work. Emphasise nature of surveillance being hidden and therefore largely unverifiable. Bit like God, eh?

Within a matter of seconds of typing the above paragraph, the entire screen on my iPhone went blank and my phone had become totally unresponsive. I immediately thought that the 'Joint Threat Research Intelligence Group' (JTRIG), a covert cyber-warfare unit based at GCHQ, had done this. According to documents leaked by the NSA whistleblower Edward Snowden, JTRIG is involved in a long list of deception and disruption activities including 'denial of telephone and computer service (to deny, delay or disrupt)'.[1] I knew this at the time, and this is precisely the point I was writing about in my notes. Other than the coincidental timing of the phone screen going blank, what made me feel that this was JTRIG is that no matter how many times I panickily pressed the home or lock buttons on my iPhone, nothing was happening. The phone had become completely unresponsive the moment I mentioned JTRIG and GCHQ in my written notes.

Eventually, I forced the phone to restart by pressing the home and power buttons together. When the phone restarted, the screen was working fine. In that moment at the service station though, I was convinced that JTRIG/GCHQ were not only monitoring my movements through my smartphone but were actively hacking my device and reading every word I typed. But what was the purpose of this surveillance? And why would this happen the moment I mention JTRIG and GCHQ in my notes? Was it a way of telling me that I had worked out the answer to a 'puzzle' of sorts? Was it the use of the word 'baby' that had triggered them and made them feel that I was not taking them seriously and therefore they had to give me an overt signal? Was it their way of confirming that I was under surveillance? Was it a threat? Perhaps a validation of what I suspected? Was it a sign? If so, what did it mean? As the questions and uncertainty raced through my mind, I stopped writing and continued driving. I was heading back to Bochum so I could return the hire car and catch my return flight that same evening. After a short while, I stopped at the service station again, for food this time.

I was eating a sandwich and an email unexpectedly appeared on my smartphone. It was from the airline Flybe: 'We are really sorry to let you know', the email read, 'that your flight scheduled to depart 15 Sep 17:50 has been cancelled.' There was no reason or explanation given for the cancellation, only an instruction telling me to go to the airline website to be issued with a refund or to rebook another flight. To my mind, this was no ordinary cancellation. This was the intelligence services working in partnership with business to send me a clear message: 'agree with what we say or be excluded from the UK'. As I sat in the car, I began considering where I would even live if I were to be denied entry to the UK and what I would do. I felt angry and upset in equal measure, but also determined to get back to the UK no matter what happened in order to show that I would not simply accept what felt like blackmail.

When I reached Aamer's home, I went on the airline website but, for some reason, it would not allow me to rebook my flight and neither my debit or my credit card worked. Again, in my mind, this was the security state working with banks and credit card companies to disrupt my travel in order to deny me entry back to the UK. I also felt my inability to book my flight was a way of making me feel disempowered and dependent on others. Even though it pained me to have to ask Aamer to book my flight for me – since he was, in my mind, representing the German intelligence service – I felt there were very few options left open if I wanted to get back to the UK. With great hesitation, I asked him to book me a flight on the condition he would let me pay him back. I did not want anything for 'free'. He agreed, and needless to say, the airline booking went through immediately on his credit card.

When I boarded the plane at Dusseldorf Airport in Germany, the seat to my left was occupied by a young brown Muslim woman, who wore a light-coloured headscarf. The first thing I noticed was the sophisticated henna pattern on her hand, which usually suggests the person had been to a wedding. But on seeing the henna, I felt triggered. In late 2014, I had seen an MI5 recruitment campaign for a 'Mobile Surveillance Officer' that was largely targeted at South Asian women. I shared a screenshot of the image at the time on Twitter. In the image, a woman whose face you cannot see, is wearing a pink traditional South Asian dress – the kind usually worn at special events such as weddings and parties – and has her arms crossed, with henna patterns visible on each of her hands. If you pay attention to the henna pattern though, you can see written into it, in English, the following words: 'If you fit in here, you'll fit in here.' If you can fit into your own community, in other words, you can also fit into MI5. When I saw the henna on my fellow passenger's hands, I felt like it was MI5's coded way of telling me they were watching me before I had even set foot back into the UK. I remained silent throughout the flight and did not leave my seat. My earphones remained in my ears even though no music was playing. I did not want the woman to speak to me. When the two of us exited the plane on landing, she went in a separate direction and I was able to breathe a little easier for that moment.

28
Dear GCHQ

On my return to the UK, I found some consolation in the fact I had made it back despite feeling that the security services were trying to disrupt my return. On the other hand, however, I felt I was now back in a country where every institution was working with the security state and where the latter could thus surveil me with much greater ease. Being at home, amongst friends, family, and familiar surroundings is meant to give you a sense of comfort and safety, but it had come to do and mean the opposite for me. I felt my mind was throbbing with the idea I was now under total surveillance. After a couple of days, I felt the need to tell somebody what I was going through but feared being called 'crazy'.

I decided to therefore publish what I was feeling on Twitter but in a 'coded' way. This would have two advantages. Firstly, only those who were paying attention to my Twitter output would pick up on what I was trying to tell them, and hopefully they would reach out. Secondly, the security services, who I felt were monitoring my account, would learn that I was not going to stop resisting them or cave in to the pressure they were subjecting me to. 'When Foucault puts you in prison', I tweeted on 18 September 2018, 'it's time to listen to Gramsci.' What I meant was that although the intelligence services may be watching me and having a coercive effect on my thoughts and behaviour (as Foucault examines in his book *Discipline and Punish*), I, just like Gramsci, would resist the coercion and control by using the same technique he did: writing. The Gramsci reference was important not only because the latter examines how invisible power can be made visible and resisted but also because he wrote *The Prison Notebooks* after being imprisoned by the fascist regime of Benito Mussolini. Though a few academic colleagues and others 'liked' the tweet, nobody seemed to have deciphered my intent or contacted me in the way I had anticipated. As soon as the tweet was posted, I therefore began to feel I was alone and at increased risk – having gone public in this way was certain to anger the security services and perhaps lead to more aggressive practices being used against me.

Despite the continuation of what can only be described as acute paranoia, I sat at my desk and tried to write this book. I was on a deadline. But every time I began typing, I felt that somebody from the intelligence services was remotely monitoring my computer and reading every word I typed on a 'live' basis. I could not therefore simply write what I wanted to write. Writer friends often said to me that writing was therapeutic and liberating for them. In that moment in late 2018, however, I experienced the total opposite. Every time I typed on my laptop, I felt like my mind was back in the security services' vice that was tightening further with every word that appeared. The writing process had become extremely debilitating and mentally exhausting, and my writing started to reflect everything except what I actually thought and wanted to write. 'Dear GCHQ/NSA', I once wrote in the middle of a sentence. 'Please stop this, man! This is private! Have some respect!' On another day, I felt that the intelligence services, rather than trying to undermine me, were on this occasion trying to make me work in partnership with them to deal with issues they could not handle on their own. 'FFS! This is just stupid!', I once angrily wrote mid-sentence. 'I can't fix the problems you have created! Please piss off!'

I realise the act of writing such messages must sound absurd. It is embarrassing to write about this today, whilst I am in control of my rational faculties and managing my trauma. But at the time, in late 2018, the fact that I wrote these 'messages' shows how my entire existence felt that it was exposed to the surveilling eyes of the security and intelligence services. And yet, I kept telling myself that I had to continue writing no matter what. My only way of resisting the security state was to write about them and the impact and effect they had and were having on me. At the same time, I wanted to demonstrate to those agents who were tasked with reading every word I typed that irrespective of their unrivalled capacity for coercion, surveillance, and violence, I would stand my ground. And then, the physical pain began.

Over the course of around two days of trying to write, I detected a pattern. Whenever I sat and wrote, I would feel an excruciating pain to the centre-left of my abdominal area. When I would stop writing and move away from my desk, the pain would subside within a matter of minutes. When I felt able enough, I would go back to my desk and begin typing and, again within a matter of minutes, the pain would restart. Initially, I tried to fight through the pain barrier, telling myself that speaking about coercive power and the security state would inevitably lead to pain. But the reality is, at that time, I did not understand how the physical pain I was experiencing was connected to, and symptomatic of, trauma.[1] Either way, the physical pain meant that the writing had to stop and I needed help.

*   *   *

Despite being told to immediately approach my doctor if there was a reoccurrence of any of the symptoms of 2013, I could still not bring myself to trust the medical profession. When I therefore visited my doctor for a medical note that I needed so I could supply it to my employer, I refused to go into any detail around what my 'problem' was. 'I am mentally drained and exhausted because of a project I am working on,' I told my doctor. 'I need to rest my mind.' Despite her best attempts to get me to share what I was feeling, I refused to be drawn into a conversation. I did, however, explain my reason for not sharing what I was feeling with her. I told her that since she was a public sector worker, she was under a professional duty to report those people who she deemed vulnerable to radicalisation and terrorism under the law. As a result, the doctor–patient code had been broken in my view and I did not consequently feel comfortable talking about my issues with her. I apologised to her and told her this was not a judgement of her. Instead, it was a result of my understanding of a deeply problematic policy area that she was caught in the middle of, whether she liked it or not. She understood and did not prod me further to share what I was experiencing.

There was also another reason why I was reluctant to engage with medical professionals from the National Health Service (NHS). Based on my previous experience with them in 2013, I reached the conclusion they did not seem to have the resources to actually deal with trauma or the distinct experiences of Muslims and people of colour who understand things from a more culturally nuanced perspective. When I had visited mental health professionals and psychiatrists in 2013, despite their being aware of my experiences of state violence and the political grounds for the way I was feeling, nobody ever mentioned to me the word 'trauma' or invoked symptoms of Post-Traumatic Stress Disorder (PTSD). I therefore knew that going to the doctors would lead to nothing more than a psychiatric assessment and the issuing of anti-psychotic medications that would deal only with the symptoms of my problems, not the root causes.

I therefore contacted a trusted friend who is professionally qualified to speak with survivors of torture and political violence, and told him what I was experiencing: the paranoia, the hypervigilance, the feeling that my laptop and smartphone were bugged, Germany, the safe house in Spain and so forth. He attentively listened and explained how my feelings and symptoms seemed to be connected to the re-enactment of 'trauma'. He helpfully summarised some key points about trauma, and how it expresses itself in a person's life. He also helped me make sense of things I was feeling in a way that nobody had ever discussed or mentioned to me before. He recommended I consult a book he felt would help me understand what I was experiencing. The book, *Trauma and Recovery*, written by American psychiatrist Judith Herman, was indeed remarkable, and helped me identify some of the things I was experiencing as being symptoms of PTSD, especially 'hyperarousal', 'intrusion', and 'constriction'. It also made me realise that if left unaddressed, these symptoms could impact a person long after a violent or abusive encounter was over. At the same time as disengaging from the writing of this book, I devised a plan in conjunction with my friend which largely consisted of unplugging from technology, especially from my smartphone and Twitter account. The reason was simple. The more I engaged with news, the more upset and triggered I felt. But despite the harm it was causing, it took me around two months to actually stop engaging with it, especially Twitter.

But there was another problem. Not working on the book, and taking a break from reading and commentating on the news, was making me feel guilty for being idle. Although I knew I had to rest, because my body was experiencing physical pains, the guilt of being inactive was causing me great anxiety. A couple of friends

I had spoken to about my situation told me I had nothing to feel guilty about. There was nothing wrong in resting the mind and body. One of them sent me an essay written by the black feminist intellectual Audre Lorde. In the essay, Lorde writes: 'caring for myself is not self-indulgence. It is self-preservation, and that is an act of political warfare.' The language and the resistive tone gave me a sense of strength and helped me understand that resting was not the same as quitting. I finally began to switch off, and learnt to ignore the news, Twitter alerts, messages, and emails that were all coming my way. I dedicated my time to my *salah*, spent time with close friends who I laughed with and talked about anything except 'politics', and binge-watched five series of the Turkish TV series *Dirilis: Ertugrul* about the Ottoman Empire.

29
Trauma Triggers

After three months of sick leave, in January 2019 I felt well enough to return to work, and slowly restart writing. However, I soon discovered that the trauma had not gone away. It was still there and would reappear when I least expected, such as, for example, in a lecture theatre. It was February 2020 and I arrived at a busy lecture theatre one morning to talk to my students about my research on counterterrorism, the methods of collecting information I have used over the last ten years, and some of the key findings of my research. As I began talking, I spotted a middle-aged man sat in the lecture, frantically taking notes of everything I said. Since this is one of the modules I lead, I knew this man was not a student. So, who was he and why was he here? Is this the first lecture he was attending, one where I happened to be talking about my research on counterterrorism, how I secured police intelligence data, discovered that I was known to MI5 before my arrest for suspected terrorism and other such things? Is he an undercover police officer? Is he an intelligence agent? Is he here to intimidate me and discipline my words and ideas? To give me a 'warning' that I am being watched? All of these questions were racing through my mind as I continued with my lecture, almost as if a parallel part of my mind was working alongside the part responsible for guiding my words through the teaching.

Despite trying my best to remain composed and calm, I could sense that my sense of psychological stress was increasing. The lecture, which is one of my favourites and often keeps students engaged due to the content matter, had become a burdensome exercise in self-disciplining and self-policing every word I uttered. It became clear to me that the safety of the lecture theatre had been compromised. The speed with which I spoke was rushed, the slides were hurriedly changed, and the details were kept to a minimum. I wanted this lecture over – and quickly. As the students began exiting the lecture theatre, I spotted this man signing each sheet of paper off with what I assume were his initials. I could no longer contain myself and approached him.

'Hi,' I said to him in as polite and non-aggressive a tone as I could find. 'Are you a student?' 'No,' he replied, raising an identification card he was wearing around his neck. As I attentively examined the ID card, he explained he had been instructed to come to this lecture to take notes for a 'client'. I found the word 'client' strange. 'Who is your client,' I asked him. He told me that he was under strict instructions not to share this information with me. When I asked if his 'client' was a student, he confirmed it was but could not share any details as to who this student was. As the person who manages and leads the module, I told him I had access to all records and can see who is entitled to receive learning support. It therefore made little sense to conceal this information from me. But he would not be drawn further on the subject. Unable to really do anything, I took down his details so I could make my own inquiries afterwards. When asking him for his contact details I noted how the tone I used – and the fact I addressed him using his title and surname – mirrored how I would address police officers, especially those who would stop and search me at the roadside and at airports; assertive yet calm. On reflection, this suggests how seriously I was taking this issue at that moment in time.

'Is this the first lecture you have attended,' I asked him. 'This is my first assignment, yes,' he replied. Whilst the word 'assignment' made me suspect that this man was a spy, the fact this was the first lecture he had attended, the one lecture where I happened to be talking about my very personal motivations for, and my methods of, researching counterterrorism had me convinced, in that moment, that he worked for the police or MI5. As I busied myself with packing my bag, the man stood outside of the lecture theatre where he was speaking and handing over the notes he made to one of my students. I knew the student was entitled to receive additional learning support, and it became quite clear on witnessing this that the man had been telling me the truth. He was a 'note-taker' for a student, not a police officer or MI5 agent.

As I walked to the seminar taking place immediately after the lecture, I felt upset and sort of ashamed. It was dawning on me that the security state had seemingly developed an ability to pierce my mind and influence my words, thoughts, and actions without even being present, and how I had internalised my own sense of powerlessness to a great extent. At the same time, I felt angry that an ordinary task – such as lecturing on my subject area – had become, in that moment, so challenging. Most importantly, it signalled to me that even though it may have been over a decade since the security state used its legally sanctioned violence against me on the pretext of protecting national security and dealing with 'terrorism', the traumatic and harmful effects were still looming over me all these years later. In the summer of 2020, realising that I needed professional help and therapy of some sort, I asked my doctor to refer me to the relevant mental health professionals for support. With the Covid-19 lockdown in full swing, I held a meeting in July with a psychologist and a psychiatrist. After a long consultation, and lots of conversations about the sorts of things I was feeling, they both went away and said they would let me know what they thought the next steps were.

30
Withdrawing Consent

When I began researching al-Qaeda for my postgraduate studies, I wanted to understand the group, what they were doing, and what they wanted to achieve. I hoped that I could play a part in identifying the root causes of the group's violence. After the police arrested, detained, and suspected me of being connected to al-Qaeda myself, and then routinely surveilled, stopped and searched me, however, I felt compelled to refocus my attention and energy towards studying and researching policing and counterterrorism. My goal was now to stop people from being impacted and harmed in the same way that I had been. I was, to put it simply, driven to resist because of the violence of the security state.

The security state recognises that the coercive exercise of power may breed resistance which is why counterinsurgents suggest that rather than relying on overtly violent counterterrorism practices such as, for instance, detentions, bombings, and targeted killings, a mix of less violent and persuasive tactics be used to fight armed Muslim groups and politically control communities. Counterinsurgents recognise that hard coercive power can be politically costly and therefore prefer exercising power through consent. Relying on influence, propaganda, and surveillance, counterinsurgency-infused counterterrorism is likely to be viewed by the public as 'the lesser of two evils' and therefore more appropriate than overt violence and force. This allows the security state to exercise power and fulfil its goals with less contestation and resistance.

Using a less violent or *different* approach to fighting armed Muslim groups and controlling communities enables the state to be seen as a legitimate holder and wielder of power. Carl Von Clausewitz, the eighteenth-century Prussian general and major influence on Western military thinking, makes an interesting point in his book *On War* in this regard. He writes that the military methods used by nation-states to fight their enemies are only a 'means' to securing a bigger objective which is 'the compulsory submission of the enemy to our will'. Getting your enemy to do what you want, in other words, is more important than what methods and means you use. If it is violence that is required, then it should be employed according to this Clausewitzian reading. If it is rewards and money that need to be used to make your enemy surrender to your will, then it is precisely these things that should be used. We can see this logic at play in the sphere of policing and counterterrorism, where a mix of methods and means are used to secure political and strategic goals to make enemies succumb to the security state's will and, if possible, maintain legitimacy in the eyes of the public whilst doing so.

In order to maintain this sense of legitimacy and consent for its power, the security state employs phrases and language that mask the coercion and violence that its practices are rooted in. Terms such as 'winning hearts and minds' are used as shorthand to describe a process that entails behavioural change induced through a mixture of manipulative and persuasive acts which seek to pacify and control people. 'Safeguarding' is used as a byword for a process that is concerned with pre-emptively intervening in the life of a person who has been surveilled by a public sector worker, such as a school teacher or doctor, and then referred to the authorities on the ground that they are 'vulnerable' to becoming a terrorist in the future. The use of these sorts of benign sounding phrases are aimed not only at hiding the physical and mental harms of the security state's activities. They are also intended to manufacture the consent of the public, including Muslims and communities of colour, and reduce the chances of contestation and resistance to the security state's activities from emerging. After all, mass resistance becomes more challenging to organise and mobilise if the security state's violence is about 'safeguarding' people and has the buy-in of the very communities who are its targets. The key point is that, because the security state needs to secure the consent of Muslims and communities of colour, there is an opportunity for us to resist its power and contest its desire to act with impunity.

When I was stopped, searched, and questioned on the streets or at airports, I did not consent to what the police did. Yes, I *complied* with the orders the officers gave but I did not agree with their course of action or their exercise of power over me. Of course, not consenting did not prevent the stop, search, and detentions from being executed. However, it did demonstrate that I was only going along with what the police were doing because there was an underlying threat of further violence being used against me. For example, when I answered the questions put to me under Schedule 7 of the Terrorism Act on my arrival from Spain in 2010, I knew that not answering the police's questions would most likely lead me to being charged for a terrorism offence akin to 'obstruction'. To minimise the risk of the police escalating matters, I complied with their orders. The same logic applies to, say, the Prevent programme. When a referral is made to the authorities because somebody is deemed to be a potential future terrorist, their consent is sought before they are formally placed onto the Channel de-radicalisation programme. Often, people may not agree or consent to participating with Channel but will comply because they are fearful that non-compliance may expose them to more intrusive and aggressive forms of police and security state intervention such as surveillance, arrest, and so forth.

The result of consenting and complying to state power, *in practice*, leads to the same outcome but withdrawing our consent and only complying serves an important symbolic function which can prove unsettling for the security state. This is because simply complying with power indicates that you are only going along with what the police and security agencies order you to do because they have the legal right to use violence against you, not because you agree with their actions, orders, and demands. The withdrawal of consent makes visible how state exercise of power is rooted in fear rather than agreement. Though the state does not require our active consent and can function simply with our compliance, the state craves validation and legitimacy. It seeks to indoctrinate individuals and communities into supporting it but in a gradual and subtle way, so people feel they have arrived at their understanding of the world organically and independently. George Orwell lucidly describes this subtle process of indoctrination as a way of minimising resistance in his dystopian novel *1984*:

We are not content with negative obedience, nor even with the most abject submission. When finally you surrender to us, it must be of your own free will. We do not destroy the heretic because he resists us: so long as he resists us we never destroy him. We convert him, we capture his inner mind, we reshape him. We burn all evil and all illusion out of him; we bring him over to our side, not in appearance, but genuinely, heart and soul.

No matter how overbearing and powerful the state's reach may seem, the security state's need to bring a person 'over to our side' in 'heart and soul' signals the existence of a space where its power can be questioned, contested, and challenged. By not actively consenting, Muslims and communities of colour can make policies harder to implement by compelling the security state to go it alone. By withdrawing their consent, communities can show that they are only complying with what the security state does because they fear the consequences of non-compliance, not because they support what it does. Though it may not bring power to its knees and force its dismantling, the withdrawing of consent challenges the ideological legitimacy the security state craves. It also serves as a useful avenue for those people who may not be as deeply engaged in resistance to take a stand against power and its coercive and abusive exercise. 'The duty of the native who has not yet reached maturity in political consciousness', writes the anti-colonial psychoanalyst Frantz Fanon, 'is literally to make it so that the slightest gesture has to be torn out of him. This is a very concrete manifestation of non-cooperation, or at least of minimum cooperation.'[1] Any action that works to make the exercise of power over us more difficult and works to disrupt the impunity with which the security state can work is a step in the right direction, especially for those on the receiving end of policing and counterterrorist violence.

31
Sharing Our Stories

Knowledge gives the powerless the understanding, impetus, and means to contest, navigate, and resist power. Finding and engaging with existing knowledge and creating new knowledge by centring our lived experiences is essential. If our personal stories of policing, counterterrorism, and fears of surveillance are not connected together to form a broader context, they will appear as individual anecdotes that can be dismissed by the security state and its advocates as exceptions to the rule. By eternalising our experiences through storytelling, we can make visible how security state violence and surveillance is the rule not the exception. At the same time, through the centring and sharing of our lived experiences of policing and counterterrorism, we can educate and empower communities by making them realise that their fears, anxieties, and traumas are more common than they may think. In creating and sharing this knowledge, we can move from individual resistance to collective struggle, standing in solidarity with those individuals and communities who are on the receiving end of state violence. At the same time, we can generate the power and critical mass necessary to take on the structures of the security state more broadly.

By connecting our lived experiences of policing and counterterrorism to the broader social and geo-political context within which they emerge, we can disrupt and challenge the deep-seated 'common-sense' assumptions that violence, coercion, and control are only used when necessary for 'public protection'. By showing how racialised identity plays a part in our treatment, we can make visible how the purported goal of 'public protection' is secured on the backs of Muslims and communities of colour. Talking about our lived experiences, in other words, can help us expose dominant representations of what counterterrorism is, what it seeks to do, whose interests and safety it serves and at whose expense.

By sharing our stories, we can also humanise ourselves and show that the violence of policing and counterterrorism is not victimless. We can reveal that this area of policy and policing induces complex forms of trauma, suffering, and harm in our bodies and minds in ways that are not as widely acknowledged or accounted for as much as they should be. I am not suggesting humanising ourselves and our stories as an appeal to white people or to the state. If through our stories, we inspire white people to stand in solidarity with us and challenge injustice and oppression in their own ways, then this is a positive development. However, since the injustices and oppressions we face operate on a structural level, our goal should be to disrupt and dismantle structures rather than try to appeal to individuals to be sympathetic to us. Change has to be led organically where communities of struggle lead the charge. The purpose of humanising ourselves is to help communities find a sense of solidarity and strength; where they can come together based on their shared and relatable experiences that are far too often rendered invisible due to a mix of fear and self-censorship. By humanising ourselves, we can educate, inspire, and empower one another to unite in resistance and struggle against injustice.

Humanising our experiences through storytelling is even more important to do because policing and counterterrorism are almost always undertaken in accordance with carefully drafted laws that construct violence as morally justified and therefore being fair and appropriate. However, the law has historically been an instrument of power repeatedly used to justify horrendous acts of violence on countless occasions against communities of colour the world over. Colonialism, genocide, and apartheid have all been considered lawful. More recently, there has been the internment of so-called 'enemy combatants' in CIA-run 'black sites' and Guantanamo Bay. All of these tyrannies were based on carefully drafted laws to authorise and legitimise what the state did, creating what Sherene Razack calls 'a place of law without law'.[1]

When state violence is 'legal', as in my case, it becomes harder to contest since the 'common-sense' assumption is that 'lawful' violence is usually done for a good reason. The law serves to legitimise and sanctify the violence and coercion people suffer, and more times than not, push the traumatic harms they suffer into the realm of the invisible. By centring our lived experiences of legally sanctioned state violence, and the harmful effects it induces within our bodies and minds, we can show that even though something may be lawful and constructed as legitimate in the public imagination, it does not morally defend the violence or lessen its harmful impact.

Whilst I did use the law to bring some accountability for the way I had been treated, my civil claim and the legal settlement I secured was an exception to the rule. How many of the 2,418 people who have been arrested and released without charge over the past twenty years[2] have gone on to secure damages for their treatment by employing the law as a tool of accountability and resistance? The use of the law to bring some semblance of accountability was only possible in my case because I had dedicated lawyers who were working on a pro-bono basis to help me formally clear my name and because I had legal insurance. Presently, with the record cuts to 'legal aid', the law has increasingly and overwhelmingly become an avenue of accountability for the rich and powerful only; not poorer and racialised people who are more likely to experience the violence of policing and the security state yet have very limited means to force accountability through the law.

An additional challenge is that the law individualises injustice rather than addressing the structural problems which give rise to it in the first place. In my case, the legal settlement I obtained did not formally compel the police or security agencies to alter their general practices. The structural oppressions of counter-terrorism, policing, and surveillance were not addressed. There was no legal precedent that was established. Whilst using the law as a tool of resistance is important, it should not be seen as a panacea to the harms, injustices, and oppressions we experience. And, it should certainly not be viewed as a replacement for the community organisation and collectivism needed to bring about social and political change on a more systematic and structural level. Through the recognition and sharing of our experiences, we can create a body of knowledge that will not only give courage to others within our communities to speak out and answer back to power but also begin to collectively disable the structural forces that shape how we are policed.

*   *   *

The coercive agencies of the state would prefer if people like me neither spoke about nor documented their experiences. But, despite their wishes, they cannot stop us from articulating our resistance, whether through art, writing, film, media, poetry, or music. Past struggles of anti-racists, anti-war movements, environmental campaigners, miners, trade unions, and women's liberation groups have compelled the state to concede power. The state cannot take away hard-won liberties without appearing highly authoritarian or triggering protest. On social media platforms like Twitter and Instagram, millions of people express resistance to state policies and practices on a daily basis through analysis, commentary, music, poetry, creative writing, or satirical memes ridiculing those responsible for governing us. There is the emergence of the Black Lives Matter movement, the shift towards a more pro-active campaign of 'decolonisation' in educational spaces, and the revitalisation of the global networks of solidarity with Palestinians through campaigns such as 'Boycott, Divestment, and Sanctions' (BDS). All of these struggles have been going on for decades but a shift is taking place in the rhetoric and discourse in favour of powerless communities and nations around the world. States are unable to fully block the evolving nature and methods of resistance made possible through the rise of technology and globalisation.

When the state cannot stop resistance in all its forms, it seeks to insidiously co-opt the existence of critique and resistance to serve its own power. Indeed, states congratulate themselves on not censoring and being receptive to dissent, protest, and critique, in an effort to legitimise themselves and reaffirm their power in the imagination of the public. When somebody has experienced state violence, the state may even trigger a formal inquiry, investigation, or review. This is done to suggest that the state is accountable and willing to learn from its critics, to ensure a fairer society is created.

These sorts of self-accountability mechanisms are rare but they serve a purpose. They weaken organisation, contestation, and resistance, and undermine movements, organisers, and activists who campaign against the structural and institutional factors that create injustice and violence in the first place. They cast these people as 'extreme', 'fringe', 'troublemakers' who are hell-bent on spreading discord for its own sake when none is necessary. Having some mechanisms of accountability therefore becomes a way for power to weaken the struggle for the systematic redistribution of political power in favour of powerless communities. Whilst this does make the political system in countries like the UK highly resilient in the face of very serious charges that are levied against it, communities, activists, and organisers should continue pointing out the systematic and structural ways in which violence and injustice are embedded, with a view to disrupting and dismantling institutions. By centring our stories of racist and Islamophobic state violence, inequality, exclusion, and trauma, we can make visible how power is exercised over us and show solidarity with others who are suffering too. We are more effective in challenging power when we organise and resist together, from the local to the global level.

32
Global Resistance

Muslims and communities of colour in the UK need to understand that the arrests and surveillance in the UK are part and parcel of the 'war on terror' taking place around the world. We need to make visible the connections and parallels between policing and counterterrorism on the streets of the UK and Europe and the torture, rendition, global surveillance, Guantanamo Bay, concentration camps, 'Shock & Awe', drone strikes and so forth. We will then be able to place our experiences in a broader global context. This will not only aid communities in making sense of why we are subjected to security state violence, surveillance, and intervention but also help us form networks of solidarity with communities around the world being targeted through the same war, though often through different and more aggressive means.

We should not be trying to perform gratefulness for our citizenship in the West by being passive and distant from the political struggles of our people and communities elsewhere. We should not be assimilating into whiteness or 'British Islam'. We must stand strong and use the small amounts of relative privilege that we *do* have – thanks to the resistive struggles of earlier generations – to mobilise in support and defence of people facing oppression, injustice, and violence in the non-West. I am not suggesting that, with our relative comfort of living in the West, we speak on behalf of those on the receiving end of harsher and more aggressive forms of securtiy state violence, such as aerial bombings and drone strikes. To do so would be artifical, inauthentic, and inappropriate. It would erase the nuance that only those who live through a particular experience can directly and truly convey and account for. What I am suggesting is that we use our own experiences of security state violence 'here' in the West in conjunction with the voices of those from the non-West suffering more naked violence in the same 'war on terror' as a way of building unity, solidarity, and connections that span the globe. If the violence of the security state is global, resistance, organisation, and solidarity must be global too.

Connecting the local to the national and then the global also serves another important purpose. It helps to reveal that counterinsurgency 'war' is not just a concentration of violent activity that impacts people 'over there' but is operational 'over here' too. Of course, whilst the methods used vary geographically, they are rooted in the same strategic logics. Mapping how local oppressions are connected to global ones can help Muslims and communities of colour not only therefore understand why they are being targeted, controlled, and vilified for their racialised and Muslim identities but also to create a sense of shared identity that could encourage a more passionate campaign of resistance.

One useful way of understanding the connection between local policing and counterterrorism activity on a national scale to the wars being fought on a global scale is through an understanding of counterinsurgency theory, doctrine, and practice. If activists and communities can understand what this form of warfare is, where it comes from, and what it seeks to achieve, they will be in a stronger position to understand that, irrespective of the difference in tactics used to control and influence people on the streets of Bradford, Baghdad, Manchester, and Musa-Qala, the security state's policies in all of these places are driven by the same strategic goals. Furthermore, by documenting how counterinsurgency has historically been a racialised form of warfare used to control, discipline, and pacify colonised peoples, communities will be able to recognise that even though the methods and locations of fighting, influencing, and co-opting may have evolved, the strategic goals of counterinsurgency warfare remain the same as they have done throughout history: to control and regulate the behaviour of Muslims and communities of colour who wish to govern their societies according to their own political desires as opposed to living in the shadow of European and Western empires.

The ideological policing and regulation of Muslims is increasingly being executed through 'Countering Violent Extremism' (CVE) policies, which aim at countering an ideology that is claimed to be at the root of terrorism. The task of implementing these policies is not restricted to the Western powers. CVE has been placed on an international footing through the United

Nations and is an area of policy that all UN member-states must implement in their own countries. The effort to surveil, influence, and regulate political organisation of Muslims and communities of colour who wish to organise the world in a way that does not reinforce Western supremacy or challenge the superiority of the 'nation-state' and its associated capitalist economic system is executed by countries in the Islamic world too. By understanding the history and mechanics of counterinsurgency, counterterrorism, and CVE, and how all three intersect to form a war that all nation-states are involved in to varying degrees, communities will be able to map the connections between domestic policing and the wars taking place overseas, and help build and strengthen networks of solidarity, support, and learning the world over. This includes navigating and managing the harms that have been created by twenty years of the 'war on terror'.

33
Healing Trauma

Documenting and addressing the emotional and psychiatric harm that state violence and surveillance embeds in our minds and bodies should not be underestimated. If we do not centre our lived experiences of mental ill health resulting from security state violence, the effects of counterinsurgency policing will be rendered invisible. There will then be less critique and contestation around what the security state is doing and an impression will be created that the police and security agencies have the consent of communities. We need to systematically document the psychiatric harms that state violence and surveillance create so that this element is not erased from public and policy conversations around policing and counterterrorism. We need to make visible how our mental ill health is not the result of mistakes or errors committed by individual officers but the inevitable consequence of integrating a wartime approach to police, control, and influence the behaviour of Muslims and communities of colour.

Documenting our experiences of state violence risks retraumatising us. This is precisely why it is essential that communities have an infrastructure in place to help us navigate our experiences and find some sense of healing. The creation of some sort of community hub to manage the harms that can be retriggered when people document their experiences is crucial before Muslims and communities of colour are asked to share their experiences of state violence. Initially, when I spoke about my experiences, I did not recognise how triggering this would be and had nobody to draw on for help or support. I just went ahead and spoke and wrote about my experiences without assessing the risk or planning for the harmful consequences.

On that April day in 2013, when I called the assistant chief constable of West Midlands Police in my broken state of mind and told him that the security services were trying to incriminate me for terrorism, I at least had my family, some close friends, and my lawyer. Their intervention saved me from even more trauma that could have resulted from that one phone call. The same applies to my traumatic relapse in 2018 during the writing of this book. If I did not have the support of my family, close friends, and a trained professional who deals with trauma that is triggered by political violence, the outcome of this breakdown could have been far worse than it was.

A community support hub will ensure that those who do not have family and friends can get the support they need if they are going through a crisis or are experiencing a retriggering. It would also create a record of what the effects of state violence and counterterrorism policing are, showing how deep the harms of this area of government policy and practice are. And it will ensure that those drawing on mental health support feel safe and secure rather than suspecting, as I did in 2013 and 2018, that their doctors are surveilling them on behalf of the police and security services. Finally, such an infrastructure could offer a way of healing trauma by documenting and sharing experiences of state violence on our own terms, and in turn, giving us a sense of recognition and validation for our suffering. This, in its own right, can help us heal and feel empowered.

* * *

The community-driven support infrastructure I am proposing needs to be autonomous of the NHS. Mental health provision within the NHS is chronically underfunded. For Muslims and communities of colour, this means that therapy is not only difficult to access but also runs the risk of being framed through whiteness. Irrespective of the good intentions of individual mental health professionals, this leads to the political and racialised drivers of mental ill health being erased.

When I used to meet with my mental health caseworker on a biweekly basis in 2013, I often found myself having to qualify and explain what I was feeling and saying, why I felt like I was under surveillance, why the police would be interested in somebody who was a Muslim person of colour and so on. The case worker, through no fault of her own, had no experience or understanding of what it meant to be a Muslim man of colour living in an age when Muslimness is associated with danger, suspicion, and potentially terrorism. The act of having to explain why I was feeling targeted was not only draining but made me doubt and question my own experiences, feelings, and emotions too. Was I being oversensitive? Was I overthinking things? Am I wrong? These sorts of questions should not be asked by a patient. The therapist should be able to understand them without the patient having to explain or qualify them.

During the two periods when my mental ill health was at its worst, in 2013 and 2018, my experiences of being arrested, detained, stopped, searched, and surveilled were never acknowledged as a possible factor contributing to the way I was feeling, even though the professionals were aware of what had happened to me. Never was the role of systemic or state violence, Islamophobia or racism highlighted or mentioned by any of the NHS professionals I spoke with. Never were the anxiety and uncertainty I was feeling connected to the surveillance I had experienced. The only time PTSD or 'trauma' came up was when I raised the subject. With the political context of my mental ill health side-lined and ignored, anti-psychotic medication seemed to become the only possible solution.

By 2020, my mental health had stabilised and, encouraged by my trauma-trained friend, I asked my doctor to refer me to the NHS's mental health service. I met with a psychologist and psychiatrist. Their conclusion was that the 2013 assessment that I was suffering from an 'acute psychotic episode' was too broad and unfocused. It was so generic a diagnosis that it did not offer any insight into what I was going through or why I was experiencing it. In this meeting, I asked the doctors whether my mental ill health could be based on having experienced security state violence and surveillance. Both of them accepted that there was certainly something central to be said about the impact of my experiences but could not provide me with much more detail at that time. They told me that they would make a referral to the Complex Trauma Team for further assessments. More than one year later I am still waiting to hear back from the NHS for an appointment.

A community support hub that works to centre the role of racial, religious, and political factors with careful consideration and empathy is therefore critical in dealing with the way we manage the effects and outcomes of state violence, policing, and counterterrorism. At the same time, such a support hub could be important in helping us understand and navigate our mental ill health and trauma, enabling our healing through the sharing of stories and experiences on our own terms. The support hub I am proposing could also serve as a blueprint for what a future, better-funded NHS might itself provide: therapy and treatments that are conscious and aware of the political and structural factors as well as state violence and surveillance that often create trauma and mental ill health amongst Muslims and communities of colour. The traumatising experience of state violence is, after all, a factor in the mental ill health not only of those targeted through counterterrorism measures but also communities affected by other categories of racist state violence: migrant communities subjected to detention, deportation, and surveillance under immigration laws; black communities stopped, searched, surveilled, or worse, as a result of racist 'gang databases' and so on; in general, the racially oppressed communities who bear the brunt of criminalisation and incarceration. I am *not* suggesting that this support hub be funded by communities themselves. There should be a central government commitment to dealing with the mental health epidemic broadly, and the trauma and harm that emerges as a result of specific government policies and state violence more specifically.

What also makes a community-driven support hub essential is the fact that the NHS has been coerced into conducting counterterrorism surveillance as a result of the duty under the Counter-Terrorism and Security Act 2015 to participate in Prevent counter-radicalisation policy. This 'duty' legally compels public sector workers, including health workers and educators, to refer people to the authorities who are suspected of being vulnerable to being 'radicalised' and becoming future terrorists. Needless to say, this duty undermines doctor–patient confidentiality and contributes to eroding the trust and confidence that patients should have when they speak with their doctor, especially when it comes to mental ill health which, amongst Muslims and communities of colour, can often be triggered by political and structural forms of discrimination such as racist policing, surveillance, and violence. In this situation, a patient should be able to express what they are experiencing, thinking, and feeling in a space that does not trigger them any more than they already are.

By piercing the entire public sector, including the NHS, the Prevent policy has removed safe spaces where the harms and traumas of state violence can be expressed. During my 2018 mental health crisis, I was reluctant to draw on the support of the mental health crisis team because, initially, I felt I could 'manage' what I was going through. When I realised I could not and my mental health began to worsen, I was still unable and unwilling to speak to my doctor or ask her for a referral to the crisis team. I only asked for an absence note on medical grounds that I could supply to my employer. I wanted to use the time away from work to figure out how I could heal and recover from the breakdown, with the support of my trauma-trained friend. I refused to go into detail with my doctor because, at that particular moment, I felt extremely afraid that my life and liberty were at risk. I could not trust medical professionals. My fear was that the doctor could interpret my state of mind, my criticisms of the government, the police, and the security state, and my Muslim and racially marked identity, as being suggestive of potential terrorism, leading to a report being made under Prevent that I was perhaps 'vulnerable to radicalisation'.

In 2013, I had felt suspicious of the doctors and mental health professionals I met. By 2018, with the Prevent duty placed into law by the Counter-Terrorism and Security Act 2015, there was no more hiding or second-guessing *if* I could be referred to the authorities. The doctor was now under a legal duty to refer people to the authorities if they were deemed a risk to themselves or society on the grounds of terrorism or future terrorism. No matter how small or unlikely this potential outcome feels at the time of writing, where I am in a stable state of mind, in that moment in 2018 this thought overpowered and terrified my mind to such an extent that I was unwilling and unable to share what I was feeling with doctors and mental health professionals. I felt an indescribable anxiety and fear that saying anything could be twisted and used against me. In that moment of complete powerlessness and vulnerability, I was unable to ask the doctor for the one thing I really needed: help.

A support hub that exists outside of the prying eyes of the sur-veillance state is not only critical in ensuring that psychiatric disorders and mental ill health triggered by racism, Islamopho-bia, and state violence can be understood and safely addressed but is also vital in resisting the damage that is being done to ordinary Muslims and communities of colour by the securitising of the public sector.

In this support hub, we can help empower one another to centre our experiences and stories and make visible how policing and counterterrorism work. We can show how they have an ability to dominate our minds and induce and embed trauma and suffering that too often goes unnoticed and unacknowledged. The state is powerful but it is not akin to God. By working together, Muslims and communities of colour can contest, disrupt, and resist power. Yes, the police and security state may have an unrivalled capacity for violence. But they cannot control and influence our minds all of the time. We have the power to push back and limit the security state's power so long as we learn, educate, and empower each other by standing united and in solidarity.

Afterword

Aamer Anwar

What I find overwhelming in the preceding pages written by Rizwaan Sabir is how similar his experiences are to that of so many Muslims who have ever had contact with our policing and state security agencies.

Sabir's story and insights show that it does not matter how educated or integrated we are into British society. It hardly matters how much social capital we have or which powerful people we have on speed-dial. When a police officer or agent of the state wants to racially profile and investigate you in the post-9/11 world, they can act with almost total impunity.

What Sabir has therefore done in his writing is validate what many Muslims have sensed, felt, and experienced for over two-decades. What is sometimes called 'paranoia' or 'oversensitivity' by some is shown to be fundamentally rooted in the state's use of exceptional violence that is embedded in law.

Sabir shows how the presumption of innocence – a bedrock of a civilised justice system and fundamental cornerstone of the rule of law – has been sidelined. Legitimate Muslim behaviour and activity has become suspicious and criminalised. So, for example, it does not matter if you have a genuine reason for possessing a document that is viewed by the state to be 'useful to terrorists'. It does not matter if you are a lawyer or an academic who has such as document for professional purposes or whether you are simply a curious person. The burden of proof is shifted to you because, as a Muslim, you are presumed guilty until proven innocent.

In the post-9/11 era, a law-abiding Muslim community, once lauded for being hard-working and respectful of the law, has been transformed into a community of potential terrorists in need of constant policing, surveillance, rendering, indefinite-detention, torture, and bombing.

For many years, I have had first-hand experience of politicians, chief constables and counter-terrorism agents trying to convince me that their officers are acting on 'intelligence'. The reality, as Sabir shows, is that the intelligence they refer to is fundamentally and intricately connected to the use of racial and religious profiling to determine guilt.

And this is not where it ends. The intelligence and profiling data that is gathered is put on computer systems and shared across the state security apparatus so that each road, airport, train station or border becomes a site of questioning and humiliation. This constant profiling, and the misery it creates, does very little to combat terrorism and seems more geared towards conducting mass-surveillance of the Muslim community. This targeting of almost every aspect of Muslim life, combined with counterterrorism laws, has created a two-tier system of justice.

The resistance to these actions has been lukewarm with some of our so-called 'moderate' community leaders, desperate to disassociate themselves from acts of terrorism for fear of being called 'terrorist-sympathisers' or 'extremists' themselves, have lined up to support and rubber-stamp policies such as 'Prevent'.

The irony of Prevent and the law and regulation that has since followed is that these moderate community leaders are now themselves being tagged as extremists since the term has come to include opposition to same-sex marriage, British foreign policy, support for Palestine, and even condemnation of the Saudi regime.

These views are held and expressed by millions of people including countless non-Muslims but the term 'extremist' and policies such as Prevent as well as counterterrorism laws seem largely reserved for Muslims.

In the years since Rizwaan Sabir was first arrested, the debate on terrorism and political violence has shifted with each attack, anti-terror arrest or case involving a so-called 'Jihadi Bride' has led to more divisive and Islamophobic rhetoric becoming normalised. In the wake of the *Charlie Hebdo* attack in France in 2015, for example, you were either with free speech or you were against it; either '*je suis Charlie*' or a freedom-hating fanatic.

What terrorist attacks have succeeded in achieving is exactly what the perpetrators wanted, creating an 'us and them' scenario that the state has been quick to use to introduce more draconian and exceptional counterterrorism laws and practices. In such a polarised society, any questioning of British power and its foreign policies leads to suspicion, surveillance, and scorn.

In the so called 'war on terror', the state has maintained that it wants to stop terrorism and challenge 'extremism' yet in recent years, by suspecting and surveilling the Muslim community en masse, it has erased trust and ignored the questions that young Muslims are quite rightly asking.

Our mosques are ill-equipped and too afraid to engage in politics in case they draw the attention of the police and security services. Our educated class are reluctant to question or critique the state in case they have their cards marked too. We, as a Muslim community, live in a climate of fear and censorship, which is increasing mistrust, exclusion, and muzzling speech.

In 2006, I represented a young Muslim man – Mohammed Atif Siddique – from a Scottish town called Alva, who was claimed to be a member of Al-Qaeda. Atif was travelling to Pakistan in April 2006 and was stopped on his departure at Glasgow Airport. The police seized his laptop computer and the next day arrested him on suspicion of terrorism.

For me, Atif was always guilty of being a foolish young man looking for answers to address his curiosity as a young politicised Muslim. In my professional view, he made a very unlikely terrorist. But the police were convinced otherwise. Over the course of the seven days I sat with him in a police interview room, I listened to some of the most profoundly stupid and insulting questions that I have ever heard in my 21 years of practicing law.

He was charged and remanded in custody until his trial started just after the Glasgow Airport attack in 2007 and concluded just after the sixth anniversary of 9/11. My client believed this was hardly the most favourable time to for a terrorism trial to take place.

As part of his case, I conducted investigations around the materials Atif possessed and a website he was thought to have launched. It quickly emerged that the website did not work. There was also no evidence or suggestion that Atif actually possessed or tried to obtain any weapons or bomb-making equipment to orchestrate an attack. The material that Atif had downloaded was also freely available on a website that belonged to an American terrorism expert, who the Crown Prosecution Service were relying upon to give expert testimony at the trial. Atif was found guilty of possessing videos and the circulation of materials that were claimed to be useful to somebody preparing an act of terrorism and was handed an eight-year prison sentence by the judge.

Many well-wishers told me not to 'rock the boat' by speaking out on behalf of my client against the draconian and unfair nature of Britain's counterterrorism laws that had allowed Atif to be convicted. But, my promise to my client and his family that I would follow his instructions and advocate on his behalf had to take precedence. I went out onto the steps of the High Court after Atif's trial concluded and read a statement on his behalf to the media which said that the trial was a tragedy for justice and free speech and that it was conducted in an atmosphere of hostility against Muslims. It was, to put it simply, a miscarriage of justice. As a result of reading this statement, the trial judge brought charges of contempt of court against me and I would eventually have to stand trial before three of Scotland's most senior judges who would determine my fate.

Apart from Claire Mitchell QC and the late Paul McBride QC, there were very few lawyers in Scotland who came out in my support. Most lawyers adopted a vow of silence for the way I had been treated. The wilderness of Scottish legal support pushed me in the direction of England where I received overwhelming support from the likes of Imran Khan QC, Gareth Pierce, Helena Kennedy QC, Michael Mansfield QC and, of course, Sabir's lawyer, Tayab Ali. They helped me prepare my defence and gave me the tools and support I needed to help bring Atif's case to the Court of Appeal.

Other lawyers and media commentators, meanwhile, attacked me; implying in no uncertain terms that my legal advocacy for Atif was based on some imagined sympathy I had with Al-Qaeda. I was suddenly transformed from a lawyer into a suspect. Some lectured me on how my statement and advocacy was not befitting of a lawyer; failing to see the irony in *not* defending a colleague who was acting on behalf of a client and challenging laws that brought the concept of the 'rule of law' itself into disrepute. Those in the Muslim community offered up prayers but did not want to be openly showing support and solidarity with neither me nor Atif for fear of being branded as terror-sympathisers too.

Eventually, I stood trial for contempt of court at Edinburgh High Court and was found not guilty. I was quietly told by my legal representatives that I should never make a statement on the steps of the High Court again. But, empowered by the victory, I did exactly the opposite. I walked outside the court and told the gathered journalists that my fight to free Atif would continue and quoted the American-Jewish legal historian Melvin Urofsky:

> If there is one right prized above all others in a democracy, it is freedom of speech. The ability to speak one's mind, to challenge the political orthodoxies of the times, to criticize the policies of the government without fear of recrimination is the essential distinction between life in a free country and in a dictatorship.

Despite having done nothing unlawful, the media were not dissuaded from attacking me or making me feel that my career and liberty were in jeopardy. The questions around my motives for defending Atif turned my family's life and my own into a living nightmare. When Sabir doubted his own sanity and felt as if he were being gaslighted, surveilled, and coerced, I recognised what he was describing only too well. I remember spending considerable time questioning what was taking place and pondering over the British legal system's seeming inability to accept that a Muslim lawyer could represent a man accused of terrorism and *not* be a terrorist-sympathiser himself.

Every Muslim lawyer who supported me during this difficult period told me that, based on their own experiences, I would spend the rest of my life looking over my shoulder. I would be a 'suspect'. It was a sad, lonely, and terrifying place to occupy.

My family, friends, and loved ones argued that I should just walk away. They demanded that I apologise for giving the statement outside of the High Court, and give up on Atif for fear of losing my career or even worse being imprisoned. I told them that I would rather go to jail than give up on Atif or refuse to speak the truth. This commitment to justice, accountability, and truth at times feels incredibly selfish and self-destructive but flows, I believe, from my own experience of racism and state violence.

In 1986, I arrived at the University of Glasgow to start a degree in engineering with the intention of joining the Royal Air Force.

Whilst at university, however, I began to witness racism being directed at fellow students of colour and became involved in anti-racism politics and organisation and so several years later began to study Social Sciences no longer wishing to 'fight for Queen and Country'. But on 6 November 1991, I was flyposting for a NUS demonstration and found myself brutally beaten-up in a racist attack by a police officer. The officer smashed out my front teeth by connecting my face with the ground, repeatedly. When I recovered consciousness at the scene, I looked up terrified to ask the officer 'why' he had done this to me. 'This is what happens to black boys with big mouths', he said, before kicking me in the stomach.

I decided to take the police to task for the brutal violence they directed at me through the courts. I was told by my lawyers that nobody had ever won a civil action against the police in Scotland; implying that I was fighting a losing battle and that I should give up.

In the four years that subsequently followed, I became even more politically active as a left-wing campaigner and was harassed with attempted arrest some 20 times, and five successful arrests. I faced court on several occasions. Sabir's writing reminds me of what it means to be at the mercy of an institutionally racist criminal justice system which doubts your innocence and questions your motives *because* of your racialised identity.

In 1995, I won my case and made legal history as the first person of colour in Scotland to win a civil action against the police for an unprovoked racist attack. The facial injuries I sustained healed with time but the trauma and PTSD are things I have had to manage and live with ever since. The violence I was subjected to then prompted me to direct all my energy and effort to change my career and return to university to study law. I knew by this stage that justice and rights were never just handed to you. You had to fight for them.

I was reminded of this idea in Atif's case in 2010, when after years of tiring legal work as he sat in prison, his case finally made it to the Court of Appeal. The three senior judges found that Atif's conviction for violating Section 57 of the Terrorism Act 2000 amounted to a miscarriage of justice and quashed his conviction.

My legal work and advocacy in defence of the powerless has earned me legal awards and accolades over the years, and I am often described as one of Scotland's leading human rights lawyers.

Yet, whilst such titles make my parents proud of my achievements, my experiences and work in the legal system and the words of survivors such as Sabir tell another, a more harrowing, story; one dominated by powerful processes, laws, and practices that ridicule, humiliate, and criminalise people based on their skin colour and religious identity, and sometimes both.

What happened to Sabir and so many others like him does not reflect the notions of freedom and liberty that countries such as Britain pride themselves on. And the history of this country shows that the violation of such principles is historically rooted, when, for example, innocent Irish men and women were interned and treated as suspects and 'terrorists'.

The lack of protest in the 1970s over the false imprisonment of innocent people such as the Birmingham Six and the Guilford Four remains a badge of shame for this country. Since 9/11, such experiences have been replicated and re-directed at a new persecuted community: the Muslims.

For all the talk of justice and liberty, the government have successively criminalised communities and created laws that outlaw the thoughts and ideas belonging to the powerless. Any civilised democracy should be judged by the manner in which its justice system treats the vulnerable, weak, and even those who are despised in society.

If Sabir's words tell us anything, it is that we are not alone in feeling the fear, emotion, anxiety, and trauma caused by the security state, its agents, policies, laws, and institutions. By raising his voice and vocalising what many of us have known to be true for far too long, his words should inspire and empower us to speak out in support of powerless and oppressed communities around the globe.

Aamer Anwar
Glasgow
November 2021

Notes

Chapter 4

1. West Midlands Counter-Terrorism Unit (2008a) Operation Minerva Forensic Arrest/Search Strategy, Restricted, 13 May, pp. 5–6. According to the following police document, the focus of the search was to look for 'terrorism related material – including items purporting to be from terrorist organisations or in support of terrorist organisations, in particular, items relating to terrorism propaganda'. In addition to this, the police were also searching for 'any material or documentation relating to the manufacture of explosive/noxious substances, improvised explosive devices or other weaponry of use to a terrorist organisation'.

2. The arrests were undertaken between 11 September 2001 until March 2021, and the breakdown of numbers is as follows: in total, 4,907 people were arrested for suspected terrorism and 2,418 of them were released without charge. See Table A-A.03 in Home Office (2021) 'Statistics on the Operation of Police Powers Under the Terrorism Act 2000 and Subsequent Legislation', year to March 2021, https://assets.publishing.service.gov.uk/government/uploads/system/uploads/attachment_data/file/991988/operation-police-powers-terrorism-mar2021-annual-tables.xlsx (accessed 26.10.21).

Chapter 5

1. Gordon, H. Phillip (2006) 'The End of Bush's Revolution', *Foreign Affairs*, Vol. 85, No. 4, pp. 75–86.

2. Witorowicz, Quentin and Katner, John (2003) 'Killing in the Name of Islam: Al Qaeda's Justification for September 11', *Middle East Policy Council Journal*, Vol. 10, No. 2, pp. 76–92.

3. Amir, Geffrey and Smith, Sara (2014) 'GMP Investigation Report: Operation Carpatus', Greater Manchester Police (GMP) and The Independent Police Complaints Commission (IPCC), 1 May 2014, IPCC Reference No: 2012-12475, Marked as 'Restricted', pp. 37–38.

4. Thornton, Rod (2011) 'Counterterrorism and the Neo-Liberal University: Providing a Check and Balance?', *Critical Studies on Terrorism*, Vol. 4, No. 3, pp. 421–429; Thornton, Rod (2009) 'The "Al-Qaeda Training Manual" (Not)', *Teaching Terrorism*, 11 July, https://nottinghamwhistleblower.files.wordpress.com/2011/06/footnote-37.pdf (accessed 26.08.21).

5. Ibid.
6. *Cryptome* (2006) 'Cryptome Introduction to the Al-Qaeda Training Manual', https://cryptome.org/alq-terr-man.htm (accessed 26.08.21).
7. Blackwells (2021) 'Military Studies in the Jihad Against the Tyrants: The Al-Qaeda Training Manual', Blackwells Book Shop, https://blackwells.co.uk/bookshop/product/9781907521249 (accessed 21.01.21).
8. Post, M. Jerrold (2004) 'Military Studies in the Jihad Against the Tyrants: The Al-Qaeda Training Manual', US Airforce Counterproliferation Center, Alabama, August, www.airuniversity.af.edu/Portals/10/CSDS/Books/alqaedatrainingmanual2.pdf (accessed 12.01.21).
9. Gus, Martin (2020) *Understanding Terrorism: Challenges, Perspectives, and Issues*, 7th edition. London: Sage Publishing, pp. 368–369; Laqueur, Walter (2004) *Voices of Terror: Manifestos, Writings, and Manuals of Al-Qaeda, Hamas, and Other Terrorists from Around the World and Throughout the Ages*. New York: Reed Press, pp. 402–409; Gunaratna, Rohan (2002) *Inside Al-Qaeda: Global Network of Terror*. New York: Colombia University Press.
10. Academic Services Division (2010) Hand delivered letter to Rizwaan Sabir by Hannah Robinson, University of Nottingham, 5 January 2010. I repeatedly asked the University of Nottingham, including via my MP Vernon Coaker, to disclose any documents they held which could support their claims that a 'risk-assessment' had been conducted prior to the police being called. I was told in a hand-delivered written letter that 'no such documents' exist.

Chapter 6

1. Hamilton, Fiona (2007) 'Man Charged Over Terrorist Training Book', *The Times*, 21 May, www.thetimes.co.uk/article/man-charged-over-terrorist-training-book-p7h2jxd25c0. (accessed 13.01.21).
2. The two additional publications in Khaled Khaliq's possession were 'Zaad-e-Mujahid' and 'The Absent Obligation'.

Chapter 7

1. At the time of the Magistrate's Court hearing, the police were legally authorised to detain us in pre-charge detention, if they could make a case and the courts supported it, for a total of twenty-eight days. The Labour government under Tony Blair wanted to increase this pre-charge detention period from twenty-eight days to three months

but failed to secure a majority in Parliament. When Tony Blair was later replaced by Gordon Brown as PM, the Labour government again asked for the pre-charge detention period to be increased to forty-two days. That attempt also failed. It was under the Conservative–Liberal Democrat coalition government that the pre-charge detention period was reduced to fourteen days, where it remains at time of writing. Fourteen days sounds like an improvement but even this time period is quite exceptional given that suspects in non-terrorism cases can only be held for a maximum of three days in pre-charge custody. Even during the height of the UK war in the North of Ireland, suspects could only be detained for a maximum period of seven days in pre-charge custody. The fourteen-day period thus signals quite an aggressive shift in the policing of armed Muslim groups and terrorism in the post-9/11 age.

2. Amir and Smith (2014), p. 82.

3. The 'Mosaic' variety of intelligence is random and disparate pieces of information on subjects and issues that are relatively meaningless in isolation, but when merged with other pieces of information, can become helpful in generating a broad-based socio-political picture of a detainee. For more on this, see Laleh Khalili (2013) *Time in the Shadows: Confinement in Counterinsurgencies*. Stanford, CA: Stanford University Press, p. 74 and pp. 128–129.

4. Police Interview 3 (2008) Police Interview Transcript 3 of 8 with Rizwaan Sabir, Bridewell Police Station, Nottingham, West Midlands Counter-Terrorism Unit, Tape Reference No. RW/5, Restricted, 12:57-13:29 (32 minutes), 16 May.

5. Ibid.

6. Ibid.

7. Ibid.

8. Police Interview 5 (2008) Police Interview Transcript 5 of 8 with Rizwaan Sabir, Bridewell Police Station, Nottingham, West Midlands Counter-Terrorism Unit, Tape Reference No. RW/9, Restricted, 11:46-12:15 (29 minutes), 18 May.

9. Police Interview 7 (2008) Police Interview Transcript 7 of 8 with Rizwaan Sabir, Bridewell Police Station, Nottingham, West Midlands Counter-Terrorism Unit, Tape Reference No. RW/13, Restricted, 12:34-13:19 (46 minutes), 19 May.

10. Police Interview 2 (2008) Police Interview Transcript 2 of 8 with Rizwaan Sabir, Bridewell Police Station, Nottingham, West Midlands Counter-Terrorism Unit, Tape Reference No. RW/03, Restricted, 19:26-19:49 (23 minutes), 15 May.

11. Police Interview 7 (2008).

12. Police Interview 2 (2008).
13. Ibid.
14. Police Interview 4 (2008) Police Interview Transcript 4 of 8 with Rizwaan Sabir, Bridewell Police Station, Nottingham, West Midlands Counter-Terrorism Unit, Tape Reference No. RW/7, Restricted, 12:51-13:37 (46 minutes), 17 May, p. 7.
15. Ibid., p. 7.
16. Ibid., p. 7.
17. Police Interview 4 (2008), pp. 15–16.
18. Police Interview 7 (2008), p. 11.
19. Ibid., p. 11.

Chapter 8

1. Ryan, Maria (2010) Statement of Dr Maria Ryan, in the Central London Country Court Between Rizwaan Sabir (Claimant) and The Chief Constable of Nottinghamshire Police (Defendant), Statement No. 1, Case No: 9CL03969, Bhatt Murphy Solicitors, 15 July, Para 13.
2. Ibid., Para 13.
3. Ibid., Para 21.
4. Ibid., Para. 11.
5. Ibid., Para. 18.
6. Ibid., Para 18.
7. Ibid., Para. 19.
8. West Midlands Police (2008) Bettina Renz Witness Statement to West Midlands Police, 17 May, p. 6.
9. Renz, Bettina (2010) Statement of Dr Bettina Renz, in the Central London Country Court Between Rizwaan Sabir (Claimant) and The Chief Constable of Nottinghamshire Police (Defendant), Statement No. 1, Case No: 9CL03969, Bhatt Murphy Solicitors, 15 July, Para. 14(f).
10. Renz (2008), p. 4.
11. Ibid., p. 6.
12. Amir and Smith (2014), p. 121.
13. Eskridge, Chris (2021) 'Encyclopedia of Afghan Jihad', University of Nebraska, www.unl.edu/eskridge/encyclopedia.html (accessed 26.08.21).
14. Thornton, Rod (2010) Statement of Dr Ian Roderick Thornton, in the Central London Country Court Between Rizwaan Sabir (Claimant) and The Chief Constable of Nottinghamshire Police (Defendant), Statement No. 1, Case No: 9CL03969, Bhatt Murphy Solicitors, 15 July, Para 23 and Para 24.

15. West Midlands Counter-Terrorism Unit (2008b) Notes of Gold Group: Operation Minerva, 17 May.
16. Thornton, Rod (2008) 'Rod Thornton Witness Statement to West Midlands Police', West Midlands Police, 16 May, p. 5.
17. Ibid., p. 4.
18. The exact words I used were: 'This document is brilliant for my research. If I can reference it for my dissertation, then it's going to get me some really good marks because it's a primary document that I thought wasn't even available.' Police Interview 1 (2008) Police Interview Transcript 1 of 8 with Rizwaan Sabir, Bridewell Police Station, Nottingham, West Midlands Counter-Terrorism Unit, Tape Reference No. RW/01, Restricted, 20:52–21:35 (43 minutes), 14 May, p. 5.
19. Ryan (2010), Para. 16.
20. Thornton (2008), p. 5.
21. Ibid., p. 5.
22. Thornton (2010), Para. 28.
23. Ibid., Para. 27.
24. McGuirk, Bernard (2008) Witness Statement of Bernard Joseph McGuirk, West Midlands Police, 18 May, p. 3.
25. Police Interview 6 (2008) Police Interview Transcript 6 of 8 with Rizwaan Sabir, Bridewell Police Station, Nottingham, West Midlands Counter-Terrorism Unit, Tape Reference No. RW/11, Restricted, 18:13–18:59 (46 minutes), 18 May, p. 19.
26. Ibid., p. 20.
27. Ibid., pp. 20–21.
28. Amir and Smith (2014), p. 60.
29. Ibid., p. 123.

Chapter 9

1. Charges for offences that violate Section 58 total to 129 from 2002 until 2019 (See table A.05a). Convictions for violating Section 58 for the same time-period total to 92 (see Table A – A.08a at the following source: Home Office (2020) Operation of Police Powers under the Terrorism Act 2000 and subsequent legislation: Arrests, outcomes and stops and searches, Great Britain, year ending December 2019, Bulletin Number 07/20 https://assets.publishing. service.gov.uk/government/uploads/system/uploads/attachment_ data/file/869780/police-powers-terrorism-dec2019-hosb0720.pdf (accessed 26.08.21).
2. Walker, Clive (2009) Blackstone's Guide to the Anti-Terrorism Legislation, 2nd edition. Oxford: Oxford University Press, p. 191.
3. Ibid., p. 191.

4. Amir and Smith (2014), p. 24.
5. Ibid., p. 94.
6. Ibid., pp. 94–95.
7. In total, 1,939 Asians were arrested for terrorism (40%) and 591 black people were arrested for terrorism (12%) out of a total of 4,907 people from 9/11 until March 2021. See Table A.11 in Home Office (2021).

Chapter 10

1. Police Interview 7 (2008), p. 10.

Chapter 11

1. My records indicate that across a twenty-six-month period (March 2009 to May 2011), I was stopped, searched, and/or detained for questioning either at the roadside or at ports for a total of fourteen times. The reasons were always varied: from 'matching the description of somebody who is wanted', to speeding, to my car being 'similar to another car involved in an incident', to suspected involvement in terrorism, to search for 'prohibited articles' such as firearms and bladed weapons, to being given no reason at all for a stop. Whatever the initial reason, matters almost always ended up – on more than a few occasions – back to my arrest for suspected terrorism and my political views either at the roadside or on the intelligence entries written by officers after the stop had concluded. This was perhaps unsurprising considering I was always open, when asked, how and why I was 'known to the police'. Any cursory search of my name on the Police National Computer (PNC) lists me for ninety-nine years as having been involved in 'offences against the state'. There was therefore little point in staying silent in this regard. Of course, whilst I had the right to *not* explain why I was known to police on grounds of privacy, exercising this right led to more questions and curiosity by the police, and a larger intelligence file that was being maintained on me. Being stopped, searched, and detained at the roadside and at ports had therefore become one of the main avenues through which I was being surveilled and monitored by the police.

Chapter 14

1. Home Affairs Committee (2013) Written Evidence submitted by the Home Office, Letter from James Brokenshire MP, Security Minister, to the Chair of the Committee, CT 04B, 3 October, pp. 20–21, www.parliament.uk/documents/commons-committees/homeaffairs/ (accessed 27.08.21).

Chapter 15

1. Nottinghamshire Police (2010) Unlinked Intelligence 20/05/08 – 10/08/2011, CIRR01170750, Grading E41, 22 February.
2. Intelligence is graded by five letters (A to E). It is evaluated with a score of 1 to 5. And it is given a handling code from 1 to 5 (5x5x5) The intelligence entry I have just cited is graded as 'E41'. According to the National Intelligence Model grading system, 'E' means 'Untested source', '4' means the content 'Cannot be Judged' and 1 means that the intelligence 'may be disseminated to other law enforcement and prosecuting agencies, including law enforcement agencies within the EEA, and EU compatible [countries]'. See HM Revenue & Customs (2014) 'MLR3C - Money Laundering Regulation: Compliance Manual, Appendix 3: The National Intelligence Model (5x5x5)', Ref: MLR3C14000, www.hmrc.gov.uk/manuals/mlr3cmanual/MLR3C14000.htm (accessed 27.08.21).
3. Since I am more interested in the processes and context of intelligence collection, and how the details of the source demonstrate how surveillance is undertaken through the Prevent policy, I have decided *not* to disclose the names of the two informants I strongly suspect of supplying the intelligence to the police which forms the content of this one intelligence entry. For convenience and clarity, however, I shall refer to them using the aliases of Adam and Mr Khan only.
4. Goodfellow, Andrew (2011) Re: Your request for information, FOI Reference IGO–92, Letter to Rizwaan Sabir from Nottingham City Council, Nottingham City Council, 19 October.
5. In order to refresh my memory ahead of writing this book, I tried to retrieve the MSN log of our conversation but was unable to find it. Regrettably, I had, in early 2009, disabled the option of keeping a record of my chat-logs in the interest of my privacy.
6. Kundnani, Arun (2009) 'Spooked: How Not to Prevent Violent Extremism', Institute of Race Relations, www.irr.org.uk/pdf2/spooked.pdf (accessed 13.10.10).
7. Hitch, Gillian (2011) Request under the Freedom of Information Act 2000 (FOIA), Ref: 002401/11, Letter to Rizwaan Sabir from Nottinghamshire Police, Nottinghamshire Police, 18 October.
8. Ibid.
9. See section 'Backdoor Surveillance' (pp. 8–12) in Sabir, Rizwaan (2017a) 'Blurred Lines and False Dichotomies: Integrating Counterinsurgency into the UK's Domestic "War on Terror"', *Critical Social Policy*, Vol. 37, No. 2, pp. 1–23.

10. Qurashi, Fahid (2018) 'The Prevent Strategy and the UK "War on Terror": Embedding Infrastructures of Surveillance in Muslim Communities', *Palgrave Communications*, Vol. 4, No. 1, www.nature.com/articles/s41599-017-0061-9 (accessed 28.08.21); see also Sabir (2017a).

Chapter 16

1. MacLean, K. (2012) File Note re: [redacted] and RIZWAN SABIR (Operation Minerva), Data Protection Act 1998 – Subject Access Request, Ref: 02/12/DPA, Crown Prosecution Service (CPS), 14 February.
2. Hemming, Susan (2012) Letter to Rizwaan Sabir, Information held by the Crown Prosecution Service, Crown Prosecution Service (CPS), 28 May.
3. Nottinghamshire Police (2007) Nottinghamshire Police Intelligence Report, CIRR00970346, Grading B11, 30 November.
4. Nottinghamshire Police (2008a) Nottinghamshire Police Intelligence Report, CIRR00984999, Grading E41, 30 January.
5. It is worth pointing out that this police intelligence report mentions an intelligence report by the reference of CIRR00972009. Neither my lawyers nor I were given a copy of this intelligence report during the course of the legal case. Since the second intelligence entry was produced on 30 January 2008, this means a total of four intelligence entries were created on the Nottingham University Palestinian Society before Operation Minerva was launched, of which I received access to only three. The police surveillance of the student Palestinian Society, in other words, is even more extensive than what is indicated by the records I have access to.
6. Nottinghamshire Police (2008b) Nottinghamshire Police Intelligence Report, CIRR01008654, Grading B11, 24 April.
7. Nottinghamshire Police (2008c) Nottingham University Palestinian Society, Report Unique Reference Number 13-2008-05-17-A-133, Grading B21, 13:58, 17 May.
8. Ibid.
9. Ibid.
10. Ibid.
11. Ibid.
12. Hemming (2012).

Chapter 17

1. Beresford, Shaun (2012a) Email of 10 September 2010 at 14:43 between [redacted] and [redacted], released under Subject Access

Request ACRO/SAR/002 to Rizwaan Sabir, Association of Chief Police Officers (ACPO), 5 April.

2. Pottinger, Diana (2012a) Email of 25 August 2011 between officials, released under Subject Access Request, Ref: SA11935 to Rizwaan Sabir, Home Office, 26 April.

3. Pottinger, Diana (2012b) Email of 24 August 2011 between officials, released under Subject Access Request, Ref: SA11935 to Rizwaan Sabir, Home Office, 26 April.

4. Ibid.

5. Beresford, Shaun (2012b) ACPO Freedom of Information Referral Template V2 – Initial Submission by force 003009/11, 31 October 2011 at 10:49, released under Subject Access Request ACRO/SAR/002 to Rizwaan Sabir by Association of Chief Police Officers (ACPO), 5 April.

6. The agencies my FOI requests were sent to and were subsequently logged were as follows: the Home Office, the Cabinet Office, the Department for Business, Innovation and Skills (BIS) and the National Policing Improvement Agency (NPIA). See Beresford, Shaun (2012c) Annex A – Requests for Information submitted to forces by Mr Rizwaan Sabir, released under Subject Access Request ACRO/SAR/002 to Rizwaan Sabir by Association of Chief Police Officers (ACPO), 5 April.

Chapter 18

1. Rawlinson, Kevin (2012) 'Police Face New Questions Over Approach to Protest Groups', *The Independent*, 6 January, www.independent. co.uk/news/uk/home-news/police-face-new-questions-over-approach-to-protest-groups-6285707.html (accessed 27.08.21); Sabir, Rizwaan (2012) 'How Police Branded OccupyLSX and UKUNCUT as "Terrorists"', *Ceasefire Magazine*, 7 January, https:// ceasefiremagazine.co.uk/police-branded-occupylsx-ukuncut-terrorists/ (accessed 12.01.21).

Chapter 22

1. Khalili (2013), p. 31; Miller, Carl (2018) 'Inside the British Army's Secret Warfare Machine', *Wired*, 14 November, www.wired.co.uk/article/inside-the-77th-brigade-britains-information-warfare-military (accessed 27.08.21).

Chapter 23

1. Hocking, Jenny (1988) 'Counterterrorism as Counterinsurgency: The British Experience', *Social Justice*, Vol. 15, No. 1, pp. 83–97.

2. Khalili (2013).
3. McCulloch, Jude and Pickering, Sharon (2009) 'Pre-Crime and Counterterrorism: Imagining Future Crime in the "War on Terror"', *British Journal of Criminology*, Vol. 49, p. 634.
4. Gwynn, Charles (1934) *Imperial Policing*. London: Macmillan and Co. For an analysis of Gwynn's ideas around the military's role in policing, see chapter 1 in Khalili (2013).
5. McCulloch, Jude (2004) 'Blue Armies, Khaki Police, and the Cavalry: On the New American Frontier: Critical Criminology for the 21st Century', *Critical Criminology*, Vol. 12, pp. 310–312.
6. Trafford, James (2020) *The Empire at Home: Internal Colonies and the End of Britain*. London: Pluto; Turner, Joe (2017) 'Internal Colonisation: The Intimate Circulations of Empire, Race and Liberal Government', *European Journal of International Relations*, Vol. 24. No. 4, pp. 765–790; Hocking (1988).
7. Churchill, Ward and Wall, Jim (2012) *Agents of Repression: The FBI's Secret Wars Against the Black Panther Party and the American Indian Movement*. Boston, MA: South End Press.
8. Balko, Radley (2014) *Rise of the Warrior Cop: The Militarisation of America's Police Forces*. New York: Public Affairs; Harcourt, Bernard (2018) *The Counterrevolution: How our Government Went to War Against its Own Citizens*. New York: Basic Books.
9. Bazian, Hatem (2012) 'Muslims – Enemies of the State: The New Counterintelligence Program (COINTELPRO)', *Islamophobia Studies Journal*, Vol. 1, No. 1, pp. 163–206; Kundnani, Arun (2014) *The Muslims are Coming: Islamophobia, Extremism, and the Domestic War on Terror*. London: Verso Books.
10. Hocking (1988).
11. Whyte, David (2015) 'Policing for Whom?', *The Howard Journal of Crime and Justice*, Vol. 54, No. 1, February, pp. 73–90; Evans, Rob and Lewis, Paul (2013) *Undercover: The True Story of Britain's Secret Police*. London: Faber and Faber; Lubber, Eveline (2012) *Secret Manoeuvres in the Dark: Corporate and Police Spying on Activists*. London: Pluto; Milne, Seamus (2004) *The Enemy within: Thatcher's Secret War Against the Miners*. London: Verso; Bunyan, Tony (1980) *The History and Practice of the Political Police in Britain*. London: Quartet Books; Sabir, Rizwaan (2017b) 'Policing Austerity through the "War on Terror"', in D. Whyte and V. Cooper (eds), *The Violence of Austerity*. London: Pluto; Sabir (2017a).
12. Jackson, William (2012) 'Countering Extremism in the Name of Security: Criminalizing Alternative Politics', in E. Taylor, J. Darlington and D. Cookney (eds), *Extremity and Excess*. Salford: University

of Salford Press, pp. 129–156; Nijjar, S. Jasbinder (2018) 'Echoes of Empire: Excavating the Colonial Roots of Britain's "War on Gangs"', *Social Justice*, Vol. 45, No. 2, pp. 147–161; Cooper, Adam (2021) *Black Resistance to British Policing*. Manchester: Manchester University Press; Williams, Patrick (2015) 'Criminalising the Other: Challenging the Race–Gang Nexus', *Race & Class*, Vol. 56, No. 3, pp. 18–35.

13. Bonilla-Silva, Eduardo (2013) *Racism without Racists: Color-blind Racism and the Persistence of Racial Inequality in America*, 4th edition. Lanham, MD: Rowman & Littlefield Publishers; Younis, Tarek and Jadhav, Sushrut (2019) 'Keeping Our Mouths Shut: The Fear and Racialized Self-Censorship of British Healthcare Professionals in PREVENT Training', *Culture, Medicine, and Psychiatry*, Vol. 43, p. 3.

14. Home Office data, for example, shows that from 2013 (which is when data on 'ideology' started to be centrally collected) until 2019, there have been 109 far-right nationalists and 1,026 Muslims taken into 'custody' (see Table P.01). That is a difference of 162%. If we look at the breakdown of terrorism convictions based purely on 'ethnicity' from the 11 September 2001 attacks until 2019, we can see that 281 white people have been convicted for terrorism offences compared to 540 Black and Asian people. Over an eighteen-year period, that is a difference of 63% based purely on 'ethnicity' (see Table A.11) which shows, relative to the size of the population, a disproportionate security state response towards Muslim, black and Asian people. See Home Office (2021) for the data set.

15. Mythen, Gabe, Walklate, Sandra and Khan, Fatima (2009) '"I'm a Muslim, but I'm not a Terrorist": Victimization, Risky Identities and the Performance of Safety', *The British Journal of Criminology*, Vol. 49, No. 6, November, pp. 736–754.

16. The MacPherson report made the argument that institutional racism should be measured by both institutional culture *and* intentions. Historically, it was only measured by a person's intention. See Home Department (1999) The Stephen Lawrence inquiry: Report of an inquiry by Sir William Macpherson of Cluny, CM 4262-I, February, London: Stationery Office, https://assets.publishing. service.gov.uk/government/uploads/system/uploads/attachment_ data/file/277111/4262.pdf (accessed 12.01.21).

17. Ali, Nadya (2020) 'Seeing and Unseeing Prevent's Racialized Borders', *Security Dialogue*, Vol. 51, No. 6, pp. 579–596; Abu-Bakare, Amal (2020) 'Counterterrorism and Race', *International Politics Reviews*, https://doi.org/10.1057/s41312-020-00074-x (accessed 27.08.21).

18. Taylor, Keeanga-Yamahtta (2018) 'The White Power Presidency: Race and Class in the Trump Era', *New Political Science*, Vol. 40, No. 1, pp. 103–112.

19. The main supporters of the 'new' terrorism thesis are Bruce Hoffman, Walter Laqueur, Steve Simon and Daniel Benjamin. See their work for more on the theory: Hoffman, Bruce (1998) *Inside Terrrorism*. New York: Columbia University Press; Lesser, Ian O., Hoffman, Bruce, Arquilla, John, Ronfeldt, David and Zanini, Michele (1999) *Countering the New Terrorism*. Santa Monica, CA: RAND; Laqueur, Walter (1999) *The New Terrorism, Fanaticism and the Arms of Mass Destruction*. New York: Oxford University Press; Simon, Steve and Benjamin, Daniel (2000) 'America and the New Terrorism', *Survival*, Vol. 42, No. 1, Spring, pp. 59–75. For a broader discussion and analysis on the 'new terrorism' thesis, see Spencer, Alexander (2006) 'Questioning the Concept of "New Terrorism"', *Peace, Conflict and Development*, Vol. 8, pp. 1–33; Tucker, David (2001) 'What's New About the New Terrorism and How Dangerous Is It?', *Terrorism and Political Violence*, Vol. 13, Autumn, pp. 1–14; and Crenshaw, Martha (2007) 'The Debate Over "New" vs. "Old" Terrorism', presented at the Annual Meeting of the American Political Science Association, 30 August–2 September 2007 in Chicago. Available at: www.start. umd.edu/start/publications/New_vs_Old_Terrorism.pdf (accessed 27.08.21).

20. Clarke, Peter (2007) 'DAC Peter Clarke's Speech on counter terror-ism: Learning from Experience – Counter Terrorism in the UK since 9/11', Colin Cramphorn Memorial Lecture, Policy Exchange, 24 April, https://policyexchange.org.uk/wp-content/uploads/2016/09/learning-from-experience-jun-07.pdf (accessed 12.01.21).

21. Khalili (2013), p. 5.

22. Khalili (2013), p. 5. See also p. 220 where the Khalili draws on Eqbal's Ahmed's work.

Chapter 24

1. Kilcullen, David (2010) *Counterinsurgency*. London: C. Hurst & Co., p. 4.

2. Ministry of Defence (2009) British Army Field Manual. Volume 1, Part 10: Countering Insurgency, Army Code 71876, October, http://news.bbc.co.uk/1/shared/bsp/hi/pdfs/16_11_09_army_manual.pdf (accessed 12.01.21), pp. 3–13.

3. See pp. 35–36 in Mockaitis, T. (2003) 'Winning Hearts and Minds in the "War on Terror"', *Small Wars and Insurgencies*, Vol. 14, No. 1, pp. 21–38.

4. Cited in Khalili (2013), p. 27.

5. Thornton, Rod (2004) 'The British Army and the Origins of Its Minimum Force Philosophy', *Small Wars & Insurgencies*, Vol. 15, No. 1, pp. 83–106.

6. Ministry of Defence (2009), pp. 3–15.

7. Khalili (2013), p. 67.

8. Ibid.

9. Ibid., p. 33. See also chapter 1 for quite a comprehensive breakdown of Frank Kitson's career and impact on counterinsurgency thinking.

10. Ibid., p. 30.

11. Kitson, Frank (1971) *Low Intensity Operations: Subversion, Insurgency and Peacekeeping*. London: Faber & Faber, p. 69.

12. At one stage, the total time-period a person could be held in pre-charge detention was twenty-eight days. In 2008, there was a significant campaign by politicians such as Tony Blair to increase this to three months.

13. McCulloch and Pickering (2009), p. 629.

14. HM Government (2021) 'Revised Prevent Duty Guidance: For England and Wales', Home Office, updated 21 April 2021, www.gov. uk/government/publications/prevent-duty-guidance/revised-prevent-duty-guidance-for-england-and-wales, (accessed 28.08.2021).

15. Qurashi, Fahid (2017) 'Just Get On With It: Implementing the Prevent Duty in Higher Education and the Role of Academic Expertise', *Education, Citizenship and Social Justice*, Vol. 12, No. 3, pp. 197–212.

16. For an assessment of how entire population groups are subject to coercive and punitive policies and practices in counterinsurgency warfare, see p. 17 in Branch, David (2010) 'Footprints in the Sand: British Colonial Counterinsurgency and the War in Iraq', *Politics and Society*, Vol. 38, No. 1, pp. 15–34; pp. 370–371 in Dixon, Paul (2009a) '"Hearts and Minds"? British Counter-Insurgency from Malaya to Iraq', *Journal of Strategic Studies*, Vol. 32, No. 3, pp. 353–381; and pp. 23–24 in Dixon, P. (2009b) '"Hearts and Minds"? British Counter-Insurgency in Northern Ireland', *Journal of Strategic Studies*, Vol. 32, No. 3, pp. 445–474.

Chapter 25

1. See Kilcullen (2010); Mockaitis (2003); Cassidy, Robert (2008) *Counterinsurgency and the Global War on Terror: Military Culture and Irregular War*. Stanford, CA: Stanford University Press; Mackinlay, John (2008) 'Counter-Insurgency in Global Perspective: An

Introduction', *The RUSI Journal*, Vol. 152, No. 6, pp. 6–7; Morris, Michael (2005) 'Al Qaeda as Insurgency', *Joint Force Quarterly*, Vol. 39, pp. 41–50.

2. Miller, David and Sabir, Rizwaan (2012) 'Propaganda & Terrorism', in Des Freedman and Daya Kishan Thussu (eds), *Media & Terrorism*. London: Sage Publishing.

3. Ibid.; D'Ancona, Matthew (2007) 'Brown is Leading the Way in Counter-Terrorist Thinking', *The Guardian*, 2 August, www.guardian.co.uk/commentisfree/2007/aug/02/comment.politics1 (accessed 27.08.21); Miliband, David (2009) '"Accidental Terrorists"'. FCO Bloggers: Global Conversations', Foreign and Commonwealth Office, 31 March, www.powerbase.info/images/a/aa/Miliband_blog_screengrab.jpg (accessed 28.08.21).

4. Ministry of Defence (2009), 6-2.

5. Kilcullen (2010), p. 200.

6. Ibid.

7. Ibid.

8. The purpose of this challenge posed by Al-Qaeda, S. Sayyid observes, is 'geared towards the formation of a [Muslim] people rather than the liberation of a [Muslim] people'. See p. 284 in Sayyid, Salman (2014) 'The Dynamics of a Postcolonial War', *Defence Studies*, Vol. 13, No. 3, pp. 277–292.

9. See Sayyid (2014), p. 284.

10. Lawrence, Bruce (2005) *Messages to the World: The Statements of Osama Bin Laden*, translated by James Howarth. London: Verso.

11. Al-Zawahiri, Ayman (2005) Letter from Ayman al-Zawahiri to Abu Musab al-Zarqawi, 9 July, https://fas.org/irp/news/2005/10/letter_in_english.pdf (accessed 12.01.21); See also Ingram, J. Haroro (2016) 'A Brief History of Propaganda During Conflict: Lessons for Counter-Terrorism Strategic Communications', International Centre for Counter-Terrorism (ICCT) – The Hague, June, www.icct.nl/app/uploads/2016/06/ICCT-Haroro-Ingram-Brief-History-Propaganda-June-2016-4.pdf (accessed 27.08.21), p. 4; Ciovacco, J. Carl (2009) 'The Contours of Al Qaeda's Media Strategy', *Studies in Conflict & Terrorism*, Vol. 32, No. 10, pp. 853–875.

12. Ryan, Maria (2019) *Full Spectrum Dominance: Irregular Warfare and the War on Terror*. Stanford, CA: Stanford University Press.

13. Ibid.

14. Kilcullen, David (2009) *The Accidental Guerrilla: Fighting Small Wars in the Midst of a Big One*. London: C Hurst & Co.

15. Kilcullen (2010), p. 214. The new and existing links exploited by al-Qaeda according to David Kilcullen are based on eight areas:

shared ideology, language and culture, personal history, family, finance, operational and planning links, propaganda, and doctrine, techniques and procedures. See pp. 175–180.

16. Kilcullen, David (2005) 'Countering Global Insurgency', *Journal of Strategic Studies*, Vol. 28, No. 4, p. 615.

17. Kilcullen (2010), p. 214.

18. Kilcullen, David (2007a) 'Subversion and Countersubversion in the Campaign against Terrorism in Europe', *Studies in Conflict & Terrorism*, Vol. 30, No. 8, August, p. 662; Neumann, R. Peter (2006) 'Europe's Jihadist Dilemma', *Survival*, Vol. 48, No. 2, pp. 71–84.

19. Kilcullen (2007a), p. 662.

20. Mills, Tom, Griffin, Tom and Miller, David (2011) *The Cold War on British Muslims*. London: Public Interest Investigations; see also Kitson (1971), p. 3.

21. Kitson (1971).

22. Bunyan (1980); Evans and Lewis (2013); Lubber (2012); Milne (2004).

23. Kilcullen (2011), pp. 7–8.

24. During the 1990s, there were at least fourteen attempted or actual attacks that were undertaken by the Algerian-based Armed Islamic Group (GIA) in France. Nesser, Petter (2008) 'Chronology of Jihadism in Western Europe 1994–2007: Planned, Prepared, and Executed Terrorist Attacks', *Studies in Conflict & Terrorism*, Vol. 31, No. 10, pp. 924–946.

25. Neumann (2006), p. 71.

26. Curtis, Mark (2010) *Secret Affairs: Britain's Collusion with Radical Islam*. London: Serpent's Tail.

27. Spaaij, Ramon (2010) 'The Enigma of Lone Wolf Terrorism: An Assessment', *Studies in Conflict and Terrorism*, Vol. 33, No. 9, pp. 854–870.

28. HM Government (2015) Press-Release: Counter-Extremism Bill: National Security Council meeting, 13 May, www.gov.uk/government/news/counter-extremism-bill-national-security-council-meeting (accessed 27.08.21).

29. Kilcullen (2007a), p. 653.

30. Ibid, p. 655.

31. The phrase 'agents and objects of surveillance' is inspired by a journal article title written by Sophia Hoffman where she examines the recruitment of Arab students by the Stasi in East Germany. See Hoffman, Sophia (2020) 'Arab students and the Stasi: Agents and objects of intelligence', *Security Dialogue*, Vol. 52, No. 1, February, pp. 62–78.

Chapter 26

1. Omand, D. (2010) *Securing the State*. London: C. Hurst & Co., p. 22.
2. Kilcullen, David (2006) 'Counter-insurgency Redux', *Survival*, Vol. 48, No. 4, pp. 111–130.
3. Clutterbuck, Richard (1990) *Terrorism and Guerrilla Warfare*. London: Routledge, p. 12.
4. Ibid.
5. Ibid.
6. Dixon (2009b), p. 465.
7. Ibid., p. 465 and p. 448; Jeffery, Keith (1987) 'Intelligence and Counter-Insurgency Operations: Some Reflections on the British Experience', *Intelligence and National Security*, Vol. 2, No. 1, p. 118.
8. RICU (2008) The following information is background information and core lines to take on recent arrests in Nottingham: to be used – if needed – in communications activity if and when the issue is raised, Research, Information, and Communications Unit (RICU), 30 May. https://nottinghamwhistleblower.files.wordpress.com/2011/06/ricu-research-information-and-communication-unit-30-may-08.pdf (accessed 28.08.21).
9. Ibid.
10. Association of Chief Police Officers (Terrorism and Allied Matters) (2008) Business Area. Police PREVENT Strategy – Partners Briefing: 27 March 2008, Restricted, Version 1.7., www.scribd.com/doc/35833660/ACPO-Police-Prevent-Strategy (accessed 12.08.21).
11. Qureshi, Asim (2019) 'My Schedule 7 Stop: Power and Coercion Presented as "Choice" and a "Friendly Chat"', *5Pillars*, 31 July, https://5pillarsuk.com/2019/07/31/my-schedule-7-stop-power-and-coercion-presented-as-choice-and-a-friendly-chat/ (accessed 29.08.21); CAGE (2019) 'SCHEDULE 7: HARASSMENT AT BORDERS: The Impact on the Muslim Community', CAGE Advocacy UK, www.cage.ngo/wp-content/uploads/2019/10/CAGE-Schedule-7-report.pdf (accessed 28.08.21).
12. Metropolitan Police Authority (2008) MPS Prevent delivery strategy, Assistant Commissioner Specialist Operations on behalf of the Commissioner, Report 8, 24 July, http://policeauthority.org/metropolitan/committees/mpa/2008/080724/08/index.html, (accessed 12.01.21).
13. Dick, Cressida (2012) Rich Picture, letter to Rizwaan Sabir from Cressida Dick, Assistant Commissioner Specialist Operations, Metropolitan Police Service, Ref: ACSO/534A/2011, 3 January 2012.
14. Sabir (2017a).
15. Kitson (1971), p. 131.

16. Ibid., p. 92.

17. House of Commons (2010) 'The Home Office's Response to Terrorist Attacks', Home Affairs Committee, Sixth Report of Session 2009–10, HC 117-II, 26 January, Stationery Office, Question Number 129, https://publications.parliament.uk/pa/cm200910/cmselect/cmhaff/117-ii/9111004.htm (accessed 28.08.21).

18. House of Commons (2009) 'Project CONTEST: The Government's Counter-Terrorism Strategy', Ninth Report of Session 2008–09, Home Affairs Committee, HC 212, 7 July, www.publications.parliament.uk/pa/cm200809/cmselect/cmhaff/212/212.pdf, (accessed 28.08.21), Ev 14. According to a senior counterterrorism police officer Bob Quick, CTU's also have military personnel embedded within them and work jointly with the military on counterterrorism investigation and inquiries. See Ev 17 in House of Commons (2009). When I requested more information on this matter under the Freedom of Information Act 2000 by contacting all the four CTUs, the Ministry of Defence, as well as Counterterrorism Command at New Scotland Yard, no information was disclosed on the grounds that doing so would undermine national security and law enforcement.

19. Chin, Warren (2015) 'Colonial Wars, Post-Colonial States: A Debate on the War on Terror', *ReOrient: The Journal of Critical Muslim Studies*, Vol. 1, No. 1, p. 99.

20. McFate, Montgomery (2005) "Anthropology and Counterinsurgency: The Strange Story of their Curious Relationship', *Military Review*, March–April, pp. 24–38, www.hsdl.org/?abstract&did=452717 (accessed 28.08.21), p. 24.

21. Price, David (2016) *Cold War Anthropology: The CIA, the Pentagon, and the Growth of Dual Use Anthropology*. Durham, NC: Duke University Press.

22. McFate (2005), p. 24.

23. Kilcullen (2006), p. 11.

24. Kilcullen (2010), p. 222.

25. Kilcullen (2006), p. 11.

26. American Anthropological Association (2007) 'American Anthropological Association's Executive Board Statement on the Human Terrain System Project', press release, 6 November, http://s3.amazonaws.com/rdcmsaaa/files/production/public/FileDownloads/pdfs/pdf/EB_Resolution_110807.pdf (accessed 28.08.21); González, J. Roberto (2008) '"Human Terrain": Past, Present and Future Application", *Anthropology Today*, Vol. 24, No. 1, pp. 1–32, https://rai.

onlinelibrary.wiley.com/doi/pdf/10.1111/j.1467-8322.2008.00561.x (accessed 28.08.21).

27. MacKay, Andrew and Tatham, Steve (2011) *Behavioural Conflict: Why Understanding People and their Motives Will Prove Decisive in Future Conflict*. Saffron Walden: Military Studies Press, pp. 121–124; Miller and Sabir (2012).

28. Tatham and Mackay (2011), pp. 118–119.

29. Ibid., pp. 120–121.

30. House of Commons (2009), Ev 20–21.

31. RICU (2008).

32. Sabir (2017a).

33. Ibid., pp. 14–17; see also Hayes, Ben and Qureshi, Asim (2016) '"We Are Completely Independent": The Home Office, Breakthrough Media and the PREVENT Counter Narrative Industry', *CAGE*, www.cageuk.org/wp-content/uploads/2016/05/CAGE_WACI. pdf (accessed 28.08.21); Cobain, Ian, Ross, Alice, Evans, Rob and Mahmood Mona (2016) 'Inside RICU, the Shadowy Propaganda Unit Inspired by the Cold War', *The Guardian*, 2 May, www. theguardian.com/politics/2016/may/02/inside-ricu-the-shadowy-propaganda-unit-inspired-by-the-cold-war (accessed 12.01.21).

34. Rowland, Lee and Tatham, Steve (2010) 'Strategic Communication & Influence Operations: Do We Really Get It?', *Defence Academy of the United Kingdom*, Special Series, 10/08, July, www.files.ethz.ch/ isn/119385/2010_08.pdf, (accessed 28.08.21), p. 3.

35. Ibid.

36. Ministry of Defence (2009), 6–9.

37. Ministry of Defence (2012) Strategic Communication: The Defence Contribution, Joint Doctrine Note 1/12, January, https://assets. publishing.service.gov.uk/government/uploads/system/uploads/ attachment_data/file/33710/20120126jdn112_Strategic_CommsU. pdf (accessed 12.01.21), pp. 1–3.

38. Mackay and Tatham (2011), p. 34.

39. Ministry of Defence (2009), 6-2.

40. Kilcullen (2010), p. 222; Kilcullen, David (2007b) 'Email from David Kilcullen to the Blogger Fabius Maximus', posted on *Small Wars Council Bulletin*, 7 January, http://council.smallwarsjournal. com/showpost.php?p=7530&postcount=80 (accessed 12.01.21).

41. Ramesh, Randeep and Halliday, Josh (2015) 'Student Accused of Being a Terrorist for Reading Book on Terrorism', *The Guardian*, 24 September, www.theguardian.com/education/2015/sep/24/student-accused-being-terrorist-reading-book-terrorism (accessed 28.08.21).

42. Ibid.

43. Ibid.
44. Falvey, Dan (2015) 'UEA Student Questioned by Special Branch over ISIS Course Reading', 5 December, www.concrete-online.co.uk/uea-student-questioned-by-special-branch-over-isis-course-reading/, (accessed 28.08.21).
45. Ibid.
46. Ibid.
47. It should be noted that it is currently unknown whether police were alerted of the student's reading by the university or through other sources/avenues.

Chapter 27

1. Dhami, K. Mandeep (2011) Behavioural Science Support for JTRIG's (Joint Threat Research and Intelligence Group's) Effects and Online HUMINT Operations, Human Systems Group, Information Management Department, Defence Science Technology Laboratory (DSTL), 10 March, 2011, TOP SECRET, www.statewatch.org/media/documents/news/2015/jun/behavioural-science-support-for-jtrigs-effects.pdf (accessed 11.01.21), see p. 9; GCHQ (date unknown) Full-Spectrum Cyber Effects: SIGINT Development as an Enabler for GCHQ's "Effects" Mission, Joint Threat Research and Intelligence Group (JTRIG), GCHQ, UK TOP SECRET STRAP1, https://edwardsnowden.com/wp-content/uploads/2014/04/full-spectrum-cyber-effects-final.pdf (accessed 28.08.21); see also Greenwald, Glen and Fishman, Andrew (2015) 'Controversial GCHQ Unit Engaged in Domestic Law Enforcement, Online Propaganda, Psychology Research', The Intercept, 22 June, https://theintercept.com/2015/06/22/controversial-gchq-unit-domestic-law-enforcement-propaganda/ (accessed 11.01.21).

Chapter 28

1. Van Der Kolk, Bessel (2015) The Body Keeps the Score: Brain, Mind, and Body in the Healing of Trauma. London: Penguin Books.

Chapter 30

1 Fanon, Frantz (1963) The Wretched of the Earth. New York: Grove Press, pp. 294–295.

Chapter 31

1. Sherene H. Razack (2008) Casting Out the Eviction of Muslims from Western Law & Politics. Toronto: University of Toronto Press, p. 34.
2. Home Office (2021), Table A-A.03.

Bibliography

Abu-Bakare, Amal (2020) 'Counterterrorism and Race', *International Politics Reviews*, https://doi.org/10.1057/s41312-020-00074-x (accessed 27.08.21).

Academic Services Division (2010) Hand delivered letter to Rizwaan Sabir by Hannah Robinson, University of Nottingham, 5 January.

Al-Zawahiri, Ayman (2005) Letter from Ayman al-Zawahiri to Abu Musab al-Zarqawi, 9 July, https://fas.org/irp/news/2005/10/letter_in_english.pdf (accessed 12.01.21).

Ali, Nadya (2020) 'Seeing and Unseeing Prevent's Racialized Borders', *Security Dialogue*, Vol. 51, No. 6, pp. 579–596.

American Anthropological Association (2007) 'American Anthropological Association's Executive Board Statement on the Human Terrain System Project', Press Release, 6 November, http://s3.amazonaws.com/rdcmsaaa/files/production/public/FileDownloads/pdfs/pdf/EB_Resolution_110807.pdf (accessed 28.08.21).

Amir, Geffrey and Smith, Sara (2014) 'GMP Investigation Report: Operation Carpatus', Greater Manchester Police (GMP) and the Independent Police Complaints Commission (IPCC), 1 May, IPCC Reference No: 2012-12475, Marked as 'Restricted'.

Association of Chief Police Officers (Terrorism and Allied Matters) (2008) 'Business Area. Police PREVENT Strategy – Partners Briefing: 27 March 2008', Restricted, Version 1.7., www.scribd.com/doc/35833660/ACPO-Police-Prevent-Strategy (accessed 12.08.21).

Balko, Radley (2014) *Rise of the Warrior Cop: The Militarisation of America's Police Forces*. New York: Public Affairs.

Bazian, Hatem (2012) 'Muslims – Enemies of the State: The New Counterintelligence Program (COINTELPRO)', *Islamophobia Studies Journal*, Vol. 1, No. 1, pp. 163–206.

Beresford, Shaun (2012a) Email of 10 September 2010 at 14:43 between [redacted] and [redacted], released under Subject Access Request ACRO/SAR/002 to Rizwaan Sabir, Association of Chief Police Officers (ACPO), 5 April.

Beresford, Shaun (2012b) 'ACPO Freedom of Information Referral Template V2 – Initial Submission by force 003009/11', 31 October 2011 at 10:49, released under Subject Access Request ACRO/SAR/002 to Rizwaan Sabir by Association of Chief Police Officers (ACPO), 5 April.

Beresford, Shaun (2012c) 'Annex A – Requests for Information submitted to forces by Mr Rizwaan Sabir', released under Subject Access Request ACRO/SAR/002 to Rizwaan Sabir by Association of Chief Police Officers (ACPO), 5 April.

Blackwells (2021) 'Military Studies in the Jihad Against the Tyrants: The Al-Qaeda Training Manual', Blackwells Book Shop, https://blackwells.co.uk/bookshop/product/9781907521249 (accessed 21.01.21).

Bonilla-Silva, Eduardo (2013) *Racism without Racists: Color-blind Racism and the Persistence of Racial Inequality in America*, 4th edition. Lanham, MD: Rowman & Littlefield Publishers.

Branch, David (2010) 'Footprints in the Sand: British Colonial Counterinsurgency and the War in Iraq', *Politics and Society*, Vol. 38, No. 1, pp. 15–34.

Bunyan, Tony (1980) *The History and Practice of the Political Police in Britain*. London: Quartet Books.

CAGE (2019) 'SCHEDULE 7: HARASSMENT AT BORDERS: The Impact on the Muslim Community', CAGE Advocacy UK, www.cage.ngo/wp-content/uploads/2019/10/CAGE-Schedule-7-report.pdf (accessed 28.08.21).

Cassidy, Robert (2008) *Counterinsurgency and the Global War on Terror: Military Culture and Irregular War*. Stanford, CA: Stanford University Press.

Chin, Warren (2015) 'Colonial Wars, Post-Colonial States: A Debate on the War on Terror', *ReOrient: The Journal of Critical Muslim Studies*, Vol. 1, No. 1, pp. 93–107.

Churchill, Ward and Wall, Jim (2012) *Agents of Repression: The FBI's Secret Wars Against the Black Panther Party and the American Indian Movement*. Boston, MA: South End Press.

Ciovacco, J. Carl (2009) 'The Contours of Al Qaeda's Media Strategy', *Studies in Conflict & Terrorism*, Vol. 32, No. 10, pp. 853–875.

Clarke, Peter (2007) 'DAC Peter Clarke's Speech on Counter Terrorism: Learning from Experience – Counter Terrorism in the UK since 9/11', Colin Cramphorn Memorial Lecture, Policy Exchange, 24 April, https://policyexchange.org.uk/wp-content/uploads/2016/09/learning-from-experience-jun-07.pdf (accessed 12.01.21).

Clutterbuck, Richard (1990) *Terrorism and Guerrilla Warfare*. London: Routledge.

Cobain, Ian, Ross, Alice, Evans, Rob and Mahmood, Mona (2016) 'Inside RICU, the Shadowy Propaganda Unit Inspired by the Cold War', *The Guardian*, 2 May, www.theguardian.com/politics/2016/may/02/

inside-ricu-the-shadowy-propaganda-unit-inspired-by-the-cold-war (accessed 12.01.21).

Cooper, Adam (2021) *Black Resistance to British Policing*. Manchester, Manchester University Press.

Crenshaw, Martha (2007) 'The Debate over "New" vs. "Old" Terrorism', presented at the Annual Meeting of the American Political Science Association, 30 August–2 September, Chicago, IL. Available at: www.start.umd.edu/start/publications/New_vs_Old_Terrorism.pdf (accessed 27.08.21).

Cryptome (2006) 'Cryptome's introduction to the Al-Qaeda Training Manual', https://cryptome.org/alq-terr-man.htm (accessed 26.08.21).

Curtis, Mark (2010) *Secret Affairs: Britain's Collusion with Radical Islam*. London: Serpent's Tail.

D'Ancona, Matthew (2007) 'Brown is Leading the Way in Counter-terrorist Thinking', *The Guardian*, 2 August, www.guardian.co.uk/commentisfree/2007/aug/02/comment.politics1 (accessed 27.08.21).

Dhami, K. Mandeep (2011) 'Behavioural Science Support for JTRIG's (Joint Threat Research and Intelligence Group's) Effects and Online HUMINT Operations', Human Systems Group, Information Management Department, Defence Science Technology Laboratory (DSTL), 10 March, TOP SECRET, www.statewatch.org/media/documents/news/2015/jun/behavioural-science-support-for-jtrigs-effects.pdf (accessed 11.01.21).

Dick, Cressida (2012) 'Rich Picture', letter to Rizwaan Sabir from Cressida Dick, Assistant Commissioner Specialist Operations, Metro-politan Police Service, Ref: ACSO/534A/2011, 3 January.

Dixon, Paul (2009a) '"Hearts and Minds"? British Counter-Insurgency from Malaya to Iraq', *Journal of Strategic Studies*, Vol. 32, No. 3, pp. 353–381.

Dixon, Paul (2009b) '"Hearts and Minds"? British Counter-Insurgency in Northern Ireland', *Journal of Strategic Studies*, Vol. 32, No. 3, pp. 445–474.

Eskridge, Chris (2021) 'Encyclopedia of Afghan Jihad', University of Nebraska, www.unl.edu/eskridge/encyclopedia.html (accessed 26.08.21).

Evans, Rob and Lewis, Paul (2013) *Undercover: The True Story of Britain's Secret Police*. London: Faber and Faber.

Falvey, Dan (2015) UEA student questioned by Special Branch over ISIS course reading, 5 December, www.concrete-online.co.uk/uea-student-questioned-by-special-branch-over-isis-course-reading/ (accessed 28.08.21).

Fanon, Frantz (1963) *The Wretched of the Earth*. New York: Grove Press.

GCHQ (date unknown) Full-Spectrum Cyber Effects: SIGINT Development as an Enabler for GCHQ's 'Effects' Mission, Joint Threat
Research and Intelligence Group (JTRIG), GCHQ, UK TOP SECRET
STRAP1, https://edwardsnowden.com/wp-content/uploads/2014/04/
full-spectrum-cyber-effects-final.pdf (accessed 28.08.21).

Goodfellow, Andrew (2011) Re: Your request for information, FOI Reference IGO–92, Letter to Rizwaan Sabir from Nottingham City Council,
Nottingham City Council, 19 October.

González, J. Roberto (2008) '"Human Terrain": Past, Present and Future
Application', Anthropology Today, Vol. 24, No. 1, pp. 1–32, https://rai.
onlinelibrary.wiley.com/doi/pdf/10.1111/j.1467-8322.2008.00561.x
(accessed 28.08.21).

Gordon, H. Phillip (2006) 'The End of Bush's Revolution', Foreign Affairs,
Vol. 85, No. 4, pp. 75–86.

Greenwald, Glen and Fishman, Andrew (2015) 'Controversial
GCHQ Unit Engaged in Domestic Law Enforcement, Online
Propaganda, Psychology Research', The Intercept, 22 June, https://
theintercept.com/2015/06/22/controversial-gchq-unit-domestic-law-
enforcement-propaganda/ (accessed 11.01.21).

Gwynn, Charles (1934) Imperial Policing. London: Macmillan and Co.

Gunaratna, Rohan (2002) Inside Al-Qaeda: Global Network of Terror.
New York: Colombia University Press.

Gus, Martin (2020) Understanding Terrorism: Challenges, Perspectives,
and Issues, 7th edition. London: Sage Publishing.

HM Government (2015) Press-Release: Counter-Extremism Bill:
National Security Council meeting, 13 May, www.gov.uk/government/
news/counter-extremism-bill-national-security-council-meeting
(accessed 27.08.21).

HM Government (2021) Revised Prevent Duty Guidance: For England
and Wales, Home Office, updated 21 April, www.gov.uk/government/
publications/prevent-duty-guidance/revised-prevent-duty-guidance-
for-england-and-wales (accessed 28.08.2021).

HM Revenue & Customs (2014) 'MLR3C – Money Laundering Regulation: Compliance Manual, Appendix 3: The National Intelligence
Model (5x5x5)', Ref: MLR3C14000, www.hmrc.gov.uk/manuals/
mlr3cmanual/MLR3C14000.htm (accessed 27.08.21).

Harcourt, Bernard (2018) The Counterrevolution: How our Government
Went to War Against its Own Citizens. New York: Basic Books.

Hayes, Ben and Qureshi, Asim (2016) '"We Are Completely Independent": The Home Office, Breakthrough Media and the PREVENT
Counter Narrative Industry', CAGE, www.cageuk.org/wp-content/
uploads/2016/05/CAGE_WACI.pdf (accessed 28.08.21).

Hamilton, Fiona (2007) 'Man Charged Over Terrorist Training Book', 21 May, *The Times*, www.thetimes.co.uk/article/man-charged-over-terrorist-training-book-p7h2jxd25c0, (accessed 13.01.21).

Hemming, Susan (2012) Letter to Rizwaan Sabir, Information held by the Crown Prosecution Service, Crown Prosecution Service (CPS), 28 May.

Hitch, Gillian (2011) Request under the Freedom of Information Act 2000 (FOIA), Ref: 002401/11, Letter to Rizwaan Sabir from Nottinghamshire Police, 18 October.

Hocking, Jenny (1988) 'Counterterrorism as Counterinsurgency: The British Experience', *Social Justice*, Vol. 15, No. 1, pp. 83–97.

Hoffman, Bruce (1998) *Inside Terrrorism*. New York: Columbia University Press.

Hoffman, Sophia (2020) 'Arab students and the Stasi: Agents and objects of intelligence', *Security Dialogue*, Vol. 52, No. 1, February, pp. 62–78.

Home Affairs Committee (2013) Written evidence submitted by the Home Office, Letter from James Brokenshire MP, Security Minister, to the Chair of the Committee, CT 04B, 3 October, pp. 18–25, www.parliament.uk/documents/commons-committees/homeaffairs/ (accessed 27.08.21).

Home Office (1999) *The Stephen Lawrence Inquiry: Report of an Inquiry by Sir William Macpherson of Cluny*, CM 4262-I, February. London: Stationery Office, https://assets.publishing.service.gov.uk/government/uploads/system/uploads/attachment_data/file/277111/4262.pdf (accessed 12.01.21).

Home Office (2020) 'Operation of Police Powers under the Terrorism Act 2000 and Subsequent Legislation: Arrests, Outcomes and Stops and Searches', Great Britain, year ending December 2019, Bulletin Number 07/20, https://assets.publishing.service.gov.uk/government/uploads/system/uploads/attachment_data/file/869780/police-powers-terrorism-dec2019-hosb0720.pdf (accessed 26.08.21).

Home Office (2021) Statistics on the operation of police powers under the Terrorism Act 2000 and subsequent legislation, year to March 2021, https://assets.publishing.service.gov.uk/government/uploads/system/uploads/attachment_data/file/991988/operation-police-powers-terrorism-mar2021-annual-tables.xlsx (accessed 26.10.21).

House of Commons (2009) 'Project CONTEST: The Government's Counter-Terrorism Strategy', Ninth Report of Session 2008–09, Home Affairs Committee, HC 212, 7 July, www.publications.parliament.uk/pa/cm200809/cmselect/cmhaff/212/212.pdf (accessed 28.08.21).

House of Commons (2010) *The Home Office's Response to Terrorist Attacks*, Home Affairs Committee, Sixth Report of Session 2009–10,

HC 117-II, 26 January. London: Stationery Office, https://publications.
parliament.uk/pa/cm200910/cmselect/cmhaff/117-ii/9111004.htm
(accessed 28.08.21).

Ingram, J. Haroro (2016) 'A Brief History of Propaganda During
Conflict: Lessons for Counter-Terrorism Strategic Communications',
International Centre for Counter-Terrorism (ICCT), The Hague,
June, www.icct.nl/app/uploads/2016/06/ICCT-Haroro-Ingram-Brief-
History-Propaganda-June-2016-4.pdf (accessed 27.08.21).

Jackson, William (2012) 'Countering Extremism in the Name of
Security: Criminalizing Alternative Politics', in E. Taylor, J. Darlington and D. Cookney (eds), *Extremity and Excess*. Salford: University
of Salford Press, pp. 129–156.

Jeffery, Keith (1987) 'Intelligence and Counter-Insurgency Operations:
Some Reflections on the British Experience', *Intelligence and National
Security*, Vol. 2, No. 1, pp. 118–149.

Kilcullen, David (2005) 'Countering Global Insurgency', *Journal of Strategic Studies*, Vol. 28, No. 4, pp. 597–617.

Kilcullen, David (2006) 'Counter-insurgency Redux', *Survival*, Vol. 48,
No. 4, pp. 111–130.

Kilcullen, David (2007a) 'Subversion and Countersubversion in the
Campaign against Terrorism in Europe', *Studies in Conflict & Terrorism*, Vol. 30, No. 8, pp. 647–666.

Kilcullen, David (2007b) Email from David Kilcullen to the Blogger Fabius
Maximus, posted on Small Wars Council Bulletin, 7 January, http://
council.smallwarsjournal.com/showpost.php?p=7530&postcount=80
(accessed 12.01.21).

Kilcullen, David (2009) *The Accidental Guerrilla: Fighting Small Wars in
the Midst of a Big One*. London: C Hurst & Co.

Kilcullen, David (2010) *Counterinsurgency*. London: C. Hurst & Co.

Kitson, Frank (1971) *Low Intensity Operations: Subversion, Insurgency
and Peacekeeping*. London: Faber & Faber.

Kundnani, Arun (2009) 'Spooked: How Not to Prevent Violent Extremism', Institute of Race Relations, www.irr.org.uk/pdf2/spooked.pdf
(accessed 13.10.10).

Kundnani, Arun (2014) *The Muslims are Coming: Islamophobia, Extremism, and the Domestic War on Terror*. London: Verso Books.

Laleh, Khalili (2013) *Time in the Shadows: Confinement in Counterinsurgencies*. Stanford, CA: Stanford University Press.

Laqueur, Walter (1999) *The New Terrorism, Fanaticism and the Arms of
Mass Destruction*. New York: Oxford University Press.

Laqueur, Walter (2004) *Voices of Terror: Manifestos, Writings, and Manuals of Al-Qaeda, Hamas, and Other Terrorists from Around the World and Throughout the Ages*. New York: Reed Press.

Lawrence, Bruce (2005) *Messages to the World: The Statements of Osama Bin Laden*, translated by James Howarth. London: Verso.

Lesser, Ian O., Hoffman, Bruce, Arquilla, John, Ronfeldt, David, Zanini, Michele and Jenkins, Brian Michael (1999) *Countering the New Terrorism*. Santa Monica, CA: RAND.

Lubber, Eveline (2012) *Secret Manoeuvres in the Dark: Corporate and Police Spying on Activists*. London: Pluto.

MacKay, Andrew and Tatham, Steve (2011) *Behavioural Conflict: Why Understanding People and their Motives Will Prove Decisive in Future Conflict*. Saffron Walden: Military Studies Press.

MacLean, K (2012) File Note re: [redacted] and RIZWAN SABIR (Operation Minerva), Data Protection Act 1998 – Subject Access Request, Ref: 02/12/DPA, Crown Prosecution Service (CPS), 14 February.

Mackinlay, John (2008) 'Counter-Insurgency in Global Perspective: An Introduction', *The RUSI Journal*, Vol. 152, No. 6, pp. 6–7.

McCulloch, Jude (2004) 'Blue Armies, Khaki Police, and the Cavalry: On the New American Frontier: Critical Criminology for the 21st Century', *Critical Criminology*, Vol. 12, pp. 309–326.

McCulloch, Jude and Pickering, Sharon (2009) 'Pre-Crime and Counterterrorism: Imagining Future Crime in the "War on Terror"', *British Journal of Criminology*, Vol. 49, pp. 628–645.

McFate, Montgomery (2005) 'Anthropology and Counterinsurgency: The Strange Story of their Curious Relationship', *Military Review*, March–April, pp. 24–38, www.hsdl.org/?abstract&did=452717 (accessed 28.08.21).

McGuirk, Bernard (2008) Witness Statement of Bernard Joseph McGuirk, West Midlands Police, 18 May.

Metropolitan Police Authority (2008) MPS Prevent delivery strategy, Assistant Commissioner Specialist Operations on behalf of the Commissioner, Report 8, 24 July, http://policeauthority.org/metropolitan/committees/mpa/2008/080724/08/index.html, (accessed 12.01.21).

Ministry of Defence (2009) British Army Field Manual. Volume 1, Part 10: Countering Insurgency, Army Code 71876, October, http://news.bbc.co.uk/1/shared/bsp/hi/pdfs/16_11_09_army_manual.pdf (accessed 12.01.21), 3–13.

Ministry of Defence (2012) Strategic Communication: The Defence Contribution, Joint Doctrine Note 1/12, January, https://assets.publishing.service.gov.uk/government/uploads/system/uploads/

attachment_data/file/33710/20120126jdn112_Strategic_CommsU. pdf (accessed 12.01.21).

Mills, Tom, Griffin, Tom and Miller, David (2011) *The Cold War on British Muslims*. London: Public Interest Investigations.

Miliband, David (2009) Accidental Terrorists. FCO bloggers: Global Conversations, *Foreign* and Commonwealth Office, 31 March, www. powerbase.info/images/a/aa/Milband_blog_screengrab.jpg (accessed 04.12.09).

Miller, David and Sabir, Rizwaan (2012) 'Propaganda and Terrorism', in Des Freedman and Daya Kishan Thussu (eds), *Media & Terrorism*. London: Sage Publishing.

Milne, Seamus (2004) *The Enemy Within: Thatcher's Secret War Against the Miners*. London: Verso.

Mockaitis, T. (2003) 'Winning Hearts and Minds in the "War on Terror"', *Small Wars and Insurgencies*, Vol. 14, No. 1, pp. 21–38.

Morris, Michael (2005) 'Al Qaeda as Insurgency', *Joint Force Quarterly*, Vol. 39, pp. 41–50.

Mythen, Gabe, Walklate, Sandra and Khan, Fatima (2009) '"I'm a Muslim, but I'm Not a Terrorist": Victimization, Risky Identities and the Performance of Safety', *The British Journal of Criminology*, Vol. 49, No. 6, pp. 736–754.

Nesser, Petter (2008) 'Chronology of Jihadism in Western Europe 1994–2007: Planned, Prepared, and Executed Terrorist Attacks', *Studies in Conflict & Terrorism*, Vol. 31, No. 10, pp. 924–946.

Nijjar, S. Jasbinder (2018) 'Echoes of Empire: Excavating the Colonial Roots of Britain's "War on Gangs"', *Social Justice*, Vol. 45, No. 2, pp. 147–161.

Nottinghamshire Police (2007) Nottinghamshire Police Intelligence Report, CIRR00970346, Grading B11, 30 November.

Nottinghamshire Police (2008a) Nottinghamshire Police Intelligence Report, CIRR00984999, Grading E41, Nottinghamshire Police, 30 January.

Nottinghamshire Police (2008b) Nottinghamshire Police Intelligence Report, CIRR01008654, Grading B11, Nottinghamshire Police, 24 April.

Nottinghamshire Police (2008c) Nottingham University Palestinian Society, Report Unique Reference Number 13-2008-05-17-A-133, Grading B21, 13:58, Nottinghamshire Police, 17 May 2008.

Nottinghamshire Police (2010) Unlinked Intelligence 20/05/08– 10/08/2011, CIRR01170750, Grading E41, Nottinghamshire Police, 22 February.

Omand, David (2010) *Securing the State*. London: C. Hurst & Co.

Police Interview 1 (2008) Police Interview Transcript 1 of 8 with Rizwaan Sabir, Bridewell Police Station, Nottingham, West Midlands Counter-Terrorism Unit, Tape Reference No. RW/01, Restricted, 20:52–21:35 (43 minutes), 14 May.

Police Interview 2 (2008) Police Interview Transcript 2 of 8 with Rizwaan Sabir, Bridewell Police Station, Nottingham, West Midlands Counter-Terrorism Unit, Tape Reference No. RW/03, Restricted, 19:26–19:49 (23 minutes), 15 May.

Police Interview 3 (2008) Police Interview Transcript 3 of 8 with Rizwaan Sabir, Bridewell Police Station, Nottingham, West Midlands Counter-Terrorism Unit, Tape Reference No. RW/5, Restricted, 12:57–13:29 (32 minutes), 16 May.

Police Interview 4 (2008) Police Interview Transcript 4 of 8 with Rizwaan Sabir, Bridewell Police Station, Nottingham, West Midlands Counter-Terrorism Unit, Tape Reference No. RW/7, Restricted, 12:51–13:37 (46 minutes), 17 May.

Police Interview 5 (2008) Police Interview Transcript 5 of 8 with Rizwaan Sabir, Bridewell Police Station, Nottingham, West Midlands Counter-Terrorism Unit, Tape Reference No. RW/9, Restricted, 11:46–12:15 (29 minutes), 18 May.

Police Interview 6 (2008) Police Interview Transcript 6 of 8 with Rizwaan Sabir, Bridewell Police Station, Nottingham, West Midlands Counter-Terrorism Unit, Tape Reference No. RW/11, Restricted, 18:13–18:59 (46 minutes), 18 May.

Police Interview 7 (2008) Police Interview Transcript 7 of 8 with Rizwaan Sabir, Bridewell Police Station, Nottingham, West Midlands Counter-Terrorism Unit, Tape Reference No. RW/13, Restricted, 12:34–13:19 (46 minutes), 19 May.

Post, M. Jerrold (2004) 'Military Studies in the Jihad Against the Tyrants: The Al-Qaeda Training Manual', US Airforce Counterproliferation Center, Alabama, August, www.airuniversity.af.edu/Portals/10/CSDS/Books/alqaedatrainingmanual2.pdf (accessed 12.01.21).

Pottinger, Diana (2012a) Email of 25 August 2011 between officials, released under Subject Access Request, Ref: SA11935 to Rizwaan Sabir, Home Office, 26 April.

Pottinger, Diana (2012b) Email of 24 August 2011 between officials, released under Subject Access Request, Ref: SA11935 to Rizwaan Sabir, Home Office, 26 April.

Price, David (2016) Cold War Anthropology: The CIA, the Pentagon, and the Growth of Dual Use Anthropology. Durham, NC: Duke University Press.

230 · THE SUSPECT

Qurashi, Fahid (2018) 'The Prevent Strategy and the UK "War on Terror": Embedding Infrastructures of Surveillance in Muslim Communities', *Palgrave Communications*, Vol. 4, No. 1, www.nature.com/articles/s41599-017-0061-9 (accessed 28.09.21).

Qurashi, Fahid (2017) 'Just Get On With It: Implementing the Prevent Duty in Higher Education and the Role of Academic Expertise', *Education, Citizenship and Social Justice*, Vol. 12, No. 3, pp. 197–212.

Qureshi, Asim (2019) 'My Schedule 7 Stop: Power and Coercion Presented as "Choice" and a "Friendly Chat"', *5Pillars*, 31 July, https://5pillarsuk.com/2019/07/31/my-schedule-7-stop-power-and-coercion-presented-as-choice-and-a-friendly-chat/ (accessed 29.08.21).

Ramesh, Randeep and Halliday, Josh (2015) 'Student Accused of Being a Terrorist for Reading Book on Terrorism', *The Guardian*, 24 September, www.theguardian.com/education/2015/sep/24/student-accused-being-terrorist-reading-book-terrorism (accessed 28.08.21).

Rawlinson, Kevin (2012) 'Police Face New Questions Over Approach to Protest Groups', *The Independent*, 6 January, www.independent.co.uk/news/uk/home-news/police-face-new-questions-over-approach-to-protest-groups-6285707.html (accessed 27.08.21).

Renz, Bettina (2010) Statement of Dr Bettina Renz, in the Central London Country Court Between Rizwaan Sabir (Claimant) and The Chief Constable of Nottinghamshire Police (Defendant), Statement No. 1, Case No: 9CL03969, Bhatt Murphy Solicitors, 15 July.

Renz, Bettina (2008) Bettina Renz Witness Statement to West Midlands Police, West Midlands Police, 17 May.

RICU (2008) The following information is background information and core lines to take on recent arrests in Nottingham: to be used – if needed – in communications activity if and when the issue is raised, Research, Information, and Communications Unit (RICU), 30 May, https://nottinghamwhistleblower.files.wordpress.com/2011/06/ricu-research-information-and-communication-unit-30-may-08.pdf (accessed 28.08.21).

Rowland, Lee and Tatham, Steve (2010) 'Strategic Communication & Influence Operations: Do We Really Get It?', *Defence Academy of the United Kingdom*, Special Series, 10/08, July, www.files.ethz.ch/isn/119385/2010_08.pdf (accessed 28.08.21).

Ryan, Maria (2010) Statement of Dr Maria Ryan, in the Central London Country Court Between Rizwaan Sabir (Claimant) and The Chief Constable of Nottinghamshire Police (Defendant), Statement No. 1, Case No: 9CL03969, Bhatt Murphy Solicitors, 15 July.

Ryan, Maria (2019) *Full Spectrum Dominance: Irregular Warfare and the War on Terror*. Stanford, CA: Stanford University Press.

Sabir, Rizwaan (2012b) 'How Police Branded OccupyLSX and UKUNCUT as "Terrorists"', *Ceasefire Magazine*, 7 January, https://ceasefiremagazine.co.uk/police-branded-occupylsx-ukuncut-terrorists/ (accessed 12.01.21).

Sabir, Rizwaan (2017a) 'Blurred Lines and False Dichotomies: Integrating Counterinsurgency into the UK's Domestic "War on Terror"', *Critical Social Policy*, Vol. 37, No. 2, pp. 1–23.

Sabir, Rizwaan (2017b) 'Policing Austerity through the "War on Terror"', in D. Whyte and V. Cooper (eds) *The Violence of Austerity*. London: Pluto.

Sayyid, Salman (2014) 'The Dynamics of a Postcolonial War', *Defence Studies*, Vol. 13, No. 3, pp. 277–292.

Simon, Steve and Benjamin, Daniel (2000) 'America and the New Terrorism', *Survival*, Vol. 42, No. 1, Spring, pp. 59–75.

Spaaij, Ramon (2010) 'The Enigma of Lone Wolf Terrorism: An Assessment', *Studies in Conflict and Terrorism*, Vol. 33, No. 9, pp. 854–870.

Spencer, Alexander (2006) 'Questioning the Concept of "New Terrorism"', *Peace, Conflict and Development*, Vol. 8, pp. 1–33.

Taylor, Keeanga-Yamahtta (2018) 'The White Power Presidency: Race and Class in the Trump Era', *New Political Science*, Vol. 40, No. 1, pp. 103–112.

Thornton, Rod (2004) 'The British Army and the Origins of Its Minimum Force Philosophy', *Small Wars & Insurgencies*, Vol. 15, No. 1, pp. 83–106.

Thornton, Rod (2008) Rod Thornton Witness Statement to West Midlands Police, West Midlands Police, 16 May 2008.

Thornton, Rod (2009) 'The "Al-Qaeda Training Manual" (Not)', *Teaching Terrorism*, 11 July, https://nottinghamwhistleblower.files.wordpress.com/2011/06/footnote-37.pdf (accessed 12.01.21).

Thornton, Rod (2010) Statement of Dr Ian Roderick Thornton, in the Central London Country Court Between Rizwaan Sabir (Claimant) and The Chief Constable of Nottinghamshire Police (Defendant), Statement No. 1, Case No: 9CL03969, Bhatt Murphy Solicitors, 15 July.

Thornton, Rod (2011) 'Counterterrorism and the Neo-Liberal University: Providing a Check and Balance?', *Critical Studies on Terrorism*, Vol. 4, No. 3, pp. 421–429.

Trafford, James (2020) *The Empire at Home: Internal Colonies and the End of Britain*. London: Pluto.

Tucker, David (2001)'What's New About the New Terrorism and How Dangerous Is It?', *Terrorism and Political Violence*, Autumn, Vol. 13, pp. 1–14.

Turner, Joe (2017) 'Internal Colonisation: The Intimate Circulations of Empire, Race and Liberal Government', *European Journal of International Relations*, Vol. 24. No. 4, pp. 765–790.

Van Der Kolk, Bessel (2015) *The Body Keeps the Score: Brain, Mind, and Body in the Healing of Trauma*. London: Penguin Books.

Walker, Clive (2009) *Blackstone's Guide to the Anti-Terrorism Legislation*, 2nd edition. Oxford: Oxford University Press.

West Midlands Counter-Terrorism Unit (2008a) Operation Minerva Forensic Arrest/Search Strategy, Restricted, 13 May.

West Midlands Counter-Terrorism Unit (2008b) Notes of Gold Group: Operation Minerva, 17 May 2008.

Whyte, David (2015) 'Policing for Whom?', *The Howard Journal of Crime and Justice*, Vol. 54, No. 1, February, pp. 73–90.

Williams, Patrick (2015) 'Criminalising the Other: Challenging the Race-Gang Nexus', *Race & Class*, Vol. 56, No. 3, pp. 18–35.

Witorowicz, Quentin and Katner, John (2003) 'Killing in the Name of Islam: Al Qaeda's Justification for September 11', *Middle East Policy Council Journal*, Vol. 10, No. 2, pp. 76–92.

Younis, Tarek and Jadhav, Sushrut (2019) 'Keeping Our Mouths Shut: The Fear and Racialized Self-Censorship of British Healthcare Professionals in PREVENT Training', *Culture, Medicine, and Psychiatry*, Vol. 43, pp. 404–424.

Index

diag refers to a diagram; *n* to a note

Thanks to our Patreon subscriber:

Ciaran Kane

Who has shown generosity and comradeship in support of our publishing.

Check out the other perks you get by subscribing to our Patreon – visit patreon.com/plutopress.

Subscriptions start from £3 a month.